Web Analytics For Du...

D0523373

Top Web Analytics Blogs and Forums

Go to these blogs and forums, and you'll get a wealth of practical information from people who have gone before you on the Web measurement journey.

- ✔ **Matt Belkin's blog:** www.omniture.com/blog
- ✔ **Web Analytics Blog:** http://analytics.thekarchergroup.com
- ✔ **Visistat:** www.visistat.com/wordpress/
- ✔ **Hitwise Intelligence:** http://weblogs.hitwise.com
- ✔ **The Web Analytics Forum:** http://tech.groups.yahoo.com/group/webanalytics/
- ✔ **Applied Insights Blog:** www.applied-insights.co.uk/news/category/blog/
- ✔ **Analytics Guide:** www.analyticsguide.com/
- ✔ **Web Analytics Demystified:** www.webanalyticsdemystified.com/weblog/

Your A to Z Guide to Free and Low-Cost Web Analytics Tools . . .

Get into the systems for a song and a smile (and maybe a few bucks). Chapter 5 tells you how to choose the right Web analytics vendor for your needs.

- ✔ **Analog:** http://analog.cx/
- ✔ **AWStats:** www.awstats.org/
- ✔ **ClickTracks Appetizer:** http://clicktracks.com/products/appetizer/
- ✔ **Crazyegg:** http://crazyegg.com/
- ✔ **Enquisite:** www.enquisite.com/
- ✔ **eXTReME Tracking:** http://extremetracking.com/
- ✔ **Google Analytics:** www.google.com/analytics/
- ✔ **HitBox Professional:** www.websidestory.com/products/web-analytics/hitbox-professional/
- ✔ **Measure Map:** www.measuremap.com/
- ✔ **OneStatFree:** www.onestatfree.com/
- ✔ **ShinyStat:** www.shinystat.com
- ✔ **Site Meter:** www.sitemeter.com/
- ✔ **StatCounter:** www.statcounter.com/
- ✔ **The Webalizer:** http://webalizer.com/

Web Analytics Courses, Classes, and Education Programs

Need more help interpreting the mountains of data? Check out these reputable Web Analytics courses, classes, and education programs.

- ✔ The University of British Columbia offers an Award of Achievement in Web Analytics.
- ✔ The Institute of Direct Marketing offers several courses pertinent to your Web Analytics education.
- ✔ The Web Analytics Association offers training summits at various locations across the country.

And here are some Web Analytics vendors that offer training. Some courses are free, others will cost you a few hundred bucks.

- ✔ The ClickTracks Virtual Classroom offers
- ✔ WebTrends Training Courses
- ✔ WebSideStory Digital Marketing Courses
- ✔ Omniture offers Web Analytics education

For Dummies: Bestselling Book Series for Beginners

Web Analytics For Dummies®

Your 1-Hour Web Analytics-Driven Web Site Makeover Checklist

Various chapters offer tips to fine-tune your Web site. Ask yourself the following questions.

- Are my most popular pages designed to convert visitors into customers?
- Does my site offer visitors a compelling reason to come back often?
- Does my Web site copy make use of the most popular keywords and keyphrases?
- Does the average visitor look at several pages, or leave after just one?
- Which particular group of users generates the most conversions?
- Are my keywords and keyphrases driving targeted traffic?
- Are there broken pages or graphics that are hurting my Web site's credibility?
- Do most visitors tend to exit on a particular page? What might be causing them to leave on that page?
- Are my landing pages converting visitors into customers?
- Are visitors naturally navigating between sections of the site that lead to cross-selling and up-selling opportunities?
- Are visitors abandoning the sale at the shopping cart?
- Are visitors finding answers on the customer service and FAQ pages?

Tips for Taking a Quick Pulse of Your Site's Performance

- View your Site Summary. Glancing at this report will give you a quick overview of unique visitors, number of visits, average visits per visitor, number of pages viewed, and other pertinent data.
- Review your Monthly History report. You can compare your unique visitors this month to last month or six months ago or the same month from a year ago.
- Examine Days of Month report. This will tell you which days brought you the most traffic. Was that special promotion you launched last week effective?
- Review your Robots/Spider Visitors report. Are Googlebot and MSNBot crawling over your pages? If not, you may need to go register with them.
- View your Visits Duration report. Are most visitors leaving within 30 seconds? It may be time to revamp your Web site.
- Check out your Top Pages report. What pages are visitor favorites? Now try to figure out why.
- View your Site Referrer report. Where is your traffic coming from?
- View your Keywords and Keyphrases report. Which words are working for you?
- View your HTTP Error Codes report. Are there problems on your site you need to fix?

Generating Site Referrer Ideas

Chapter 9 gives you the skinny on site referrers that build traffic. Here's a quick list of some site referrers you may not have thought of — and a few you may need to be reminded of.

- Mainstream search directories
- Niche search engines
- Association Web sites
- Submit content to free article banks
- Content exchanges
- Webrings
- Press releases
- Affiliate marketing
- Strategic alliances with other companies
- Newsletters
- E-mail campaigns
- Offer free content on your site
- Search engine marketing
- Link exchanges
- Blogging
- Online forums
- Contests and awards
- Online PR
- Offline PR
- Link-building services
- Banner ads
- Promote a charitable cause
- Friends, family, and employees

For Dummies: Bestselling Book Series for Beginners

Web Analytics FOR DUMMIES®

**by Pedro Sostre
and Jennifer LeClaire**

Wiley Publishing, Inc.

Web Analytics For Dummies®

Published by
Wiley Publishing, Inc.
111 River Street
Hoboken, NJ 07030-5774
www.wiley.com

Copyright © 2007 by Wiley Publishing, Inc., Indianapolis, Indiana

Published by Wiley Publishing, Inc., Indianapolis, Indiana

Published simultaneously in Canada

For general information on our other products and services, please contact our Customer Care Department within the U.S. at 800-762-2974, outside the U.S. at 317-572-3993, or fax 317-572-4002.

For technical support, please visit www.wiley.com/techsupport.

Wiley also publishes its books in a variety of electronic formats. Some content that appears in print may not be available in electronic books.

Library of Congress Control Number: 2007920021

ISBN: 978-0-470-09824-0

Manufactured in the United States of America

10 9 8 7 6 5 4 3 2 1

About the Authors

An accomplished affiliate marketer with several successful Internet properties relying heavily on Web analytics to stay on top of the charts, **Pedro Sostre III** is a New Media entrepreneur who understands how to blend art and business to reap financial rewards.

Pedro fell in love with the World Wide Web, its opportunities, and its challenges in 1999. Since then he's done everything from freelance design and marketing consulting to multimedia design for a major dot-com to launching his own Web development and consulting firm, Sostre & Associates. In the course of his career, he's managed Web projects for companies like CBS Sportsline, BMW Motorcycles, Reebok, and Motorola, among others. Web analytics were an important factor in all of those projects.

Recognized as an Internet business and marketing guru, Pedro is a columnist for *Revenue* magazine and is regularly quoted in media outlets, including *Microsoft.com, Web Host Industry Review,* and Internet advertising hot spot *Adotas.* Pedro's coveted knowledge has also landed him invitations to judge design awards at Content Week. The Yahoo! Search Marketing Ambassador and Google Adwords Qualified Professional is also a regular presenter at industry events like eComExpo and the Affiliate Summit. You can find him online at www.sostreassoc.com.

Jennifer LeClaire has been chronicling e-commerce since its humble beginnings. She has witnessed the rise, fall, and resurrection of Dot-com Land. Jennifer's tech news credits include *NewsFactor, E-Commerce Times, Information Week* and *Inc.com,* among others. In fact, tens of millions of readers rely on Jennifer for straight-up business and technology news and insightful special reports each year.

Jennifer is also a veteran business news journalist, with credits including the Associated Press, *The New York Times,* and CBS and ABC News. Jennifer is a weekly guest technology analyst on CBS Radio's KMOX, where she shares the real news behind technology headlines with millions of listeners nationwide. Jennifer is also an active blogger on AnalyticsInsider.com.

Jennifer is a member of the American Society of Authors and Journalists and the Public Relations Society of America. Jennifer's personal Web site is www.jenniferleclaire.com. She also heads Revelation Media Networks, an integrated marketing communications firm.

Dedication

This book is dedicated to my leadership team at Sostre & Associates, Lisa Ramos and Chris Rivera. If it hadn't been for the willingness of this dynamic duo to take on new levels of responsibility for the day-to-day operations of the firm, I would not have been able to dedicate myself to writing this book.

— Pedro Sostre

I would like to dedicate this book to the ECT News Network's publisher, Ric Kern, and his hard-working editorial staff. These devoted tech news specialists offered me tremendous support through the long process of dissecting Web analytics.

— Jennifer LeClaire

Authors' Acknowledgments

Between the two of us, we've written plenty of articles, designed plenty of Web sites, and analyzed plenty of stats, but writing a book that applies those skills and that knowledge is an entirely different story. Blair Pottenger is the project editor of this book and deserves a hearty round of applause for his careful reading, incisive comments, and patience. Blair is a pro who shows no signs of cracking even under deadline pressure. Whatever you throw his way, he catches it and runs with it. Thanks, Blair!

We tried to make Teresa Artman's copy editing job easy, but we appreciate her keen eye. She made us look good by ridding our pages of unclear techie stuff and a few typos along the way. With an entire new language called Web analytics to learn over a few short months, we're convinced Teresa could copy edit books in any tongue.

Many thanks to Steve Hayes for launching this project and cultivating its first seeds. Steve held our hands through the beginning stages of developing the outline and sample chapter. His advice and experience in the publishing arena made this project an experience to remember (a good one!).

As for Paul Chaney, the technical editor, he had an unusually difficult job with this book because of the myriad of analytical concepts within its pages. His insights were invaluable.

Every single pair of eyes and hands who played a role in bringing this book to fruition should be congratulated. This is an important topic for online businesses large and small and the editorial team deserves a place in the Web analytics hall of fame for deciding to make this complex topic understandable to even Web analytics newbies.

Publisher's Acknowledgments

We're proud of this book; please send us your comments through our online registration form located at www.dummies.com/register/.

Some of the people who helped bring this book to market include the following:

Acquisitions, Editorial, and Media Development

Project Editor: Blair J. Pottenger

Senior Acquisitions Editor: Steven Hayes

Senior Copy Editor: Teresa Artman

Technical Editor: Paul Chaney

Editorial Manager: Kevin Kirschner

Media Development Manager: Laura VanWinkle

Editorial Assistant: Amanda Foxworth

Sr. Editorial Assistant: Cherie Case

Cartoons: Rich Tennant (www.the5thwave.com)

Composition Services

Project Coordinator: Erin Smith

Layout and Graphics: Carl Byers, Denny Hager, Joyce Haughey, Stephanie D. Jumper, Barbara Moore

Proofreaders: Aptara, John Greenough, Christy Pingleton

Indexer: Aptara

Anniversary Logo Design: Richard Pacifico

Publishing and Editorial for Technology Dummies

    Richard Swadley, Vice President and Executive Group Publisher

    Andy Cummings, Vice President and Publisher

    Mary Bednarek, Executive Acquisitions Director

    Mary C. Corder, Editorial Director

Publishing for Consumer Dummies

    Diane Graves Steele, Vice President and Publisher

    Joyce Pepple, Acquisitions Director

Composition Services

    Gerry Fahey, Vice President of Production Services

    Debbie Stailey, Director of Composition Services

Contents at a Glance

Table of Contents

Part IV: Knowledge Is Power — Making Analytics Work for You....................................199

Chapter 12: Sifting through Search Data 201

Chapter 13: Increasing Web Site Visibility 221

Introduction

What would you pay for a book that could help you tap into the mindsets of your Web site visitors, show you where you're missing golden sales opportunities, and save you big bucks on online advertising initiatives? How about less than $30? (It's quite the bargain for a wealth of knowledge, isn't it?)

Web Analytics For Dummies is the book you've been waiting for. See, Web analytics tools are essential, vital, and even critical for anyone who wants to improve his success on the World Wide Web. In fact, from entrepreneurs to mega corporations, the need for Web analytics has never been stronger. The truth is, what you don't know about your Web site could be hurting your business.

Web Analytics For Dummies is an introduction to the wonderful world of Web site statistics. The book will help you understand and unleash the power of Web analytics. It will take you on a journey with a colorful map that shows you the sign posts ahead as well as the right and left turns to lead you to greater profitability. Indeed, by the time you're done reading this book, no one will be able to call you a dummy anymore. You'll have confidence in your abilities to use these practical techniques that get results.

About This Book

This book takes the mystery out of Web metrics. You find out what you need to do to get the inside scoop on visitor behavior, measure your Web site's performance against your business goals, and make adjustments to help you meet those objectives.

In this book, we show you how to

- Understand the language of Web analytics.
- Choose the right Web analytics software for your business.
- Get the nitty-gritty on what your visitors are doing on your Web site.
- Calculate your conversion rate and set goals for your Web site.
- Identify your most popular — and most profitable — pages.

✔ Get the lowdown on where your traffic is coming from and discover which site referrers you want to get cozier with.

✔ Fine-tune your Web site and reduce shopping cart abandonment.

✔ Avoid common data interpretation mistakes and implement proven best practices.

And plenty more!

Foolish Assumptions

You know what they say about people who make assumptions, but because you bought this book, we have to presume a few things about your present circumstances — things such as

✔ You own a Web site, are planning very soon to build a Web site, or are in the business of helping other people improve their Web sites.

✔ You know how to use a Web browser.

✔ You know how to do some simple math: for example, calculating a percentage.

Of course, if you bought a book like this, we have to figure you know a little more than the basics about how to manage a Web site — or that you have access to someone who does. Because this book deals with statistics galore and how to use those stats to improve your site, we have to assume that you can take action on what you glean from this book. Specifically, you'll probably need to know how to

✔ **Do vendor research (compare and contrast).**

✔ **Download and install software.**

✔ **Fix any Web site errors that your Web analytics software identifies.**

✔ **Make changes to your Web site.** The Holy Grail of Web analytics is not merely accessing and interpreting the data but also using what you discover to optimize your Web site and your Internet marketing campaigns.

We don't get into coding in this book. This isn't a primer on fixing errors or using HTML to make changes to your site. In order to get the most out of this book, however, you or someone you know needs to have some basic HTML skills so you can fine-tune your Web site. That may mean moving a picture from the top to the bottom of the screen or adding new content to certain pages. If you need more information about HTML, pick up a copy of *HTML 4 For Dummies,* 4th Edition, by Ed Tittel and Natanya Pitts (Wiley).

How This Book Is Organized

This book isn't anything like the boring reference books you relied on for your high school term papers, but it is organized like a reference book. In other words, you can start at any chapter and get the information that you need on the spot. You don't necessarily have to read the chapters in order like you would a mystery novel.

This book is divided into several parts: the basics, choosing the tools you need to succeed, tips on searching for statistical treasure, how to make good with the knowledge you've acquired, and the Part of Tens. If you want to understand the differences between client-side, server-side, and hosted solutions, read Chapter 4. If you need some insight into *key performance indicators (KPIs)* — metrics that illustrate how well your site is performing against goals — read Chapter 11. If all you need is some quick info on how to determine who is sending traffic to your site, go right to Chapter 9. You get the idea.

With all that said, Web analytics is a complex topic, and each chapter sort of builds on the other as you strive to erect your Web-based empire. Yes, you can skip ahead to Chapter 5 and start the process of comparing and contrasting Web analytics vendors. If you don't know the difference between the basic tool types, though, you might choose the wrong software. You can start with Chapter 3 and take a sneak peek at the data, but if you don't speak the language of analytics, you might not have a clue what you're really looking at. We recommend that you take the time to read the entire book from cover to cover, and then use it as an ongoing reference guide as needed. We believe that you'll better understand how to set benchmarks, interpret the data properly, and use the right data to guide you down the path of Web optimization.

Part I: Getting Started with Web Analytics

In this part, we give you the keys you need to start the Web analytics engine and keep it humming. Like a foreman setting out to build a skyscraper, this part of the book lays a strong foundation that will support your efforts as your Web site grows. Why is Web analytics important to your business? And for that matter, what is Web analytics? What's the difference between a hit, a pageview, and a unique visitor? In this part, you'll find out the basics of Web analytics: how it can benefit you, how to speak the language, and how to access your data and start recording some simple KPIs.

Part II: Choosing the Right Web Analytics Solution

It's been said there's more than one way to skin a cat. (Gruesome thought, isn't it?) Well, there's also more than one way to capture Web analytics. In fact, as you'll discover in this part, there are three ways to be exact. Each has its pros and cons — and all three together offer synergies that no individual tool offers alone. That's why you need to know the difference between client-side, server-side, and hosted solutions.

But that's not all you need to know as you assess tool types. There are dozens, even scores, of Web analytics vendors on the market. Some offer free tools. Others offer low-cost tools. And still others charge a small fortune for their ability to tell you just about anything you could ever possibly want to know about your visitors. You'll find even niche solutions that measure RSS feeds and let you eavesdrop, so to speak, on visitor navigation — live.

Part III: Searching for Statistical Treasure

After you settle on a Web analytics tool that suits your specific needs, you can start searching for statistical treasure. First, though, you have to take out the *trash:* that is, the data generated from non-human users, referrer spam, and other data that block the view of your gold mine. In this part, you'll discover a dizzying array of KPIs. We'll help you figure out which ones matter most to you. We'll also roll into the real world of shopping cart abandonment — the four-letter word of e-commerce — and talk about conversion funnels. (Don't worry, you'll understand all this and more as you read Part III.)

And your treasure hunt doesn't end there. We also show you how to explore search engine and non-search engine traffic as you identify who you can thank for sending visitors your way. Then you'll see how to analyze your data so you can get better acquainted with your visitors and the pages they love to return to again and again.

Part IV: Knowledge Is Power — Making Analytics Work for You

If knowledge is power, Web analytics offers the thrust of a jet engine, taking you soaring above the clouds so you can see your site from 10,000 feet. Then it swoops down and lets you land on individual pages to see exactly what's happening on ground level. In this part, you'll read how to make Web analytics work for you. It all starts with chronicling your Web analytics history. You don't need to be a historian to appreciate this data. In fact, you might be surprised by some of the keyphrases that drive traffic — and it could open the door to a whole new set of customers and partners. Or, you might discover that it's time to revisit your online advertising strategy. We give you actionable information to help you decide. Finally, we demonstrate some practical ways to fine-tune your Web site by using your data to guide page, section, and site redesigns that help reduce shopping cart abandonment. What more could a Web site owner dream of?

Part V: The Part of Tens

All *For Dummies* books have The Part of Tens. In this part, you'll find ten myths, mistakes, and pitfalls that you want to avoid at all costs. You'll also discover a list of reasons why Web analytics will revolutionize e-business. Finally, we leave you with some Web analytics best practices that will help you avoid those myths, mistakes, and pitfalls in the first place. The rest is up to you.

Appendix

Don't forget to check out the Appendix, where you'll find a Web analytics glossary that will serve you well regardless of which vendor you choose.

Icons Used in This Book

Like all *For Dummies* books, this book uses icons to highlight certain paragraphs and to alert you to especially useful information. Here's the lowdown on what those icons mean:

A Tip icon means that we're giving you a valuable tidbit of information that can help you on your journey or provide some extra insight into the concepts being discussed.

When you see the Remember icon, take note. These mean that we're offering information that's worth remembering.

The Technical Stuff icon alerts you that you are about to enter the Geek Zone. If you'd rather not venture into that realm, simply skip it. If you want to know the every last detail, though, you'll love these sections.

The Warning icon does just that — it warns you. This icon helps you avoid common mistakes, misconceptions, myths, and pitfalls. The bomb symbol sort of gets your attention, doesn't it? Be sure to look for it so you don't do more harm than good as you wade through the world of Web analytics.

Part I

Getting Started with Web Analytics

The 5th Wave   By Rich Tennant

"The top line represents our revenue, the middle line is our inventory, and the bottom line shows the rate of my hair loss over the same period."

In this part . . .

The basics of Web analytics are, well, anything but basic. Learning the ins and outs of Web analytics software may not be as daunting as understanding complex computer programming languages — but it's not as easy as firing off a document in Microsoft Word, either. The Web analytics guru is one part statistician, one part psychologist, and one part prophet. The good news is you can glean valuable insights without being any one of the three.

This part starts with the basics. We begin by explaining what Web analytics is, who should use it, and why you can't afford not to use this seemingly all-knowing software in today's competitive online environment. Whether you are a small but growing e-commerce vendor, a successful and growing affiliate marketer, a professional online lead generator, a media/content portal, blogger — or anyone else with any other type of Web site we didn't mention — you'll be fascinated to learn what Web analytics software reveals about your visitors.

The only catch is you'll have to learn a new language — the language of Web analytics. That's why we spell out the ABCs of analytics in clear terms you can understand. You'll discover the difference between hits, pageviews, and unique visitors. You'll learn to decipher commonly used acronyms like CRT, KPI, and PPC. You'll even get familiar with some Internet marketing lingo. There is no industry standard terminology, so interpreting Web analytics can be confusing even when you think you speak the language fluently. But don't worry, we've got you covered.

This part of the book also gives you an opportunity to get your hands dirty with Web data. We'll show you how to find your stats, tell you what to do if your Web host doesn't provide them, and walk you through some of the basics of analyzing your visitor behavior. Finally, we'll help you set some goals to keep in mind as you begin to enter the world of Web analytics.

Chapter 1

Understanding Web Analytics

A long time ago, in a World Wide Web far, far away, *Web counters* — those rudimentary software programs that indicate the number of online visitors — were the only way to tally how many eyeballs viewed your Web site. You knew nothing about where those visitors came from, what brought them there, what they did while they were there, or when they left. You could experience the thrill of watching the Web counter jump from 100 to 1,000 in January but then drive yourself crazy trying to repeat the performance in February.

Today, even free *Web analytics tools* — software that analyzes the behavior of site visitors — offer the nitty-gritty details about what, when, from where, and why visitors come to your site. And top-dollar solutions, with their ultra-sophisticated technologies, are getting so detailed that you may soon know what your visitor ate for breakfast. (Okay, not really, but an online grocer could at least collect data about what visitors like to eat by analyzing their *clickstreams,* the recorded paths that a visitor takes through your Web site.) So as far as the Web goes, George Orwell's prophecies are true: Big Brother is indeed watching.

The overarching goal of monitoring your Web analytics is to make improvements to both your promotional initiatives and your Web site design. If you know how visitors find your site and then how they subsequently use your site, you can take measured steps to make the most of your promotional campaigns and your visual presentation. The bottom line is this: The easier it is for visitors to find your site — and the more comfortable they feel while they cruise around it — the better your chances to convert that traffic into paying customers and repeat visitors.

This chapter gives you an overview of Web analytics, what these tools measure, who should use them, why they are valuable in your quest to generate revenue, and what you could be losing by not paying attention to the wealth of visitor data that this software compiles.

Web Analytics: Why Bother?

Maybe you need a little more convincing. After all, there is an admitted learning curve with Web analytics programs, and you're already undoubtedly busy enough just keeping your site updated, much less dissecting statistics, charts, and graphs. Why bother, you ask? The answer is clear: Understanding Web analytics can unlock business strategies that pay dividends even while you sleep.

There are already millions and millions of Web sites, and that number grows day by day. An August 2006 Netcraft survey reveals more than 92 million Web sites are up. Netcraft is an Internet services company that provides security services and research data and analysis. That's 4 million Web sites more than in July and 8 million more than in June. It's more than likely that thousands — or even hundreds of thousands — of Web sites are competing for the same traffic you are. Web analytics can help you build strategies that make you stand out from the pack.

Who should use Web analytics?

Anyone who hopes to use the World Wide Web to generate income or leads should use Web analytics. Major e-commerce brands use Web analytics data to make real-time changes to their sites. Affiliate marketers use analytics to discern what programs are paying off as well as which ones merely take up space. Online lead generators tap Web analytics to measure how keywords are working, and information portals depend on these metrics to offer traffic figures to their advertisers.

Consider the following questions to determine whether you should invest in Web analytics software:

- Is my Web site a channel for revenue generation?
- Do I have high traffic counts but low conversions?
- Am I investing in paid-search campaigns through Google, Yahoo!, or some other search engine?
- Am I actively pursuing link building campaigns and link exchanges?
- Do I engage in e-mail marketing?
- Am I planning a site redesign?

Browser blues?

When you look at the Browser section of your Web analytics report (as shown in the figure), you might be surprised to see how many browser brands there really are. Most people use Microsoft Internet Explorer or Mozilla Firefox, but many others are available, including Safari, Opera, and Netscape. What you need to know is that your Web analytics report lists these browsers, in part, so you can make sure your site design is optimized for the most common browser. Sometimes a Web site looks much different on an Apple browser than it does on an open source browser or a Microsoft browser. In fact, the site can look skewed and jumbled on some browsers. Make sure that your designer tests the site on the most popular browsers so you can make the best possible impression.

You can read more about the browser section of your report in Chapter 9.

Statistics of freebookclubs.com (2007-02) - Microsoft Internet Explorer

File   Edit   View   Favorites   Tools   Help

Browsers (Top 10) – Full list/Versions – Unknown

Browsers	Grabber	Hits	Percent
MS Internet Explorer	No	67204	90.9 %
Firefox	No	3879	5.2 %
Unknown	?	995	1.3 %
Safari	No	909	1.2 %
Netscape	No	438	0.5 %
LibWWW	No	235	0.3 %
Mozilla	No	158	0.2 %
Opera	No	42	0 %
Links	No	7	0 %
Konqueror	No	4	0 %
Others		4	0 %

Internet

If you answered "yes" to any one of the preceding questions, you should begin to use Web analytics today. The truth is that your competition is already using Web analytics. You could be missing golden opportunities to turn the traffic you've worked so hard to generate into sales, subscribers, or members.

You can't afford not to invest in this software. Neglecting Web analytics in today's information-based society is akin to working in a retail store wearing a blindfold and earplugs. You might make some sales just because the doors are open, but you won't know who your customers are, where they came from, or how long they stayed — you get the picture.

Why you should use Web analytics

Here is a list of the top ten compelling reasons to use Web analytics:

1. **You can identify which site referrers generate the most traffic and revenue.** The *site referrer,* or *referring page,* is the URL of the previous Web page from which a link was followed. This is a good way to identify which Web site owners you should foster relationships with, and which ones you can afford to forget about. See Figure 1-1 to see how your Referrer report looks in the free server-side analytics application AWStats.

2. **You can determine what products have the highest browse-to-buy ratios.** That way, you can get rid of products — or content, in the case of an informational portal — that has the lowest revenue-generating potential.

3. **See which campaigns work — and which ones don't.** You can cut off promotional campaigns that aren't working and beef up campaigns that bear fruit.

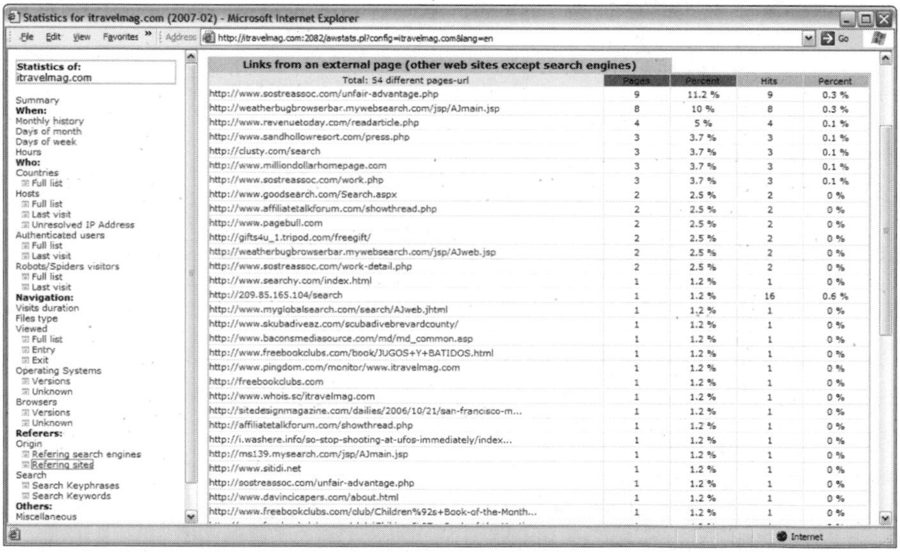

Figure 1-1: Referrer report from AWStats.

4. **You can measure the impact of the online channel on your overall business.** If your e-commerce Web site is generating more revenues than your bricks-and-mortar business, then it may be time to close up shop and concentrate all your efforts on the Web. If your Web site is generat-

ing more leads than other forms of advertising, then you may want to sink more into the former and less into the latter. By contrast, if your Web site is not making much of an impact on your business, then you need to consider some strategies to boost traffic or convert the traffic you already have. It could be poor design, poor content, or just poor marketing efforts. Your Web analytics program can give you some clues.

5. **You can discover which visitor groups are most likely to become customers, subscribers, or members.** Then you can adjust your marketing efforts accordingly.

6. **You can analyze your visitor clickstreams.** From this information, you can make changes to your site *hierarchy* (how you arrange your Web site) to improve your rate of *conversion*. Conversion occurs when you close the deal — when you convert a visitor to a buyer, subscriber, or member.

7. **You can identify cross-selling opportunities.** Use this information to increase sales to the same customer by introducing other similar or complementary products. Amazon has championed this concept in the online space as it uses massive stores of analytics data to identify and recommend related products, as shown in Figure 1-2.

Figure 1-2:
Amazon.com page, which recommends related products.

8. **You can determine the effect of adding new content to the site.** If the new content you added causes visitors to stay on your site longer and/or increases your conversion rates, then your wordsmithing is to be congratulated. If the new content has the opposite effect, revert back to what you were doing — quick!

9. **Track the keywords that visitors search for within your site.** Then you can develop new product lines, services, or content based on those keywords.

10. **Find errors in your site.** With this information in hand, you can eradicate errors that could frustrate customers, such as broken links and pages that no longer exist.

Of course, there are many other benefits to keeping tabs on customer behavior, and in the end, careful attention to your analytics, and actions based on that data will result in converting more visitors into customers, subscribers, or members. When the right analytics tools are in place, you will have new information to work with daily, or even in real-time depending on how sophisticated your Web analytics software is.

The importance of benchmarking

You won't know how far you've come if you don't record where you were — *benchmarking* — and compare that with where you are now. Before you invest your time, energy, and money into generating more traffic, be sure to set specific goals based on the available metrics. For example, if you want to

- ✔ **Generate more international traffic:** Record how many countries you reach.

- ✔ **Boost your weekend traffic:** Record the average daily visitors before you begin.

- ✔ **Beef up your newsletter subscriptions:** Tally your current subscribers now.

Benchmarking your starting point allows you to measure your specific goals. For more on benchmarking, see Chapter 15.

Web Analytics 101

Web analytics isn't about gathering data for the sake of gathering data any more than a police detective collects clues for the sake of collecting clues. In both cases, the goal is to solve a mystery. Instead of detailing criminal activities at the scene of a crime, Web analytics details visitor activities on a Web site.

There are two sides to your Web analytics story; the software and the human element:

- ✔ **Web analytics software** collects data on Web site users' behavior.
- ✔ **The human element** involves sifting through data about a visitor's online experience to determine which site changes could improve that experience.

Maybe you've stumbled upon your Web analytics tools by accident and couldn't make heads or tails of the charts, graphs, lists, and icons. Or maybe you never even knew about a way to go behind the scenes and examine a visitor's pathway through your site.

Either way, if you aren't sure what to measure or how to start thinking about Web metrics, you can't benefit from the valuable clues that they provide. Taking a moment to review the basic language of Web analytics software can put you on a path to knowledge that leads to power.

Thinking like a journalist

You've probably heard the journalist's rule to tell the reader who, what, when, where, and why. That's just what Web analytics does at its most fundamental level. The following sections outline the basics of what you can expect to glean from your Web analytics software.

Who

The Who category gives you the inside scoop. First, you can see what countries visitors came from. This is where you see the *world* in the World Wide Web. You might be surprised to discover that your visitors live in such far away places as Singapore, Algeria, or Switzerland. This category might also reveal the Internet service provider (ISP) of the visitor as well as whether the visit is from an authenticated user or a search engine spider.

- ✔ **Authenticated users** are users who were required to log in, such as subscribers or members.
- ✔ Also known as *Web crawlers, robots,* or *bots,* a **search engine spider** is an automated script or program that browses the Web. Search engines use spiders to gather up-to-date data as they index the Web.

Benefit: Knowing who your visitors are can help you cater to their specific needs. If most of your users are members or subscribers, you can do member polling and make changes to your product, service, or content offerings accordingly. If most of your users are from Japan, you may consider translating your site into Japanese or making design changes that appeal to their cultural preferences. If most of your visitors are search engine spiders, you've got major issues! You need to launch some online and perhaps offline promotional campaigns to get the word out. You can get some ideas of the different types of online strategies you could employ, along with tips on how to measure their effectiveness, in Chapter 16.

What

The What category tells you what the visitor did during his time on your site. You can discover how long the visitor stayed, what types of files he viewed (images, static pages, JavaScript files, and so on), what specific URLs were visited, and which operating systems and browsers were used to navigate your site.

Benefit: Knowing what the visitor did on your site can help you understand what his interests are. If a high percentage of your visitors spent most of their time on a handful of pages, then you can quickly discern what their interests are and add more of the same to your site. If most of your visitors are downloading one white paper over all the others you've posted or reading certain articles more than others, you can safely assume that you've struck content gold. If your visitors are spending lots of time on your FAQ pages, you might conclude that they are confused and need better online customer support. The point is to pay attention to what visitors did on your site to look for trends — positive or negative — and make any necessary adjustments to your site.

When

The When category tells you just that — when visitors traveled across your virtual domain. You can see this data broken down by the number of unique visitors, how many visits as well as how many pages and how many hits were tracked each month, each day of the month, and each hour of the day (see Figure 1-3). You can also break this data down to determine which days of the week and which times of day see the most traffic.

Figure 1-3: Visitor report broken down by time of day.

Hours	Pages	Hits	Bandwidth	Hours	Pages	Hits	Bandwidth
00	476	2414	9.57 MB	12	705	4450	16.45 MB
01	374	1760	7.46 MB	13	817	5015	18.16 MB
02	260	1274	5.05 MB	14	808	4881	18.49 MB
03	99	443	1.85 MB	15	775	4884	23.41 MB
04	99	542	1.97 MB	16	640	4044	15.78 MB
05	105	570	2.19 MB	17	713	4722	17.63 MB
06	225	653	2.96 MB	18	766	4941	17.68 MB
07	195	1038	4.03 MB	19	792	4427	18.07 MB
08	370	1966	8.77 MB	20	725	4380	17.93 MB
09	440	2767	10.11 MB	21	655	3914	16.26 MB
10	697	3638	14.83 MB	22	682	3912	15.17 MB
11	616	3677	14.54 MB	23	557	3563	13.01 MB

What's up with error codes?

If you're alarmed at the number of *HTTP (HyperText Transfer Protocol)* error codes you find in your Web analytics report (shown in the figure), don't be. Common HTTP error codes include

- ✔ `Document Not Found`: This error occurs if the file that a visitor is trying to access has been moved or deleted.

- ✔ `Too many users`: This error usually means too many visitors were trying to access your site at the same time or that you have run out of bandwidth, in either case, you should speak with your Web hosting company to determine what you can do to remedy these errors.

- ✔ `Internal server error`: This error requires a little more investigation; it could be caused by any number of reasons. Although this metric is not included in your other charts and does not skew your overall numbers, you need to identify and correct these errors because you could be frustrating visitors, losing sales opportunities, or both.

You can read more about identifying and correcting error codes in Chapter 10.

http://freebookclubs.com:2082 - Statistics of freebookclubs.com (2007-02) - Microsoft Internet Explorer

File Edit View Favorites Tools Help

HTTP Error codes			
HTTP Error codes*	Hits	Percent	Bandwidth
404 Document Not Found	403	82.4 %	4.52 MB
206 Partial Content	74	15.1 %	334.08 KB
403 Forbidden	5	1 %	0
301 Moved permanently (redirect)	3	0.6 %	768 Bytes
302 Moved temporarily (redirect)	3	0.6 %	667 Bytes
400 Bad Request	1	0.2 %	0

* Codes shown here gave hits or traffic "not viewed" by visitors, so they are not included in other charts.

Internet

Benefit: Knowing when your visitors enter your site can help you track the effectiveness of special promotions or seasonal sales.

Where

The Where category tells you where the visitor came from. These are as *site referrers*. Referrers could be search engines, Web ring partners, link partners, affiliate marketers, or a host of others. You can read more about site referrers in Chapter 9.

Benefit: Knowing where your visitor came from helps you strategize link partner and paid-search campaigns. You can also learn more about your visitors by seeing what types of sites they frequent.

Why

The Why category tells what drew them to your site. That could include site referrers (such as search engines) or keywords and keyphrases that visitors used to find you in those search engines.

Benefit: Knowing why the visitor came — and what she was looking for — gives you the knowledge you need to make adjustments to your products, services, and content.

As you put on your journalist's cap, be sure to do what any good journalist would do on a breaking news story: Take notes. Although your Web analytics software will chronicle and store your site's data, you'll want a quick reference of the top visitors, keywords, and site referrers at the tip of your fingers so you can compare them with a glance to identify trends.

The language of Web analytics

As you venture into the world of Web analytics, you'll quickly notice that it has a language of its own. You might even feel as if you've been submersed in a foreign culture without a translator as you begin to hear words like *hits, traffic,* and *sessions* that have totally different meanings online than they do offline.

Like any new language, the best way to become fluent is to begin with the fundamentals. In Web analytics, those fundamentals — or core metrics — are found in the five Ws in the journalist's toolbox. Specifically, the heart of Web analytics is captured in the following terms:

- ✔ **Hits**
- ✔ **Pageviews**
- ✔ **Visits**
- ✔ **Unique visitors**
- ✔ **Referrers**
- ✔ **Keywords and keyphrases**

Take a look at each one of these terms and what they mean in the big picture.

For more on the language and terminology of Web analytics, be sure to check out the Appendix at the end of this book.

Hits

People love to boast about this metric. A *hit,* or impression, is created when your Web server delivers a file to a visitor's browser. PDF, sound files, Word documents, and images are a few examples of files that generate hits. A request for a page with five images would count as six hits: one hit for the page itself plus one hit for each of the five images. This has been a popular metric with sites hoping to score advertising, but it can be deceiving. See Chapter 2 for an in-depth look at common terminology confusion.

Pageviews

A *pageview* is recorded each time a visitor views a Web page on your site. This metric reveals how well your site captured the interest of your visitor. Simple analytics programs divide the number of visitors by the number of pageviews to determine the average number of pages each visitor viewed. If that number is low, you might need to rethink your content, design, or hierarchy.

Visits

Sometimes called a *session* or *user session,* a *visit* describes the activity of an individual user on your site. You could also say that a visit is a series of views by the same visitor. It's interesting to note that most analytics tools will end the session if the visitor remains idle for 30 minutes although that time limit can often be adjusted in your software's options.

Unique visitors

The *unique visitors* metric represents the number of individual people who visit your Web site. Each individual is counted only once, so if a person visits your site five times in the reporting period, that behavior might count as five sessions but only as one unique visitor. Most analytics programs track unique visitors by their *IP address,* which is the unique string of numbers that identifies a computer or server on the Internet.

Some users are assigned dynamic IP addresses from the ISP. That means that their IP address changes daily, or sometimes even every few hours or minutes. These types of users might skew your number of unique visitors slightly.

Site referrers

The *site referrer,* or *referring page,* is the URL of the previous Web page from which a link was followed. A referrer could be a search engine, a blog, a banner ad, an e-mail, an affiliate marketer, a Web ring, a link partner, or some other Web site. Your Web analytics program will record the exact URL of the site that referred traffic so you that can measure the success of your various traffic-building initiatives.

Keywords and keyphrases

Keywords and *keyphrases* are appropriately named because they hold the key to potentially significant traffic. People use these words to search for products, services, and information on the Web. You can pay search engines to display your advertisement in the results of a user's search based on the keywords and keyphrases you choose. If you are selling helium balloons, for example, you might pay Google to display a link to your Web site when searchers enters the keyphrase *helium balloons* into that engine.

Don't wait until the end of the month to view your Web analytics report. You could be losing valuable opportunities to convert customers — and you could be wasting your paid-search ad dollars. By monitoring your Web analytics software weekly — or even daily — you can reap the full potential of this intelligent tool.

The Bandwidth report

Your Web host probably has a limit to the amount of *bandwidth* (the data that is transferred to and from your Web site) that you can use in a given month. Web analytics tells you precisely how many *bytes* (a unit of measurement for data) your site is sending to and receiving from users. The bottom line is this: The more traffic you get, the more bandwidth you need. If you run out of bandwidth, your visitors might not be able to view your Web site. Another metric

in the Bandwidth report (shown in the figure) is bytes per second (bps). This measures the average transfer rate. If your transfer rate is set too low by your hosting provider, your Web pages might load very slowly — and your visitors might get impatient and leave.

You can read more about the bandwidth report in Chapter 3.

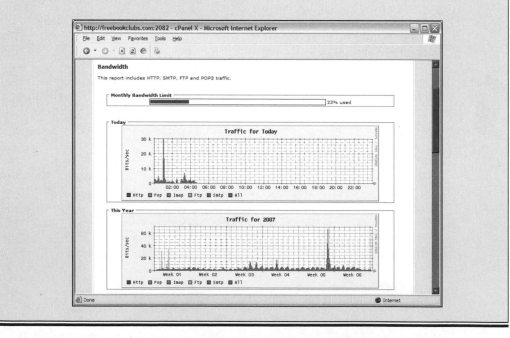

Chapter 2

Steering Clear of Common Terminology Confusion

· ·

· ·

When you apply for a driver's license, the state requires you to pass a written exam before you receive permission to hit the road. The Powers That Be give you a thick study guide that defines every sign, symbol, and flashing light on the highways and byways. The goal is to help you steer clear of accidents so you can get where you want to go safely — even in heavy rush hour traffic that can demand split-second decision making.

Just like a vehicle, your Web analytics software has a dashboard, of sorts, that displays important information about your Web site. Instead of oil, temperature, and gas, though, it offers information on visitors, length of stay, and site referrers. The *site referrer,* or *referring page,* is the URL of the previous Web page from which a link was followed.

Of course, most Web analytics control panels are far more complex than even the highest-tech car dashboard. The more sophisticated the software, the more difficult it is to navigate the charts, graphs, and other data that unlocks the secrets to visitor behavior. If you don't understand the terminology that describes the various Web measurements, you could be in for a bumpy ride as you make changes to your site based on misunderstandings of what the data really means — as well as what it doesn't mean.

Indeed, you have a lot to master about graphs, charts, symbols, and terminology as you venture into the world of Web analytics. You won't find this stuff in your friendly dictionary, and little progress has been made toward industry standard analytics language. Each vendor uses its own terminology. Think of this chapter as your study guide that defines common signs, symbols, and flashing lights on the road to successful Web analytics interpretation. With definitions, synonyms, acronyms, and the like, you can be sure to choose the right tools and use them well.

For more definitions and descriptions of the language and terminology of Web analytics, be sure to check out the Appendix at the end of this book.

Hitting the Terminology Targets

In Chapter 1, we outline some of the most common Web analytics terms, such as *hits, pageviews, visits,* and *site referrers.* Those are the fundamentals of Web metrics, as shown in Figure 2-1, but understanding these terms will hardly make you fluent in the language of analytics. In fact, without a thorough understanding of Web analytics vocabulary, you could be throwing your dart at the wrong board.

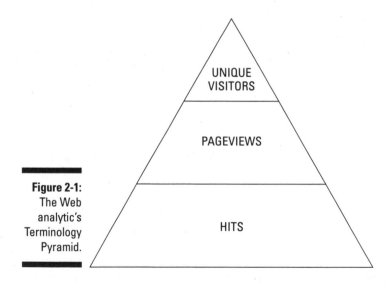

Figure 2-1:
The Web analytic's Terminology Pyramid.

Have you ever heard anyone brag about how many hits his Web site gets? A *hit,* or *impression,* is created when your Web server delivers a file to a visitor's browser. Advertising-supported sites, such as online magazines, boast the loudest and longest about this metric, but using this as a target is deceptive at best. As for *pageviews* (a record of each time a visitor views a Web page on your site), well, this metric at least hits the target. However, if you want your measurement dart to hit the bulls-eye, you need to zero in on *unique visitors,* which is the actual number of individual users who came to the Web site.

Searching for standards

Web analytics is a rare segment of the software industry because no hard and fast industry standards currently exist. That's not surprising, seeing as how it took several years for the industry to even settle on a name for itself. (Vendors toyed with monikers like *e-metrics* and *Web metrics* before deciding on *Web analytics*.) Surprisingly, debate is still ongoing as to what should be measured as well as little agreement on the best way to calculate the measurements or even what to call them. Sure, you'll find some cross-over between Web analytics vendors, but the lack of an industry standard has admittedly caused terminology confusion. The good news is several organizations are developing Web analytics standards. Britain's Audit Bureau of Circulation (www.abc.org.uk), the Joint Industry Committee for Web Standards (www.jicwebs.org) and the Web Analytics Association (www.webanalyticsasso-ciation.org) are all working to set clear definitions for this relatively young industry.

Hits: The most deceptive stat of all

Hits are the most deceptive stat of them all, and here's why. Each page on your Web site includes photographs, text, graphics, sound files, PDFs, or some other file type. Thus, a request for a page with five images counts as six hits: one hit for the page itself plus one hit for each of the images. Thirty-thousand visitors could easily rack up a million hits in a hurry on a catalog-style site that serves up 30 or 40 photos per page.

If you are trying to impress advertisers with big online "circulation" numbers, you would be tempted to let them know your hits. Be careful, though, to not deceive yourself in the process. Breaking the million-hit barrier is something to celebrate, but the inflated figures could cause you to rest on your laurels while your competition continues to launch initiatives that bring more unique visitors to their sites. More visitors mean more opportunities to make a sale, woo a member, or generate a lead. From that perspective, hits ultimately don't mean much.

Measuring the success of your Web site based on hits is like putting cheap gas in a luxury sports car: It could backfire. When you look at your Web analytics dashboard, shown in Figure 2-2, concentrate on the number of unique visitors rather than the deceptive, inflated number of hits.

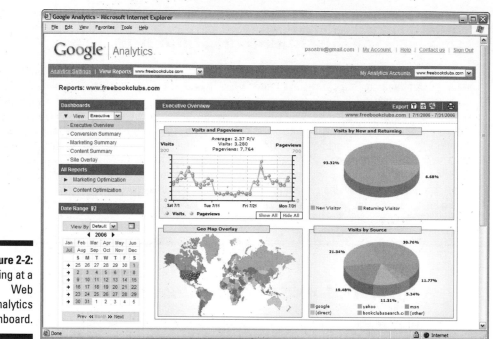

Figure 2-2:
Looking at a
Web
analytics
dashboard.

Pageviews: Getting closer to the truth

Pageviews can offer valuable information. A *pageview* reveals how well your site captured the interest of your visitor. This metric becomes the foundation for tracking a visitor's *clickstream* (the recorded path, page by page, of the pages a visitor requested while navigating through a Web site).

However, industry experts disagree about what constitutes a pageview and how this metric should be interpreted and applied. The Interactive Advertising Bureau (IAB; www.iab.net) defines a pageview as "when the page is actually seen by the user." In the next breath, it notes that pageviews can only be estimated because you can't discern whether the visitor actually viewed the page or merely clicked through it. The IAB recommends measuring *page displays* — when a page is successfully displayed on the visitor's computer screen.

Any way you define it, pageviews still get closer to the truth about a Web site's popularity. Pageviews clearly reveal the popularity of certain pages or sections of the Web site. If a shoe retailer's boot section receives the most pageviews, it becomes obvious that either boots are coming back into style or that the retailer's site offers competitive prices, selection, and so on. That allows the retailer to examine the market and tweak his offerings or advertising to leverage the popularity of those products.

 You might sell vacuums, but don't look at your pageviews in one. In other words, put the pageview metrics in perspective. Dig a little deeper to discover why certain pages are drawing visitors. Find out what referrers are sending traffic to those particular pages. A retailer might discover that he needs to increase promotion efforts for certain *landing pages* — the specific Web page where a visitor first arrives in response to a search or advertising campaign. An information portal might find out that current events drive traffic to special content sections and need a Subscribe Now button to convert that traffic.

Unique visitors: The undisputable facts

As we state earlier, tracking hits can make it seem like you have 5, 10, or even 50 times as much traffic as you really drive. Pageviews are good for determining how popular your site content is after users find your site, but they still aren't an accurate representation of how many people visit your site. By contrast, *unique visitors* represent the undisputable facts.

The three faces of unique visitors

✔ **Anonymous:** Not all unique visitors are created equal; some browse your Web site in relative obscurity. Your Web analytics software can tell you where they came from, which pages they visited, and some other standard metrics, but information related to their location or network is hidden. These anonymous visitors purposely hide behind *proxies* (computers that allow multiple users to surf the Internet using their IP address in order to hide the users' real IP address and maintain privacy) that do the following:

✔ *Cloak their IP address.* An *IP address* is a unique numeric code assigned by the user's Internet service provider (ISP).

   and

✔ *Disable cookies. Cookies* are small text files that allow a Web server to store information about a visitor and recognize them when they return.

✔ **Partially anonymous:** Other visitors are partially anonymous. They might not be hiding, but they aren't volunteering any personal information, either. If you don't require them to log in or give them an incentive to ante up their personal data, they will remain in the Web analytics shadows.

✔ **Known:** The "end all be all" are known visitors. Known visitors can be segmented into demographic segments. You can view their shopping history, and you can target them with special offers.

Unique visitors are the purest measurement of Web site traffic because an individual visitor — regardless of how many times he returns to your site during a reporting period, how many pages he views, or how many images are on a page — counts as an individual user.

Search engine spiders — programs or automated scripts that crawl the Web to update search engine indexes — are not included when calculating unique users, pageviews, or hits by the majority of analytics applications. However, look out for smaller, less-advanced applications that don't automatically exclude this traffic.

With the right analytics tools, you can measure unique visitors during any reporting period that suits you — by the day, week, or month. The unique visitors metric is important because it clearly communicates the bottom line about your traffic-generating efforts. You can understand, in no uncertain terms, whether you wooed more visitors to your site in February than you did in January, or if you attract more people during your Friday promotion than you do on an average weekday. Understanding unique visitors is the beginning of Web analytics wisdom.

The ABCs of Web Analytics

What is abandonment? Why is the average lifetime value important? What does KPI stand for? With plenty of acronyms and words like *dashboard* that have different meanings in the online and offline worlds, making the most of your Web analytics experience demands learning the ABCs of this tech terminology. Some terms have synonyms, so one Web analytics user might call a 404 error a *Page Cannot be Found* error, while another calls it a *broken page*. Some people prefer the word *crawler,* while others insist on using the term *spider.*

What's the meaning of this?

People who learn English often complain that our language has too many different meanings for the same words. In Web analytics, you'll run into your fair share of these. *Abandonment, session,* and *navigation* are fairly self-explanatory, but you'll find synonyms galore. With no industry standard Web analytics vocabulary, terms used in Software X could mean something much different than terms used in Software Y. Take *frequency, latency,* and *recency* as examples. All three terms are used to reveal the number of days since a visitor's most recent visit during a reporting period. As you choose your software vendor — and as you begin to decipher data — be sure that you're speaking the same language as your application.

Web analytics vocabulary is extensive and continues to evolve as Web metrics analysts more clearly define their measurements and as technology advances to offer deeper capabilities. However, if you take the time to review and understand these common nouns, verbs, and adjectives you will be well on your way to understanding and unleashing the power of Web analytics for your site.

Some terms, like *abandonment* or *opt-in,* describe what a visitor did on your site. *Abandonment* means just what it says: The visitor left your site in the midst of a transaction. Terms like *bounce rate* may stir images of how many times a star basketball player dribbles before passing the rock to another player. In the analytics arena, however, the *bounce rate* is a metric that shows the percentage of entrances on any individual page that resulted in the visitor's immediate exit from the site. Take a look at Figure 2-3 to see how Google Analytics displays bounce rates for your Top 5 entry pages.

Figure 2-3:
Viewing the
bounce rate
for your
entry pages.

Take a moment to review this list of the most common terms that describe visitor behavior on a Web site.

✔ **After-click tracking (ACT):** Also called *path analysis, clickstream,* or *navigational analysis,* this is simply a study of the paths that visitors take through your site. This detailed assessment begins with the referring page and ends with the exit page.

- **Clickthrough rate (CTR):** Typically, this metric is used to calculate how often a banner ad is clicked compared with how many times it is viewed, and it helps indicate how effective a particular banner ad is. This metric can also be used to indicate the rate at which visitors clickthrough from one page on a Web site to another.

- **Conversion:** This is what it's all about. *Conversion* occurs when you close the deal — when you convert a visitor to a buyer, subscriber, or member.

- **Entry page:** Sometimes called the *landing page,* the *entry page* is just what it sounds like: the page at which the visitor entered your site. Your Web analytics tools list the entry pages based how many visitors viewed that page.

- **Exit page:** The *exit page* marks the point at which the navigational path within the site ends. In other words, it's where the customer exits the site.

- **Navigation:** This describes clicking from one page to another within a Web site, or sometimes from one Web site to another.

- **Session:** Also called a *visit,* a *session* is the time from when a visitor logs on to your site to when he leaves. A site might receive 50,000 unique visitors but have 65,000 sessions. That just means that the some users visited more than once.

- **Visit duration:** This is a record of how long an individual stayed on your site. Sessions are measured in time, often in increments ranging from 0–30 seconds, 30 seconds–2 minutes, 2–5minutes, 5–15 minutes, 15–30 minutes, 30 minutes–1 hour, and 1 hour-plus. This log divides the number of visits by number of minutes visitors spent on your site to determine the average length of stay.

Much ado about landing pages

You don't have to wade through the world of Web analytics long before you start hearing about *landing pages,* which are specific Web pages that a visitor reaches after clicking a link from a search engine or an advertisement. Landing pages are typically associated with promotional campaigns. Instead of driving visitors to your home page and relying on them to navigate through the site to find the products they are looking for, your basketball gear promotion drives them to the exact page on the site that had the latest and greatest basketball equipment. Measuring the traffic to and behavior on your landing pages is critical so that you can make changes that lead to greater conversions. An entire subindustry is forming around landing page optimization, just as it did around search engine optimization.

Mastering Internet Marketing Lingo

Online advertising also has a language all its own. The Wiley book, *Search Engine Optimization For Dummies,* (Peter Kent) goes into great detail about this topic. However, before you can begin to optimize your site for search engines, you need to understand the lingo of the search world as well as the online advertising and Internet marketing initiatives that populate it. Here are a few of the most common terms that Web analytics masters use to describe these measurements:

- **Acquisition:** Just like it sounds, *acquisition* is attracting customers to a Web site by using various advertising and marketing strategies.

- **Affiliate marketing:** This is an advertising system in which Web site owners, search engine marketers, and e-mail marketers promote companies in return for a commission. This commission is often either a percentage of revenue or a flat fee, sometimes called a *bounty.* When a visitor clicks an advertisement, he is taken to the merchant site. If the visitor makes a purchase from the merchant, the affiliate receives a commission.

- **Banner ad:** A *banner ad* is an advertisement that is displayed on a Web page. Some banners allow visitors to click through the advertiser's site. This allows you to measure the effectiveness of the banner.

- **Keyword:** These are terms entered into the search box of a search engine.

- **Organic search:** This is a search that retrieves results by indexing pages based on content and keyword relevancy.

- **Pay per click (PPC):** Also called *paid search,* this method retrieves listings based on who paid the most money for keywords to appear at the top of the search results.

- **Search engine marketing (SEM):** This is a method that seeks to increases the ranking and visibility of a Web site in search engine results pages. This includes creating paid search campaigns.

- **Search engine optimization (SEO):** This is a method of improving the rankings for relevant keywords in search results by making changes to the content or navigational structure of a Web site.

- **Segment:** This is a customer group as defined by a user's activities on a Web site or other strategic data. Segmenting allows Web sites to target their visitors more effectively based on specified behaviors.

Return on investment

The bottom line on Web analytics is *return on investment (ROI)*. After all, this software isn't measuring behavior for the heck of it. The goal is to tweak your site and its content to drive more conversions. The greater the number of conversions, the greater the return on your online investment. Here are several ROI terms that you want to get straight when considering how your online strategies are paying off:

✔ **ROMI:** You can determine the Return on Marketing Investment (ROMI) by looking at site referrers and clickstreams of visitors who came in through marketing efforts such as link exchanges, posting to newsgroups and blogs, or sponsorships of online events.

✔ **ROAS:** The Return on Advertising Spend measures your conversions stemming from banner ads and paid search.

✔ **GRP:** Gross Rating Point offers the percentage of your target audience that an ad reaches. If you aren't careful, your return could fail to cover your spending. Web analytics can save you time, money, and financial headaches by making it crystal clear what is working — and what is not.

Defining Actionable Data

Actionable data offers an accurate foundation on which to make decisions about changes to your Web site, search engine marketing, or customer relationship management. Here are some terms that are associated with digging for the hidden statistical treasure in your Web analytics software:

✔ **Aggregate data:** This is a summary of the information that your Web analytics program collects. It is presented in groups rather than individual-level statistics.

✔ **Average lifetime value (ALV):** This metric defines an individual visitor's lifetime value in monetary terms by tracking past orders. This could be a helpful metric when determining to whom to send private sales or special discount offers.

✔ **Benchmark:** A *benchmark* is a clearly defined point of reference from which measurements can be made. Benchmarks become standards by which you can judge the effectiveness of your advertising and marketing initiatives.

✔ **Filters:** Using filters is a method of narrowing the scope of a report by defining statistical ranges or data types that should or should not be included.

✔ **Key performance indicator (KPI):** KPIs illustrate how well a site is performing against goals. You can read much more about KPIs in Chapter 11.

✔ **Log file:** This kind of file records transactions that occurred on the Web server. Log file data can include a visitor's IP address, site referrer, date and time of the visitor, and other analytical information.

When you dive into Web analytics, you'll quickly realize that you can slice the data 12 ways from Sunday. In other words, there are many different perspectives of what's happening on your site. Start with the simple metrics, like unique visitors, site referrers, and clickstreams before you attempt to understand some of the more advanced analytics discussed in later chapters.

Untangling Technical Terms

You don't have to attend a technical institute to take full advantage of Web analytics software, but you do need to untangle a few technical terms if you want to fully understand what you are looking at and what you are looking for. Take a few minutes to review these complex technical terms spelled out in plain language and you'll be rattling off these acronyms with the best tech geeks out there.

✔ **Active Server Pages (ASP):** This a scripting language, developed by Microsoft, that runs on a Web server. It allows developers build Web pages that present *dynamic content,* images and text that are pulled from a database, XML file, or other data source.

✔ **Application Programming Interface (API):** This is a language and format that one software program uses to communicate with another software program.

✔ **Authentication:** This process requires users to enter a username or password to identify themselves in order to gain access to a Web site's resources. Users might be asked to log in to a Member's Only section or provide details to make a payment in an e-commerce transaction.

✔ **Bandwidth:** This is the amount of data that can be transferred to and from a Web site in a given period of time. This is usually expressed as bits per second (bps) or higher units like Mbps (millions of bits per second).

✔ **Cookie:** These are small text files that allow a Web server to store information about a visitor and recognize them when they return.

✔ **JavaScript:** Not to be confused with the Java programming language, *JavaScript* is a scripting language developed by Netscape. It can be embedded into the HTML (HyperText Markup Language) of a Web page to add functionality, such as validating data or responding to a visitor's button clicks.

✔ **Platform:** This is the operating system that runs a computer. The three most common operating systems are Windows, Macintosh, and Linux.

✔ **Robot:** Also known as *Web crawlers, bots,* or *spiders,* a *robot* is an automated script or program that browses the Web. Search engines use robots to gather up-to-date data as they index the Web.

Are your spiders poisonous?

There are only a few poisonous spiders in the world (and that's more than enough), but just one Black Widow bite could cause a painful headache, among other unwanted symptoms. In the online world, *spiders* — also known as *Web crawlers, bots, or robots* — wander around the Web to gather up-to-date data as they index the Web and are typically welcomed visitors because they help your search engine rankings. There are a few "poisonous" spiders that you should be aware of, though.

Benign bots follow proper protocols, letting Web analytics programs know that they are automated scripts so that they aren't mistaken for actual human beings. Bad bots, on the other hand, masquerade themselves as real people in hopes of gathering data from your site — such as e-mail addresses — to use for their own purposes. You can tell the difference by analyzing your log analysis for high-query volumes from an IP page range. If a bot queries you 20 or 30 times in an hour, it's probably up to no good. Check with your hosting company or server administrator for ways to block them at the Web server level and stop them dead in their tracks.

Chapter 3

Getting Your Hands Dirty with Web Data

▶ Finding your Web analytics statistics

▶ Taking a sneak peek at the data

▶ Measuring your conversion rate

▶ Setting quantifiable goals

*I*f the thought of reviewing statistics on Web site visitor behavior is beginning to make you a little dizzy, don't despair. Whether you are a numerical genius or easily intimidated by double digits, we'll be right here with you as you get acquainted with your Web measurement tools and the statistics that they generate. ***Remember:*** Your goal is to improve your Web site's performance — and your profits.

Your first Web analytics assignment is not merely an exercise in overcoming a technology learning curve. This chapter yields useful results as we escort you through accessing your Web stats and recording important data. You'll see how to measure your Web site's progress toward your goals, too. So be sure to make a good record of the stats you discover while going through these motions.

Are you ready? All right, then. Take a deep breath, roll up your sleeves, and get ready to get your hands dirty with Web data. Pretty soon you'll be reading — and analyzing — your reports with the best of them and taking action to make your Web site the best it can be.

Help! I Can't Find My Stats!

Maybe you've admired your eye-pleasing Web site for many months without ever realizing that a back-end might exist that offers more tools than the average do-it-yourselfer's toolbox. Depending on your Web host, the back-end — that is, a *control panel,* which comprises site configuration and management software application — of your Web site might offer general account information about your hosting package, along with your IP (Internet Protocol) address, disk e-mail configurations, FTP (File Transfer Protocol) accounts, site management tools, databases, and, yes, Web analytics software.

In fact, you might be pleasantly surprised to discover what you can control on the front-end by visiting your Web site's control panel. One of the most popular Web control panels is cPanel. It supports many operating systems and allows you to manage and monitor almost every aspect of your Web site with an easy user interface. Other popular control panels are Ensim, Plesk, Helm, and Webmin. For the exercises in this chapter, we use cPanel (www.cpanel.com; see Figure 3-1) because it is widely available and offers several options when it comes to viewing your statistics information.

Figure 3-1:
The homepage for the cPanel Web site.

How to access your Web analytics tools

Time to take a look at a back-end. If your host offers cPanel with your hosting account, you can access your Web analytics tools by following three easy steps:

1. **Point your browser to the control panel.**

   Generally, you can access your cPanel installation by typing your URL, followed by a slash and then *cpanel*. Here's an example:

   ```
   http://www.yoururl.com/cpanel
   ```

   That URL will probably direct you to another URL that corresponds with your Web hosting provider, so don't be alarmed if the URL changes. If you know that your hosting company offers cPanel but the instructions above don't take you anywhere, you may need to contact your hosting company to get the URL for your cPanel installation.

2. **Enter your username and password and click OK to gain access to the control panel.**

   You are greeted with a pop-up box that instructs you to enter your Name and Password. (See Figure 3-2.) You may choose to select a check box that offers to remember your password so you don't have to enter it the next time around. (If you've already forgotten your Name and Password, of if you never knew what it was to begin with, contact your Web hosting provider for details.)

Figure 3-2:
The cPanel
log in
dialog box.

3. **In the Web/FTP Stats section (in the center column, the second category), click the software that you would like to use.**

   Voilà! You have access to a world of data.

You'll see several different links in this section, as shown in Figure 3-3. The options available in this area depend on what your Web host has enabled for the server. Keep reading to see what kind of information these links offer.

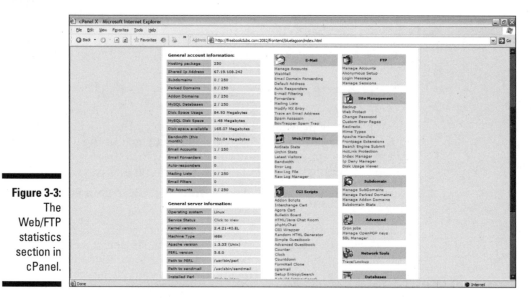

Figure 3-3:
The
Web/FTP
statistics
section in
cPanel.

If your host has enabled several different analytics applications, you're probably wondering which link to click. Don't worry: The choice is not as dramatic as taking the red pill or the blue pill. You are not in *The Matrix*. The following sections serve as a quick guide to understanding what's behind all those "doors" so that you can walk through the one you really need.

AWStats Stats

AWStats is a popular, free analytics application that displays your traffic logs graphically. Feature-rich and fast, it's generally a good option if you need to get overview data for your Web site. One of the downsides to this choice is that it displays data monthly but does not give you the flexibility to see data for one particular day or a date range. (See Figure 3-4.)

Urchin Stats

As soon as you click the Urchin link, you'll notice that the Urchin user interface is exceptionally graphical. It also parses your log files and displays the information graphically, similar to AWStats. Urchin might run slightly slower because of its graphic-rich interface, but it allows you to see data by day, week, year, or any other custom data range you care to view. Urchin is helpful because it offers a glossary of terms. (See Figure 3-5.)

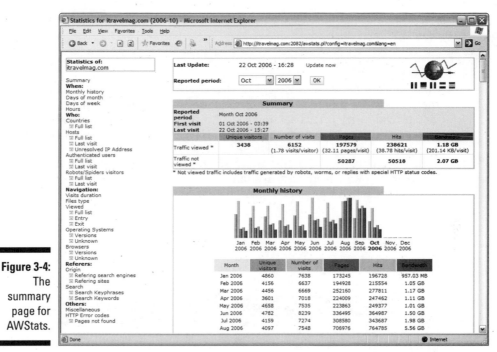

Figure 3-4:
The
summary
page for
AWStats.

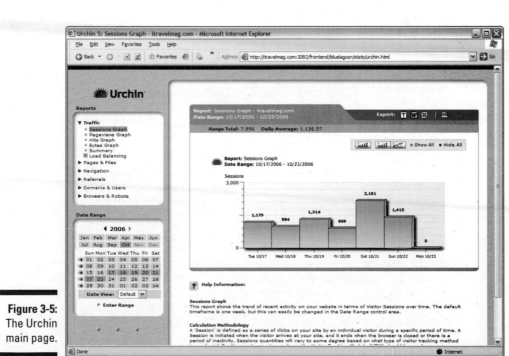

Figure 3-5:
The Urchin
main page.

TIP

For more information on how to select the right Web analytics tools for your Web site, read Chapter 4.

Latest Visitors

Click this link for a quick look at the latest visitors, which are organized by their *IP address,* a unique numeric code assigned by the user's Internet service provider (ISP). This section also shows you the HTTP (HyperText Transfer Protocol) response code. (An *HTTP response code,* or *HTTP code,* is generated each time a visitor requests a file. For more information on HTTP codes, read Chapter 10.) This area also shows you the page visited; the browser that was used; and, in some cases, the site referrer. However, this section doesn't put any of the data in context. (See Figure 3-6.)

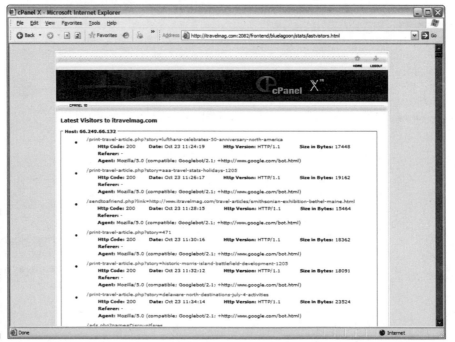

Figure 3-6:
The cPanel view of the latest visitors to the Web site.

The Latest Visitors view is ideal when you want a quick look at what your recent visitors did on your site. For example, say your business receives a phone call, and the user mentions that he Googled your Web site: You might be able to look at this log to determine the caller's exact search terms and which pages he visited on your site. That could give you some clue as to what search terms are most effective and/or what content or images on the pages he visited that spurred him to pick up the phone and call. Did the search terms he used actually match what he was calling about, or was it just an entry point of interest? Were there strong calls to action on those pages? Did he have to go to a contact page to get your phone number, or was it readily available for him? Most importantly, did you actually close the sale, or was it just a waste of time? As you can see, the Latest Visitors section can give you plenty to consider.

Bandwidth

Bandwidth is the amount of data that can be transferred to and from a Web site in a given period of time. This is usually expressed as bits per second (bps) or in higher units like Mbps (millions of bits per second). The bandwidth report may include HTTP, SMTP, FTP, and POP3 traffic.

Before you go into acronym overload, let us explain. The following are the main consumers of your bandwidth:

- **HTTP (HyperText Transfer Protocol):** The four letters before the www in a URL, this is the actual communications protocol that enables Web browsing. HTTP traffic is browser-based traffic.

- **SMTP (Simple Mail Transfer Protocol):** This is used to send and receive e-mail.

- **FTP (File Transfer Protocol):** This is the language used for file transfer for computer to computer across the World Wide Web.

- **POP3 (Post Office Protocol):** This traffic is a data format delivery of e-mail across the Internet.

Keeping an eye on bandwidth usage isn't always the most exciting activity. If your site attracts lots of traffic, though, watch your bandwidth to make sure you aren't going to exceed the quota imposed by your host. That can result in slow Web site performance, costly overage charges, or even deactivation of your hosting account. Would-be visitors might click the Stop button on their browser while they grow impatient waiting for the site to load — or, if the requested site doesn't load, they might easily go to your competitor instead.

Error Log

This list (see Figure 3-7) gives you a quick rundown of your *site errors* — that is, what has gone wrong on your site — showing the last 300 error log messages, in reverse order. You can see the exact date and time of the error, the error code, and an explanation of what it means. (Now all you have to do is fix it.) For more information on error codes, also called HTTP codes, read Chapter 10.

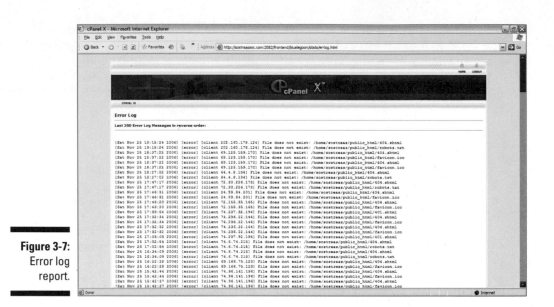

Figure 3-7:
Error log
report.

Raw Log File

Click this link to get a pop-up box from your browser asking you what you'd like to do with the file. You can open it or save it to your hard drive. Unless you are highly analytical, though, you might not be able to make sense of its contents. A *raw log file* stores information of all requests made to your Web site. These are the files that your Web analytics software uses to calculate the Web site statistics. The format looks something like this:

```
68.142.250.40 - - [30/Sep/2005:03:12:35 -0500] "GET /robots.txt HTTP/1.0" 404 -
        "-" "Mozilla/5.0 (compatible; Yahoo! Slurp;
        http://help.yahoo.com/help/us/ysearch/slurp)"
68.142.249.113 - - [30/Sep/2005:03:12:35 -0500] "GET /dog.php?breed=Chihuahua
        HTTP/1.0" 200 6321 "-" "Mozilla/5.0 (compatible; Yahoo! Slurp;
        http://help.yahoo.com/help/us/ysearch/slurp)"
```

You might need access to these files if you want to run a client-side Web analytics software package. *Client-side Web analytics* are programs that are installed on your computer, just like Microsoft Word or Adobe Photoshop. For more information on client-side, server-side, and hosted Web analytics software solutions, read Chapter 4.

Raw Log Manager

The Raw Log Manager (see Figure 3-8) allows you to control whether your raw log files are saved or deleted at the end of each month. If you choose to save your logs, you can use the Raw Log Manager to view any saved logs. You have two options here:

- ✔ *Archive logs.* If you want to save your raw logs at the end of the month, select the Archive Logs in Your Home Directory at the End of Each Month check box.

- ✔ *Remove logs.* If you want to remove the previous month's saved logs when a new month's logs are saved, select the Remove the Previous Month's Archived Logs from Your Home Directory at the End of Each Month check box.

Regardless of whether you choose to archive or remove your logs, click the Save button to put the command into effect.

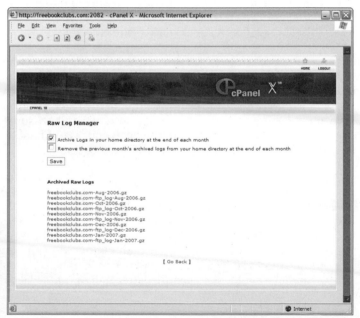

Figure 3-8: The Raw Log Manager.

Saving your logs can take up a tremendous amount of disk space. Busy sites can build up log files as large as several gigabytes in one month. These files count against your storage space on your hosting account. If you have lots of very large files, you might need to upgrade your hosting package or choose not to save log files for more than one month.

What if my host doesn't offer analytics?

Arrgh. You access your control panel only to discover that you have no Web analytics software package preinstalled on the back-end. Uh, oh. Now what are you going to do? First, don't panic. Plenty of free options are available that can get you started quickly and fairly easily. See Chapter 5 for the low-down information on choosing and setting up analytics applications.

Some hosting providers might be willing to install higher-end Web analytics applications — for a price. If you determine that you need something more robust than what you have available, check with your provider.

Taking a Sneak Peek at the Data

By now, your curiosity has probably gotten the best of you. You probably went ahead and opened your Web analytics software and looked at all the numbers, charts, graphs, and other pertinent data-oriented presentations. If you weren't that brave, take a sneak peek at the data right now.

Before you get too excited — or nervous, as the case may be — remember that you're just looking at some overall numbers here so you can get your feet wet (and your hands at least a little dirty.) Read along to see how to review the monthly history so you can see how your site has been performing. Then, delve into site referrers, measure the conversion rate, and set some goals for your site. If you want to jump right into the deep end, read Chapter 11 on key performance indicators (KPIs) and swim with the big sharks.

Recording your monthly history

It's been said that when Christopher Columbus set out for the New World, he didn't have a clue where he was going. He didn't know where he was when he got there. And he didn't know where he had been when he returned to Spain. Old Chris could have avoided at least the latter half of that legacy if he had simply recorded his monthly history.

Of course, Columbus deserves a bit of a break. After all, it was 1492 when he sailed the ocean blue. He didn't have any maps to follow nor high-tech gadgets to guide him to his discovery of America. You don't have the same excuse. As you steer the ship (your Web site) toward the land of opportunity (greater profits), you can be sure of where you are headed, you'll know when you get there, and you'll be able to tell others how you did it — that is, if you record your monthly history.

Recording your monthly history lets you set a benchmark so that you'll know how far you've come from month to month. You can compare how many unique visitors, visits, pages, and hits you've had as well as how much bandwidth you used in any given month. With that information in hand, you can compare those numbers with other months to determine historical trends, such as busy seasons. You can also use your monthly history to measure the effectiveness of campaigns.

For a more detailed review of monthly reporting, read Chapter 15.

For now, allow us to show you some of the basics as you familiarize yourself with the software. With your control panel open (see how to open this, earlier in chapter), here's what you need to do. Again, we're using AWStats.

1. **Click the AWStats Stats link.**

   It's under the Web/FTP Stats section, in the middle column.

   In the left-hand column is a list of options.

2. **Click the Monthly history link (the first option under the When category).**

   See Figure 3-9.

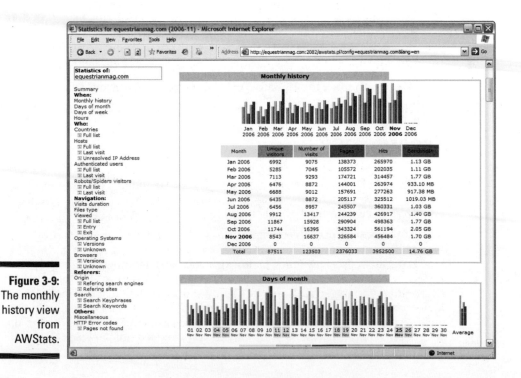

Figure 3-9: The monthly history view from AWStats.

You see a bar graph with various colors that correspond to the headings on the chart below. There are headings for Month, Unique Visitors, Pages, Hits, and Bandwidth.

3. Save this history.

Some Web analytics programs will save this data for you automatically, though perhaps only for a period of time. You could also input it into a Microsoft Excel spreadsheet or burn it to a disk. For more back up recommendations, check out Chapter 15.

Although your software will keep this record for you, plan for the worst and record it elsewhere. If you switch analytics providers or if some catastrophe occurs, you could lose your data. As you progress through the sea of Web analytics, you will want to identify KPIs and add those records to your historical data as well.

Each month of the current year is listed on your monthly history report. This is helpful, for example, when you want to compare specific months: say, this June with last June. Here's how:

1. Scroll to the top of the page.

You see a box there with two items inside, as well as the AWStats globe.

You'll see the date and time that your analytics program last updated the data. AWStats commonly processes your Web site log files automatically every night, but your host might have set this process to happen less frequently. If you're looking at data that's more than 24–48 hours old, look for an Update Now link.

2. (Optional) Click the Update Now link to get to-the-minute stats.

This option to manually update your stats is not available with all Web hosts.

3. Set the reported period.

The second, and only other, line item in the box is Reported Period. Use the two drop-down menus there to choose any month of any year of your Web site's history. Choose the month and year for which you want to receive data and then click OK.

At the bottom of each column, your handy-dandy Web analytics program tallies how many unique visitors, visits, pages, and hits you've had, year to date, as well as how much bandwidth you used, as shown in Figure 3-10.

Off the bat, you might see some trends by simply reviewing your monthly history. Hopefully, you are pleasantly rewarded by steadily increasing unique visitor counts. If your site is on the skids, though, it could be time to amp up your lead generating efforts — or maybe you need a whole new look.

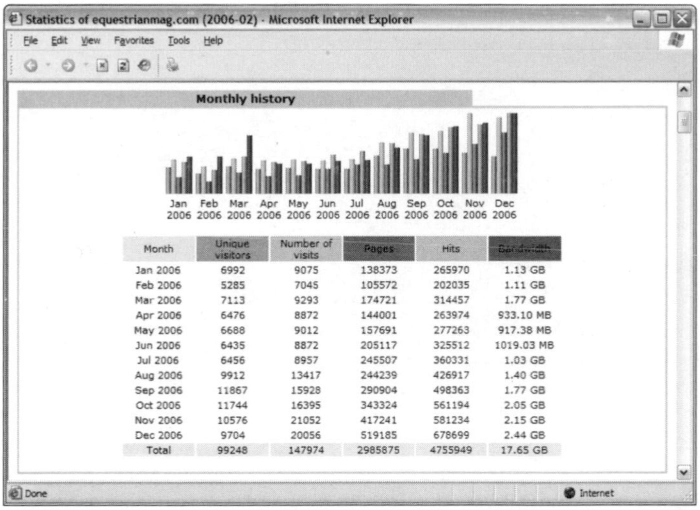

Figure 3-10:
Viewing
your year-
to-date
results.

Making note of peak days and times

Although recording monthly history gives you a good historical baseline,
making note of peak days and times offers a here-and-now point of view. You
can get fairly detailed with these charts, opting to view days of the month,
days of the week, or hours of the day.

Dealing in days of the month

How many people visited your site on October 17? Was that more or less than
the number of folks who walked through your virtual doors on October 1? You
can find out in a flash by viewing your Days of Month report. Here's how to
access and read this report. (See Figure 3-11.) With your control panel open

1. **Click the AWStats Stats link.**

   It's under the Web/FTP Stats section in the middle column.

2. **Click the Days of Month link.**

   Look for this in the left column, in the options list, under the When
   category.

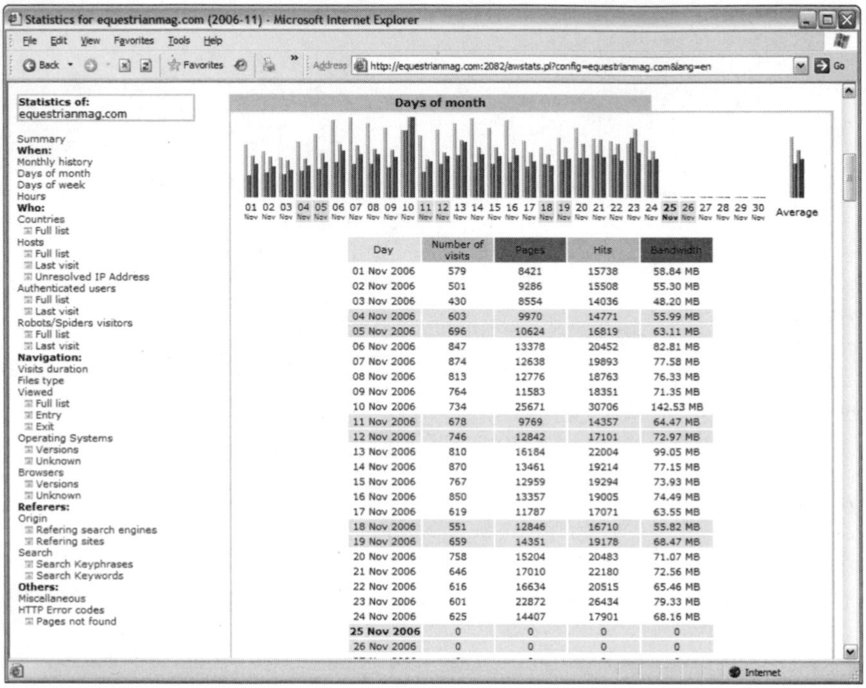

Figure 3-11:
The Days of
the Month
report from
AWStats.

3. Review the Days of Month report.

This report offers a line graph and a day-by-day chart that outlines the number of visits, pages, and hits as well as bandwidth used for each day of the month, with the current day of the month highlighted. The days highlighted in gray are weekend days. For e-commerce sites, weekends might be among the busiest of the month: comparatively, for service firms, the lightest.

What's really neat for the math-averse is that the Days of the Month report offers totals and averages so you can avoid the number crunching and the calculator pecking. Maybe you got 10,000 hits one day and 5,700 another, and only 3,200 another. This report gives you an average per day. It also reveals the average bandwidth used in a day so you can adjust your Web hosting package to get more bandwidth if you need it.

Delving into days of the week

If you want to drill down even further, check out the Days of Week report. The data is narrower, but that's the point: If you just want to see how many hits you got on Wednesday, this little chart satisfies the need. Here's how to find your Days of Week report in AWStats. (See Figure 3-12.) With your control panel open

1. **Click the AWStats Stats link.**

   It's under the Web/FTP Stats section in the middle column.

2. **Click the Days of Week link.**

   Look in the left column option list. It's under the When category.

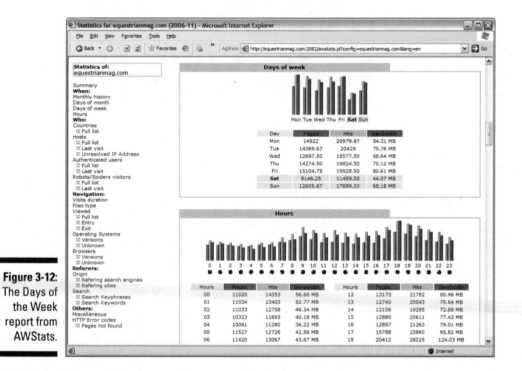

Figure 3-12:
The Days of
the Week
report from
AWStats.

3. **Review the Days of Week report.**

   You see a line graph that shows you the peaks and valleys that your Web analytics program recorded throughout the current week. Make a note of which day of the week sees the most traffic to compare it with weeks past — and get ready to compare it against weeks in the future.

Honing in on hours of the day

Honing in on hours of the day can lead to some intriguing insights. You might discover that night owls are populating your site. Or you might discover that the early birds are catching the worms that you leave out for bait. Here's how to find your Hours report in AWStats. (See Figure 3-13.) With your control panel open

1. **Click the AWStats Stats link.**

2. **Click the Hours link.**

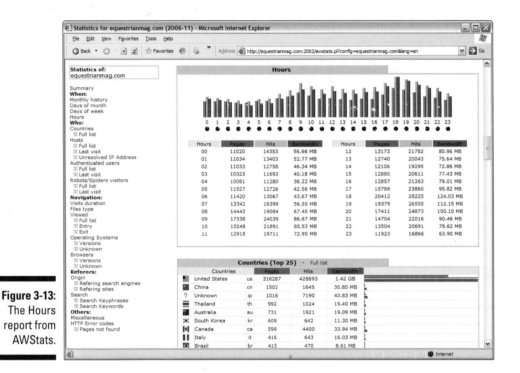

Figure 3-13:
The Hours report from AWStats.

3. **Review the Hours report.**

You'll see a line graph that shows you the peaks and valleys your Web analytics program recorded throughout the current week. Make a note of which day of the week sees the most traffic, then compare it to weeks past and get ready to compare it to weeks in the future. There are several insights you can glean from the Hours report. For example, if the bulk of your traffic comes between the hours of 9am and 5pm, then you can accurately assume that most of your users are surfing from work. This type of visitor behaves different than weeknight or weekend traffic. For example, at-work users usually prefer to visit Web sites that don't feature music or sound because they don't want their boss to find out they are goofing off at work. What's more, at-work users may be trying to take care of some personal matters on a break or at lunch, making quick checkout options a desirable characteristic for this audience.

Get creative with your Web promotions. Knowing what hours see the most traffic could help you craft special midnight sales, early-bird specials, or even lunchtime-giveaways designed to give that traffic an incentive to become regular customers, subscribers, or readers.

Where's my traffic coming from?

Half the battle of any e-business is driving traffic to your site. After all, you can't convert a visitor into a customer, subscriber, loyal reader, or qualified lead until you first get that visitor to your site. Whether you depend purely on organic search or you pull out all the stops with a combination of paid search, affiliate marketers, link building campaigns, and the like, you need to know what methods are working — and what methods are not.

Einstein is attributed with this pithy witticism: "Insanity: Doing the same thing over and over again and expecting different results." He's got a pretty good point: If your traffic-building tactics aren't working, don't go nuts. Just change your tactics.

Perhaps you need to write Web site copy that uses keywords more effectively. Maybe you need to work harder to build *reciprocal links*. In fact, it could be any number of things. You won't know where to begin, though, until you find out where your traffic is (and isn't) coming from. Here's how (see Figure 3-14). With your control panel open

1. **Click the AwStats Stats link.**

2. **Click the Origin link.**

   Look in the option list, in the left column. Toward the bottom of the list is the Referrers section. The link is there.

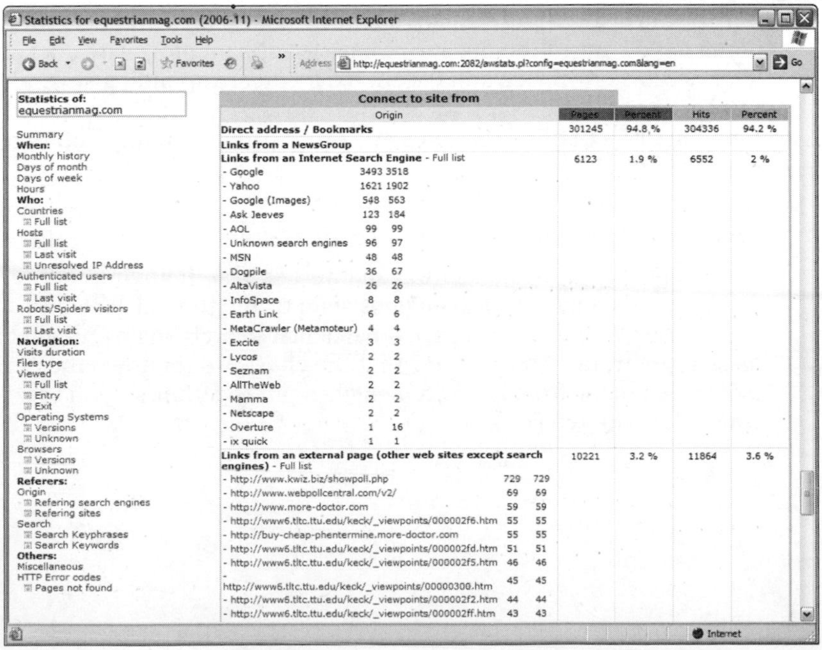

Figure 3-14: The Referrers Origin report from AWStats.

3. Review your Referrers.

In the Connect to Site From section, you will find four or five key categories. You can see your site referrers by examining these four sections. The Origin section breaks down visitors in terms of hits, pages, and percentages. In the following sections, we briefly review each section. For extensive information on where your traffic is coming from, read Chapter 9.

Direct Addresses/Bookmarks

The first origin in the list of site referrers is Direct Addresses and Bookmarks. Visitors who either typed in your URL by hand in response to some external prompt (usually an offline ad) as well as loyal visitors who have bookmarked your site are counted in this section. If you already have an established following or if you do a lot of offline advertising, a large percentage of your traffic natural falls under the Direct Address/Bookmarks section of your site referrer report.

Links from a NewsGroup

This section records how many visitors found your site through a newsgroup. A *newsgroup* is a Usenet discussion group that is related to one topic. Internet users can subscribe to many different newsgroups. Perhaps one of your traffic building strategies is to position yourself as an expert in a newsgroup on real estate. You would put your URL at the bottom of your signature, and anyone who sees it can visit you online.

Google and Yahoo!, among other industry powerhouses, have newsgroups, but they are not as powerful of a tool for generating traffic as they once were. Some have blamed the decline of newsgroups on blogs and social networking sites, such as MySpace and Facebook. If you are spending several hours a week posting on newsgroups and have little to no traffic to show for it, your time might be better spent on some other traffic-building initiative (like blogging or social networking).

Links from an Internet Search Engine

A quick glance at the Links from an Internet Search Engine section (see Figure 3-15) records which search engines send traffic to your Web site. Chances are that if your Web site is listed in a particular search engine, it will drive at least some traffic. You'll notice that the chart breaks down the percentage of traffic that came from all search engines put together so you can compare it with other site referrers.

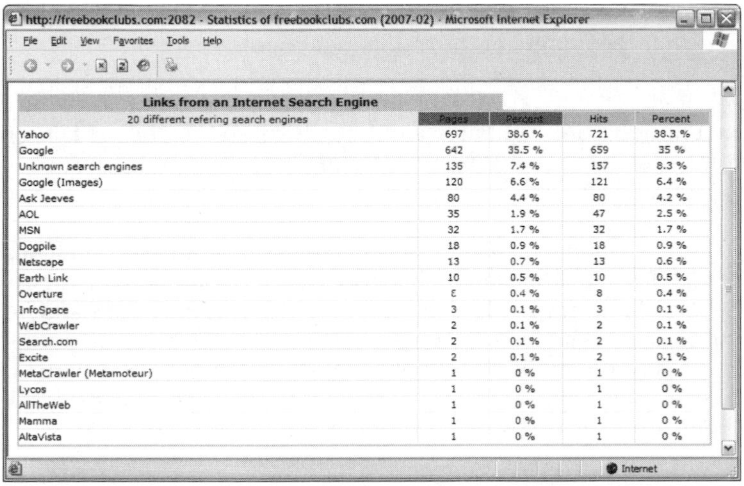

Figure 3-15: The Links from an Internet Search Engine report.

Links from an Internet Search Engine				
20 different refering search engines	Pages	Percent	Hits	Percent
Yahoo	697	38.6 %	721	38.3 %
Google	642	35.5 %	659	35 %
Unknown search engines	135	7.4 %	157	8.3 %
Google (Images)	120	6.6 %	121	6.4 %
Ask Jeeves	80	4.4 %	80	4.2 %
AOL	35	1.9 %	47	2.5 %
MSN	32	1.7 %	32	1.7 %
Dogpile	18	0.9 %	18	0.9 %
Netscape	13	0.7 %	13	0.6 %
Earth Link	10	0.5 %	10	0.5 %
Overture	8	0.4 %	8	0.4 %
InfoSpace	3	0.1 %	3	0.1 %
WebCrawler	2	0.1 %	2	0.1 %
Search.com	2	0.1 %	2	0.1 %
Excite	2	0.1 %	2	0.1 %
MetaCrawler (Metamoteur)	1	0 %	1	0 %
Lycos	1	0 %	1	0 %
AllTheWeb	1	0 %	1	0 %
Mamma	1	0 %	1	0 %
AltaVista	1	0 %	1	0 %

One engine will likely drive the majority of your traffic. That could be because you are running paid advertising campaigns on that engine or that engine has more active spiders. Also known as *Web crawlers* or *robots, spiders* are programs or automated scripts that browse the Web. You might occasionally hear spiders referred to as *ants, automatic indexers, bots,* or *worms.* Search engines use spiders to gather up-to-date data as they index the Web.

Look for any niche search engines that drive traffic to your site. This is an area that you might want to exploit. Those niche engines, or other search engines that have the potential to drive more traffic to your site, could be hidden beyond the Top 10. Right next to the Links from an Internet Search Engine heading is a blue link that reads Full List. Be sure to click that link to see every engine that's sending traffic your way.

Links from an External Page

This section shows site referrers that are not search engines. In other words, these sites referrers are other Web sites beyond Google, Yahoo!, MSN, and others. These external pages are listed first, second, third, and so on, based on how many visitors they referred to your site. The chart breaks down the percentage of traffic that came from all external pages put together so you can compare it with other site referrers.

Be sure to go beyond the Top 10 external page referrals to see who else is sending traffic your way. You can do this by clicking the Full List heading right under the section header. It could be that the quality of traffic coming from blog sites is more valuable than traffic coming from content exchanges.

You won't know unless you do a comparison. Sometimes it's not the quantity but rather the quality of the traffic that counts.

In AWStats, when you view the full list of site referrers from an external page, you'll notice a box right above it that allows you to choose Filter or Exclude Filter. Filters are applied to the information coming into your Web analytics reports.

You can use filters to manipulate the final data your Web analytics application displays so you can get reports that suit your needs. With Google Analytics for example, you could set up filters to exclude visits from certain IP addresses — such as the origins of known referrer spam (for more information on referrer spam, read Chapter 7) — or you could set filters to take dynamic page URLs and convert them into readable text strings. Here's a list of some filters you could use in Google Analytics:

- ✔ **Exclude all traffic from a domain:** You can use this filter to exclude traffic from a specific domain, such as an ISP or company network. This is helpful in fighting referrer spam.

- ✔ **Exclude all traffic from an IP address:** You could use this filter to exclude clicks from certain sources. You could enter one or many addresses. This is also helpful in fighting referrer spam.

- ✔ **Include only traffic to a subdirectory:** You might choose to use this filter if you are only interested in tracking behavior of visitors to a particular section of the site.

- ✔ **Exclude pattern:** You could use this filter to exclude hits that match the filter pattern. For example, a filter that excludes Firefox would also exclude all other information in that hit, such as visitor, path, referral and domain information. You might decide to do this if you are trying to differentiate the behavior of visitors who use one browser over another before you optimize your site for a particular browser.

- ✔ **Uppercase/Lowercase:** This filter converts the contents of the field into all uppercase or all lowercase letters.

- ✔ **Search & Replace:** You could use this filter to search for a pattern within a field and replace the found pattern with an alternate form.

You can create many different types of custom filters that meet your needs. Be sure to find out first, though, if you can keep all your raw data intact so you can go back and review the full reports without filters if you choose to. Also, remember to remove the custom filter after it has served its purpose.

Unknown Origin

You might find this difficult to believe in this high-tech age in which we live, but sometimes your Web analytics program just doesn't know where someone who visited your Web site came from. Referrers are determined by *reverse DNS look-ups* — that is, translating IP numbers to domain names to uncode the true referrer. However, many numerical addresses are of unknown origin.

When you review your site referrers, you might be disgruntled by the percentage of hits that seem to wear the cloak of anonymity. Even the best analytics programs are stumped, it seems, although this is clear: If you see a high level of use from an unresolved IP number, it could be spiders. The Unknown Origin category, though, at least shows you how many of these masked visitors you had.

Comprehending Conversion Rates

You can hardly claim that you've gotten your hands dirty with Web analytics until you measure your conversion rate. *Conversion* occurs when you close the deal — that is, when you convert a visitor into a buyer, subscriber, or member. The *conversion rate,* then, is the percentage of your Web site visitors that take the desired action. That can mean completing a retail sale for merchandise; subscribing to a newsletter, magazine, or community; filling out a form that sends you information to qualify a lead, or achieving some other goal.

The conversion rate is sort of the bottom line of Web analytics and the Web site optimization that follows. You might look at any number of KPIs in your quest to turn more traffic into customers. However, it's often the overall conversion rate that tells you whether the changes you are making to your site are helping — or hurting — your cause. For more insights into KPIs, read Chapter 11.

Calculating that all-important metric

Your conversion rate is an all-important metric. Here's where it gets fun. You can calculate more than one kind of conversion rate. For instance, you could measure the average number of visitors prior to conversion, the new visitor conversion rate, the returning visitor conversion rate, the repeat customer conversion rate, and . . . well, you get the picture.

Right now, focus on the overall conversion rate. Calculating your conversion rate is not difficult, even for mathophobic. Here's how it works:

1. **Determine the number of positive outcomes.**

   The first step in calculating the overall conversion rate is to determine how many positive outcomes you had in a defined period — usually a month. In other words, how many widgets did you sell, how many leads did you generate, and how many subscriptions did you receive? This is your *baseline number*.

2. **Determine the number of unique visitors.**

   The second step is to determine how many unique visitors you had during that same period. You can find this in your Web analytics program under the Unique Visitors label.

3. **Divide and conquer.**

   Divide the number of closings by the number of unique visitors. That is your overall conversion rate.

You're probably wondering whether your conversion rate is healthy or ill. The answer is, "That depends." Namely, that depends on several factors, including what industry you are in and what users need to surrender (information, money, or both) to buy what you are selling. According to the Fireclick Index (an index developed by hosted Web analytics provider Fireclick; www. fireclick.com), average conversion rates vary greatly. As an example, the October 16, 2006 index showed the following conversion rates:

- **Electronics Industry**

  Conversion rate = 0.40%

  Abandonment rate = 84%

- **Fashion and Apparel Industry**

  Conversion rate = 1.90%

  Abandonment rate = 69.8%

- **Catalog Industry**

  Conversion rate = 4.80%

  Abandonment rate = 65.10%

- **Outdoor and Sports Industry**

  Conversion rate = 0.40%

  Abandonment rate = 63%

- **Software Industry**

  Conversion rate = 3.50%

  Abandonment rate = 80.40%

As you can see, the catalogers do it best, followed by the software industry. The electronics and sports industry products are notably harder sells. A 2-percent conversion rate in the fashion industry is fairly standard. A 2-percent conversion rate in the software industry, though, could cause a headache.

Goal Setting 101

We assume that your goal is the same as most other Web site owners' goals: to be wildly successful and make lots of money. You'll need to get a little more specific than that if you want to achieve Web wealth status. In fact, your e-business goals should be broken down into two categories: non-financial and financial. You should also have an idea of what you expect to get out of your e-business this year, next year, and several years from now. This is typically called a *marketing plan,* or the marketing section of a *business plan.*

If you want a good lesson on how to write a business plan or a marketing plan, pick up a copy of Wiley Publishing's *Business Plans For Dummies.* Meanwhile, hear this: Your goals should always be realistic yet challenging. It doesn't matter whether you are the Amazon of your category or still playing in the Pee Wee league. Google didn't start off as the most profitable search engine. So take a look at your historical data and keep in mind your strategies and tactics as you set out to set goals.

Setting nonfinancial goals

Nonfinancial goals can be related to financial goals at a broad level. Nonfinancial goals include entering new territories; adding new products, services, content, or customer support features to your Web site; or increasing market share 25 percent per year for the next three years.

After you implement the strategies that aim to help you meet your goals, Web analytics can help you measure them. Did the Spanish-language translation of your Web site increase your market share? Web analytics will measure it for you. Do those new products help boost profits? Web analytics will tell you. Do those new customer service tools reduce calls to the call center? Web analytics can help you figure that out, too.

Setting financial goals

Your financial goals should be more definite. Maybe you want to grow sales from $100,000 last year to $125,000 this year and $150,000 the following year. Or if you are an entrepreneur who is convinced that you have the next best idea since Google, your goal might be to land venture capital investment. The latter means proving your business model, which probably means building your traffic or your conversions. Web analytics, once again, helps you measure your progress toward your financial goals.

Setting conversion rate goals

Because determining whether you met your lofty goals will be measured in some way, shape, or form by calculating the conversion rate, you might as well set a conversion rate goal, too. If you're in the catalog industry, for example, your goal should probably be a conversion rate of about four percent because that's the industry standard. If you are in some other industry, first determine what the industry standard is and then set that as your benchmark.

Generally speaking, a conversion rate of 2 percent is admirable — and that means there's plenty of room for improvement. No matter what your current conversion rate, just think of the potential profits you could generate if you could double that number.

Setting Web site goals

Increasing conversions might mean increasing visitor counts, average time on site, or some other area. With that in mind, you need to tie your financial and nonfinancial goals to the Web statistics your software measures. Maybe you need to increase the number of visitors from 5,000 per month to 15,000 per month to give yourself a fighting chance to double that conversion rate. Or maybe you need to add content or imagery to keep visitors on your site longer. Maybe you need *search engine optimization,* which covers making changes to your Web site so that it attracts more visitors from search engines. You can employ any number of strategies. Just be sure to measure them to find out whether they're doing the trick.

Ready, set, measure

Some media portals aren't waiting for visitors to enter into their virtual content shop. Instead, they push content to the people through Really Simple Syndication (RSS). *RSS* is a software system that lets users subscribe to content from their favorite Web sites. With this technology, you can put your content into a standardized format that can be viewed and organized through RSS-aware software or automatically delivered as new content on another Web site. On the reader's end, a feed reader or content aggregation software can check those subscriptions for new content and pull it into a display. Web analytics software allows media portals that rely on RSS to push content to its loyal readers to measure their efforts.

RSS is actually easier to measure than e-mail. Your goal with RSS measurement is to determine how many people subscribe to your feed and whether that number is increasing or decreasing. If your subscribers are declining, perhaps your content is boring for your target audience. In that case, you need to revamp your content strategy in a hurry because this decline could soon become apparent on your Web site, too. Web analytics can also tell you whether your subscribers are clicking the content items in the RSS feed. If your subscribers aren't actually reading the content, you might need to offer more creative headlines that will entice them. For more information on RSS analytics, read Chapter 6.

Part II

Choosing the Right Web Analytics Solution

The 5th Wave   By Rich Tennant

"Sales on the Web site are down. I figure the server's chi is blocked, so we're fudgin' around the feng shui in the computer room, and if that doesn't work, Ronnie's got a chant that should do it."

In this part . . .

Time to make some decisions. In this part we will arm
you with detailed information that will help you determine what type — or types — of Web analytics tools you
need to get the data you crave. You'll quickly learn that
while all Web analytics tools have the same objective —
to measure visitor behavior — no two software packages
are exactly alike. Understand the differences and you are
well on your way to choosing the best solution for your
Web site.

We start off with a discussion of the pros and cons of the
three basic options in Web analytics programming: server-
side, client-side, and hosted solutions. Those terms may
not mean much to you now, but soon you'll understand
what types of tools you need — and why you need them.
You may even discover that you need to use more than
one type of tool to gather all the data you desire. In this
part, we'll guide you through the ins and outs of leveraging multiple tool types, too.

Before you actually invest in a particular vendor, though,
you'll need to do some test drives. We'll show you how to
get your hands on some free analytics tools and get a
taste of what's available. We'll also introduce you to some
low-cost tools that may take you where you need to go.
And if your appetite for data is virtually insatiable, we'll
escort you straight to some enterprise-level tools that
offer more data than you may have thought possible.

With the popularity of social networking and new "push"
technologies, we wouldn't dare leave out niche Web analytics solutions. You'll discover which analytics vendors
are catering to the special needs of search marketers with
tools customized to track pay-per-click advertising, blogging, and RSS feeds. We'll help you get acquainted with
A/B and multivariate testing software and usher you into a
Web analytics world where you can watch the action live,
click by click.

Chapter 4

Web Analytics Tools You Can Use

● ●

In This Chapter

▶ Surveying server-side software

▶ Discovering desktop applications

▶ Getting the hang of hosted solutions

▶ Considering multiple tool usage

● ●

*M*ore than 100 Web analytics vendors are on the market, and while industry experts expect some consolidation in the years ahead, they also expect some new start-ups to emerge on the scene. Wading through the scores of Web analytics tools on the market can be daunting for even the most experienced Web gurus. That same task can be frustrating for those who are just learning the lingo. And it can be absolutely maddening for newbies.

Unlike many other software segments, choosing a Web analytics tool is not merely a matter of brand name or even price. Although those factors should certainly play a role in your decision, you have three distinct options in the analytics world:

✔ **Server-side:** Server-side analytics tools are software installed on the Web site's server. Server-side solutions are often the most convenient because many of them are preinstalled by your hosting company and don't require much work to start using them.

✔ **Client-side:** Client-side tools are installed on your computer. Client-side software lets you keep track of multiple domains with the same tool and can move with you if you change hosting companies.

✔ **Hosted solutions:** Hosted solutions are hosted by a service provider on its server. Hosted solutions are independent of your Web server and your desktop computer, but there is a monthly fee associated with most of these services.

Of course, this overview only describes Web analytics tools in a nutshell. Finding the right tools that work for you means cracking that shell. Before you begin reviewing Web analytics vendors, you need to understand the ins and outs of these three classes of applications. In this chapter, we review the pros and cons of server-side, client-side, and hosted solutions. We also offer some reasons why you might want to use more than one type of tool.

Before You Begin . . .

Before you set out on this three-pronged trail, take inventory of your supplies and outline a clear map of your specific needs. You may be impressed with the bells and whistles a certain program class has to offer, but your budget might not allow let you make that much noise. Consider the following factors as you begin to compare and contrast the three classes of Web analytics software.

What's my budget?

If your budget looks like a goose egg, don't fret. Some attractive options are available in both the server-side and hosted categories that cost little to nothing. In addition to the free applications, you can find a fair selection of feature-rich, hosted applications in the intermediate, or middle market, budget range (between $15–$30 per month).

Most client-side solutions worth using are going to cost you a prettier penny up front. On the low end, you could spend between $100 and $500 for an entry-level client-side solution, but then it's yours for the keeping. No monthly fees to nag you. If money is no object — if you can fork over thousands of dollars without blinking — don't hesitate to check out the enterprise-level server-side and hosted Web analytics applications.

Some people swear by the adage that you get what you pay for. Of course, to a certain extent, that is true. With so much competition in the Web analytics market, though, you can find helpful tools at any price point. Decide how you want to access your analytics and what options you need, and then begin your search for a provider that meets those needs.

What does your hosting company support?

Some estimates figure that 90 percent of Web sites are hosted on *shared servers:* that is, Web servers that host multiple clients and potentially thousands of Web sites. So, if you're like most Web site owners, your options might be limited by the resources that your Web host provides. Most Web hosting providers today offer free Web analytics tools (see Figure 4-1) such as Webalizer (www.webalizer.com), AWStats (awstats.sourceforge.net), and Urchin (www.google.com/analytics/urchin_software.html). If your host offers those tools, your Web site is probably already recording metrics on your visitors. All you need to do is access them. Because no two Web hosts are alike, you need to check your registration information or send an e-mail to customer service to get instructions.

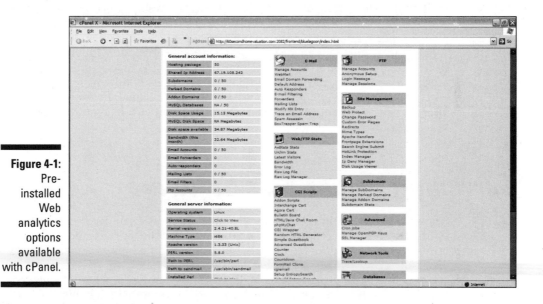

Figure 4-1:
Pre-installed Web analytics options available with cPanel.

If your host isn't quite gracious enough to offer free analytics tools as part of the package, you might have to upgrade your account or purchase an add-on package that includes the tools you need.

Server-side analytics applications require a complex installation and configuration process. A professional server administrator with specialized training typically performs this highly technical task. If your hosting company doesn't offer free analytics tools, installing a server-side analytics application on a shared server is usually not an option. Clients generally don't have the authorization to install programs at the server level on shared servers for security and performance reasons that could impact all the Web sites that share the same server.

Check which analytics applications are offered before committing to a particular Web host. If your hosting company doesn't come with analytics tools already configured and if it doesn't offer the ability to download *access logs* (the data files your analytics applications use to get the data for reports-more in the next section), your measurement options will be limited.

If you find yourself in this unwanted predicament, you might have the option to use a client-side application like ClickTracks Analyzer to process your raw logs. Of course, you need to check with your hosting provider to make sure that you can get access to your raw traffic logs. Check the FAQs or send an e-mail to customer service to get the skinny. If you can't, the only way you can get the data you crave is to use a hosted application like Google Analytics.

Hosted applications are independent of your hosting provider. All they require is that you add a small bit of code directly to the Web pages that you want to track. That means your Web hosting company doesn't have to lift a finger or give you permission to access anything in order to gather your site statistics. What's more, hosted Web analytics applications can move with you if you decide to move to another Web hosting company. If your Web site(s) operates on a dedicated server, you probably have a server administrator on staff who can configure your server to work with the Web analytics solution of your choice. A *dedicated server* is a server that you own or rent and offers you full control.

Surveying Server-Side Software

Server-side applications are generally installed on the same server on which your Web site is hosted, whether shared or dedicated. Server-side analytics applications parse your log files at regularly scheduled intervals. *Access logs,* also called raw log files or just log files, are simple data files that record visitor data such as time of visit, what files a visitor accessed, where the visitors were referred from, and more. The format looks something like this:

```
68.142.250.40 - - [30/Sep/2005:03:12:35 -0500] "GET /robots.txt HTTP/1.0" 404 -
          "-" "Mozilla/5.0 (compatible; Yahoo! Slurp;
          http://help.yahoo.com/help/us/ysearch/slurp)"
68.142.249.113 - - [30/Sep/2005:03:12:35 -0500] "GET /dog.php?breed=Chihuahua
          HTTP/1.0" 200 6321 "-" "Mozilla/5.0 (compatible; Yahoo! Slurp;
          http://help.yahoo.com/help/us/ysearch/slurp)"
66.194.6.83 - - [30/Sep/2005:11:46:48 -0500] "GET / HTTP/1.1" 200 4910 "-"
          "Mozilla/4.0 (compatible; MSIE 6.0; Windows NT 5.1; Q312462)"
216.118.213.30 - - [30/Sep/2005:11:53:17 -0500] "GET /dog.php?breed=Shih%20Tzu
          HTTP/1.1" 200 8189
          "http://search.msn.com/results.aspx?q=shi+tzu+magazine&FORM=MSNH&s
          rch_type=0" "Mozilla/4.0 (compatible; MSIE 6.0; Windows NT 5.1)"
216.118.213.30 - - [30/Sep/2005:11:53:17 -0500] "GET /css/css.css HTTP/1.1" 200
          559 "http://www.akcstandard.com/dog.php?breed=Shih%20Tzu"
          "Mozilla/4.0 (compatible; MSIE 6.0; Windows NT 5.1)"
216.118.213.30 - - [30/Sep/2005:11:53:17 -0500] "GET /pictures/header.jpg
          HTTP/1.1" 200 8854
          "http://www.akcstandard.com/dog.php?breed=Shih%20Tzu" "Mozilla/4.0
          (compatible; MSIE 6.0; Windows NT 5.1)"
```

As you can imagine, trying to analyze these log files without an analytics application to parse the data and turn it into easy-to-read charts and top ten lists would be next to impossible for the average Joe. Some of the points an analytics application could pull from the example data above are:

- ✔ **There are six hits.** A hit registers with every file that is accessed from the server. The example logfile data shows a new line for each hit, as do most log files.

- ✔ **There are four unique visitors.** This is based on the four unique IP addresses (the set of numbers at the beginning of each entry).

- ✔ **The first two hits are from Yahoo!**'s crawler. This can be determined by the user agent section in parentheses near the end of each entry, "Yahoo! Slurp; http://help.yahoo.com/help/us/ysearch/slurp" as well as the behavior in the first entry, accessing robots.txt, a text file that tells robots if any files should be excluded from the search engine's index.

These are just a few of the points that would be spelled out for you in easy-to-read reports by your analytics application.

As we mention in the preceding section, if your Web site is hosted on a shared server, there's a good chance your provider has already preinstalled the commonly free Web analytics tools, such as Webalizer, AWStats, and Urchin, for you.

If your Web site is hosted on a *dedicated server,* you might need to have your server administrator download and install this software for you.

Some hosting providers might be willing to install higher-end Web analytics applications — that is, for a price. If you determine that you need something more robust than what the free tools have to offer, check with your provider.

The selling points of server-side analytics

Although many industry analysts have predicted that hosted Web analytics solutions offered by *Application Service Providers (ASP)* — a company that hosts applications and charges a monthly fee — would overtake server-side analytics, the latter still boasts a few selling points.

- ✔ **Anywhere access:** Server-side systems allow you to view your Web metrics from any computer. Client-side systems relegate you to the computer your software is installed on. That means unless you have server-side systems, you can't check Web stats during your Hawaiian vacation unless you pay an additional license fee to install it on another computer.

✔ **Fast access:** Server-side applications automatically parse your Web server log files at regularly scheduled intervals or sometimes on-demand, as is the case with AWStats. Because your software is doing all the work for you, you only need to log in to your analytics application to see the results (see Figure 4-2).

✔ **Free and clear:** One of the most compelling selling points of server-side analytics is the cost. Many of the most popular and robust server-side analytics tools cost zero, zilch, nada . . . um, free.

✔ **Reliability:** Server-side application data is based on your server log files. The Web server records each and every access, making the data reliable and robust. Server-side solutions are often viewed as more reliable because the data is based on your server log files, which record every file (pages, images, documents, and so on) that are accessed via your Web sites. This is different from hosted applications, which rely on a bit of code placed at the bottom of your Web pages to track visitor activity. If the code is somehow removed or if the user leaves the page before the code has time to load properly, visitor access might not be tracked.

✔ **Privacy issues:** With server-side analytics, you don't have to worry about a competitor seeing your hidden treasure because the data is stored in-house. This is often the biggest fear when it comes to using tools like Google Analytics. For some Internet businesses, the idea that Google will have access to their Web site data is unnerving.

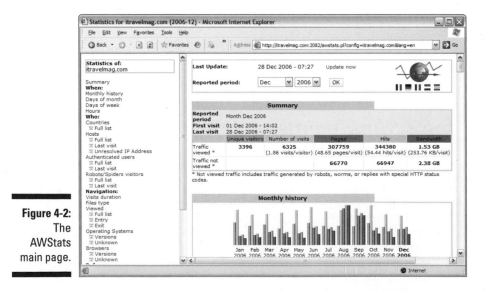

Figure 4-2:
The
AWStats
main page.

- **Site failures:** Server-side software offers insights into failed requests. Client-side software will tell you only if the page is successfully viewed. You can't fix what you don't know is broken.

- **Spider activity:** Server-side analytics offer critical information on search engine spider visitations. These visits are not lumped in with human activity: That is, they don't count as unique visitors. This spider data is key to search engine optimization (SEO) strategies. *SEO* is a method of improving the rankings for relevant keywords in search results by making changes to the content or navigational structure of a Web site.

- **Standardized log files:** Because the data is on your server, you can easily switch from program to program as you see fit, or use multiple programs that might offer slightly different features or data presentation. In other words, if you switch vendors, you won't lose your data.

Server-side shortcomings exposed

Of course, server-side tools do have their shortcomings. Client-side and hosted analytics solutions were developed to overcome some of them. Here are some server-side downsides that you should be aware of before ruling out other types of tools.

Server space shortages

Server-side analytics tools store lots of data on the Web server. If you have a hosting plan with strict limitations on space usage, you might have to limit the amount of historical data that you save on the server. Because viewing your analytics in a historical context can be vital to your success, this is a shortcoming that could make or break the deal.

Portability problems

If your Web site is on a shared hosting plan and you change hosting providers, your log files and analytics data probably won't move with you. If you aren't committed to your host, you might want to rely on a client-side or hosted solution, both of which can move when you do.

Is there an administrator in the house?

Whether your Web site is on a shared or dedicated server, there is always a chance that something will go wrong. Hard drives fail. Configurations get corrupted. You might run out of space on your hosting account. Log files could exceed their maximum defined file size. The possibilities are virtually endless.

Here's a general rule: If something can go wrong, you should plan for it. That means having a capable, responsive support staff at your hosting company, or a server administrator for your dedicated server in case your hardware stops tracking statistics for whatever reason. If you don't have someone who can respond in a hurry, you could face losing days or weeks of valuable analytics data — and corresponding opportunities.

Are server-side solutions right for me?

For many (if not most) small to medium Web site owners, server-side solutions are the simplest way to start keeping track of Web site performance and visitor activity. They come preinstalled and preconfigured, requiring little or no setup. If you are looking for simple, easy-to-use analytics data that are available at your beck and call but don't cost anything when you don't, free server-side tools are probably going to suit your needs perfectly.

On the other hand, if your hosting company offers raw log files but doesn't offer analytics tools, you might want to consider purchasing a client-side (or desktop) application to parse those log files for you. Additionally, if you think you might be changing to a different hosting provider, consider opting for an analytics solution that is completely independent of your hosting provider and get set up with a hosted analytics application so you won't have to worry about switching analytics programs ever again (unless you want to).

Discovering Desktop Applications

Like many terms in the Web analytics world, the second type of site measurement tools has various names. Some call it a *desktop solution* because, well, you can access it from your desktop. Others call it *client-side software* because the computer is known in technology circles as a *client.* Much the same as server-side analytics, there are pros and cons to using client-side solutions.

Maintaining control with client-side analytics

Client-side analytics have caught on with Web site owners for three good reasons:

- The application is installed on the user's computer.
- The stored data can be presented with lightning speed.
- The analytics can be accessed even without an active Internet connection.

Client-side analytics also offer this added bonus: The software allows you to keep original log files on your computer and store them independently of Web hosts or hosted analytics providers.

All this adds up to a level of comfort and control for users who don't have complete access to their Web server. Additionally, this software provides the data in a vehicle — namely, the desktop — that users are already comfortable with for most of their everyday computing needs.

Long-term cost versus benefits

Any assessment of software must include a look a long-term cost versus benefits. This is especially true when you look at handing over large sums of cash up front to invest in a program. Although server-side analytics offers strong data points to discern user behavior, more robust server-side solutions can become costly and difficult to implement. This is because in the server-side arena, the next step up from free is generally straight to the enterprise level. These tools can costs thousands of dollars to license and might require an in-depth level of configuration that only experts are suited for.

Client-side applications (and hosted applications, too) do a fine job of filling a void in the middle market, e-businesses that need more than what free tools provide, but don't have the money or need for costly enterprise solutions, without breaking the bank. When you need more detail than your standard server-side applications offer but you don't feel the need to invest in the enterprise-level software, your two choices are simple. You can pay $10–$50 a month for a hosted solution, or you can purchase entry-level, client-side software in the $100–$500 range.

When you're looking at a long-term solution, it might make sense to pay the one-time cost rather than commit to a long-term relationship with a hosted analytics provider. Hosted providers store all the Web analytics data on their servers. That means that if you cancel your account, you lose access to that data — forever. Without this historical data, forecasting future seasonal or product trends is more difficult. So when you're comparing paid hosted providers, total the rental expenses for a one-year, five-year, and ten-year period. After viewing the costs in light of the big picture, you might decide that purchasing a piece of software for $500 is cheaper than paying $39 per month, after all.

Managing multiple domains

If you have more than one Web site, client-side Web analytics programs offer a marked advantage over other options: the ability to manage multiple domains. Keeping track of multiple domains with sever-side and hosted solutions can be difficult. Instead of forcing you to view your precious stats in several locations, client-side application gives you one central place to view statistics for all your domains and save all your data. There is also a cost factor to consider for the frugal data miner: If you're using a paid hosted solution, the cost is usually assessed per domain. Those fees can add up in a hurry when you're managing scores of domains.

Client-side cons and desktop downsides

It's been said that every pro has its con. After you filled up the plus side of your comparison column, consider these desktop downsides.

The buck stops here

One of the first disadvantages to client-side applications is cost. Although several free options are available in both the server-side and hosted categories, the control offered by client-side analysis comes at a price. Pricing for entry-level desktop analysis tools falls within the $100–$200 range, and intermediate tools cost around $250–$500.

Getting too big for your britches

Because client-side applications rely on server log files, you have no choice but to download all those log files to your computer. When you have a Web site that serves up tons of traffic, these log files tend to get very large, very quickly. That can make downloading the files and then waiting while your applications parses the files far too time-consuming to trouble with, especially when compared with server-side and hosted solutions. With the latter two options, the parsing is accomplished behind the scenes.

All client-side software is not created equal. In fact, some client-side software cannot parse extremely large log files and might just leave you stumbling around in the dark on your search for hidden treasure. Entry-level applications might freeze or operate very slowly when presented with log files that are over 100MB.

Getting granular: Access log parsing

Client-side and server-side analytics tools rely on raw access logs located on your server to calculate your Web site traffic and visitor data. Your Web server records every single file that is accessed from your Web site, including images, PDFs, Word documents, or other file types. This data usually includes dates, times, referring information, a record of pages viewed, information about the user's computer and network, and more. Essentially, analytics applications automatically parse the access logs and present the information in easy-to-read bar charts and relevant rates and percentages.

Keeping all your eggs in one basket

Because all the data gathered by client-side analytics applications is typically saved to your local desktop computer, you have only one point of failure. However, it's a potentially devastating one. A corrupted or failed hard drive could mean the losing months — or worse, years — of analytics data that can never be recovered again even by the most sophisticated recovery programs.

Most hosted and server-side solutions are prepared for these types of night-mare-inducing failures. They keep multiple backups, so even if something happens to the data, it can be restored from a backup.

If you choose to use client-side software, save yourself some potential drama by keeping regular backups of your files.

Are client-side solutions right for me?

Client-side solutions allow you to take a more active role in the nitty-gritty Web analytics process. Simply put, you set up the domains, download the log files, and choose your options in an environment that you're already familiar with: the desktop. Client-side solutions, though, are often more costly than server-side solutions, so if you are just testing the waters, if your budget is low to non-existent, or if you really need only some simple metrics to satisfy your curiosity, client-side solutions might not be your best bet.

Hooked on Hosted Solutions

Offered by any one of many ASPs on the market, hosted analytics solutions are the newest breed of analytics application. *Hosted solutions* are called such because the data is stored on the ASP's server instead of the shared server provided by your Web host or the dedicated server in your offices. Hosted solutions require you to log in to an ASP's Web site in order to view and ana-lyze your data.

Just like server-side and client-side, hosted solutions have plenty of pros and cons that you need to understand before you can make an intelligent decision about your intelligence-gathering tool of choice.

On-demand: Let the vendor do the work

Also called *on-demand*, hosted solutions are all the rage — and for good reason: The Web analytics vendor does all the work. There's no log file pars-ing, downloading, installing, or maintenance. The vendor also gets to deal with all the trouble shooting if something goes wrong. That means you don't need to know how to do anything except interpret the data. For more information on how to interpret the data, read Chapter 8.

Keep your cash flow flowing

Hosted applications can also help regulate your cash flow. ASPs let you rent the application for small monthly payments. Payments range from $15–$60 a month for intermediate tools and $100–$250 a month for advanced tools. Compare this with handing over a large, one-time fee to actually purchase the software and call it your own. If your Web site is a revenue generator, you may want to check with a qualified tax consultant to see if you can write off the cost of the hosted tools on your taxes as an operating expense.

Anytime access

Similar to server-side tools, hosted analytics solutions don't tie you down to one-computer access. That means if you are the type who gets sudden impulses to check your Web analytics on the fly, ASPs can usually accommodate you with Web-based reports that can be accessed anywhere there is an Internet connection. (See Figure 4-3.)

Figure 4-3:
Login
screen for
Google
Analytics, a
popular
hosted
analytics
application.

Individual page tagging

Client-side analytics have caught on with Web site owners because they capture data only for pages you want to track. That reduces the amount of data you have to store or process and can make it easier for you to identify key performance indicators (KPIs) when you are looking over your data. *KPIs* illustrate how well the site is performing against goals.

One Web site, multiple servers

Occasionally, you might need your Web site to span multiple servers. Sounds techie, we know. Here's a practical example that will drive this important point home. If you're using a hosted third-party shopping cart solution, your server-side analytics tools might not work. This is a common situation e-commerce players who depend on server-side analytics find themselves in because server-side solutions record traffic only from the server on which they are installed. If you use a hosted solution, your Web site can span multiple servers and combine the data from different servers into one complete report.

Hosted analytics pitfalls

Although hosted solutions seem to be the next frontier in Web analytics, they are not without their faults. Review these common pitfalls before you take the plunge.

To tag or not to tag?

One of the advantages of hosted solutions is that you have to tag only the pages that you want to track. When you stop to think about that, though, the disadvantages are obvious. If you don't tag all the pages, you won't get an accurate clickstream. That means you can throw all the sermons about accuracy out the back door. If you have a simple site, tagging every page might take a matter of minutes. If your site is content heavy, though, you could be in for a major project.

Considering site architecture

Although adding a few lines of code onto a Web page isn't complicated, making sure that you tag every page to get the big clickstream picture can be a difficult task on certain sites. In fact, depending on how your site is architected and designed, tagging every page can be virtually impossible. If your site consists of individual HTML pages, you (or your Web developer) would have to open each page and add the code in the appropriate location for each page. Imagine the task that becomes when you are looking at hundreds of thousands of pages!

No error page information

Unless error pages and redirect pages have JavaScript embedded in the tags, you can't track page-loading errors with hosted solutions. That means you might not see the whole picture when it comes to broken pages or images on your site. Error information is important because if your customers are trying to read a thrilling article, make a purchase, or perform some other function only to click to a broken page, they might get frustrated and not return.

Are you looking for a long-term relationship?

ASPs design hosted solutions for customers who are looking for long-term relationships. Because of the time investment involved in adding the code to your pages and because all your access information is stored on the ASP's server, hopping from provider to provider is not easy or advisable. If you're considering a paid hosted solution, don't forget to weigh the long-term costs of the relationship. In other words, do you want to keep paying the monthly fees for this service in five years? Ten years?

Are hosted solutions right for me?

Hosted solutions might make the most financial sense when you consider the big picture. When you "rent" a hosted analytics solution, you can leave your problems at the vendor's doorstep. You don't have to worry about potentially costly server administrator time if something goes wrong with your server-side analytics. As we mention earlier — and it's worth mentioning again — the low monthly fees also save you from shelling out large sums of money to purchase a desktop solution.

Don't forget the tech-savvy warning: If you'd rather pull your hair out than learn how to add code to your Web site, you'll want to avoid hosted solutions like the Avian flu. And if your organization requires a high level of privacy and control, you might want to bring the task in house. Finally, don't forget to consider the long-term costs associated with the long-term commitment associated with hosted providers.

Getting the Best of All Worlds

Serious Web analytics watchers might choose to use some combination of the three available tool types to leverage synergies that could never be achieved by a single tool alone. Remember, hosted solutions mean you don't have to keep log files. Client-side software allows you to track all your domains with a single program. And server-side solutions are very convenient and oftentimes free. Here we show you what you can do by combining one or more of these tools in your search for statistical gold.

Leveraging synergies of multiple tool types

You've heard undoubtedly the phrase, "You scratch my back, and I'll scratch yours." In other words, two people help one another. In the world of Web analytics, client-side and server-side Web analytics sort of scratch one another's backs. They make up for one another's weaknesses when used to analyze the same Web site.

Keeping track of downloads — such as PDF files, Microsoft Word documents, music files, or some other type of download that your site offers — can be difficult, if not impossible, with today's hosted analytics solutions. Instead of missing out on this valuable information, just revert to your sever-side solution, which offers flawless tracking of downloads because the Web server logs every file request individually. Are you getting the picture?

If you regularly check your server-side tools for overall traffic patterns but you're limited by poor visitor segmentation, try supplementing your server-side data with a client-side tool, such as ClickTracks Analyzer (`www.click-tracks.com`). Leveraging the benefits of multiple tools could give you insights that are otherwise only available in much more expensive solutions. Getting a little creative can save you money and help you cover all your analytics bases.

Why you might want to use multiple vendors

Just as you might choose to use more than one tool, you might also choose to use more than one vendor. Think of laundry detergents: They all have their proprietary benefits. Cold water soap is extra gentle on clothing, whereas Brand A is extra tough on stains. Others offer color-safe bleach or extra whitening power. It's a value-add that distinguishes one brand of soap from another.

It's the same in the Web analytics market. Each vendor certainly offers baseline benefits, but some have developed proprietary algorithms, visitor segmentation methods, or special graphical presentations that might interest you.

Sure, it's a pity to have to use three services to get all the features and functions you need, but it's not much different than buying pre-stain remover, extra-strength detergent, softener, and wrinkle-remover for your laundry. It's a "whatever it takes to get the job done" mentality that, well, gets the job done.

If all of this has your head spinning, don't worry. Table 4-1 breaks it down for you in black and white. A quick glance will offer you a checklist of sorts of the benefits of server-side, client-side, and hosted solutions.

Table 4-1	Benefits Table for the Three Types of Analytics Applications		
Benefit	*Server-Side*	*Client-Side*	*Hosted*
Free tools available	✓		✓
Middle-market tools available		✓	✓
Enterprise tools available	✓		✓
Independent of Web server log files			✓
Independent of hosting company		✓	✓
Anywhere access (with Internet connection)	✓		✓
Available for offline viewing		✓	
No modification of Web pages required	✓	✓	
Able to track across multiple servers			✓
Independent of vendor	✓	✓	

Chapter 5

Investing in Web Analytics Tools

*W*hen it comes to word processors, choosing software is relatively simplistic. (A software giant in Redmond, Washington, has made sure of that.) Stepping into the world of Web analytics tools, though, is like venturing into your local big-box home improvement center. Walk down the power tools aisle, and you'll find cordless drills, compact drills, variable speed drills, drill combos, and a host of other borers for your consideration — large drills, small drills, red drills, yellow drills . . . . You get the picture.

In addition to the three key categories of Web analytics software — namely, client-side, server-side, and hosted — you'll also find a world of difference in the functions, capabilities, and (of course) price ranges for these data mining applications. (*Server-side analytics tools* are software installed on the Web site's server. *Client-side tools* are installed on your computer. And *hosted solutions* are hosted by a service provider on its server. Read more about all these categories in Chapter 4.)

Thus, before you invest your time and energy when purchasing a Web analytics tool, learning its distinct terminology, and benchmarking your data based on its initial assessment of your Web site, you need to know exactly what you're getting into. Most Web analytics vendors — and there are enough of them to make your head spin — offer a free trial before forcing you to fork over the dough.

So which one do you choose? That depends on your specific needs: the size of your company, how much traffic your site gets, and how much you want to spend. What is certain is this: You need the tools if you want to monitor conversion rates, learn how user groups interact with your Web site, discover where visitors are coming from and what they are looking for, and many other metrics that could help you improve your success online.

So take a hint from the savvy home improvement guru who visits the big-box store looking for that new drill. Rather than getting intimidated by shelf after shelf of choices, get excited by the possibility of choosing from the one shelf that offers several models to fit your specific needs. In this chapter, we'll help you narrow the choosing field so you can spend your time drilling through data rather than selecting the drill.

Before You Begin

You wouldn't rush into a marriage, so don't rush into a commitment with a Web analytics vendor. Take your time to compare apples with apples, so to speak, and measurements with measurements. Because being able to review historical data is immensely important and because vendor hopping can erase that history in a heartbeat, you want to be sure that the vendor you choose has the features, functions, and technologies to serve your needs for the long term.

You can't possibly know whether a vendor has what you need until you know what you need. The best way to do that is to start with a free tool and get familiar with the baseline measurements. Quite possibly, a freebie tool has everything you need and more. If it doesn't, you can quickly figure out what you're missing. While you are monitoring your Web analytics reports for trends, take some time to review the for-fee offerings on the market to discover what you might not even know that you're missing. You'll be surprised at what Web analytics can tell you about your site. Really surprised.

 Plan to take several months to choose your Web analytics vendor. If you're looking at free or low-cost solutions, ferret out which software meets your business requirements and gels with the technical specifications of your site. That may mean reviewing vendor Web sites or even picking up the phone and calling a vendor. And if you're looking at an enterprise solution, the vendor might work up a proposal to win your business. Either way, put on your investigator's cap and check out the vendor's history, stability, track record for innovation, implementation and support offerings, contract terms and (of course) pricing. Always ask for client referrals, and don't jump on the low-price bandwagon just to save a few dollars. Inaccurate results could cost you well more than a few dollars in the long run.

Don't Forget the Freebies

Before you invest a single penny in Web analytics, consider taking some of the free programs for a test drive? You might find that these tools give you a nice view of the landscape.

The advantage of free tools is clear: They are free. And plenty of free tools are out there for the installing. The downside, though, can be dark:

- ✔ **Not as full-featured:** Free tools don't pack the same informational punch as paid tools.

- ✔ **Not as much support:** Free tools don't usually offer any support, either. That means you are on your own in a sea of data. No one is there to hold your hand, explain a metric, or help you interpret the findings. (Of course, that's what you have this book for.)

Still, you should at least give the freebies a try. Who knows? You might catch on quick and begin leveraging the tool for more profits from Day One.

Before you can begin using the free tools, you need to know where to find them. And as you begin to use them, you should go in knowing what to expect — and what not to expect — or you could wind up frustrated. You wouldn't expect a Hyundai to perform the same way a Jaguar does. Much the same, you can't expect a free tool to perform the same way an enterprise tool does. What you can expect from a free tool (and a Hyundai) is to get you on the road so you can see some pretty views.

What to expect from free analytics tools

Free tools often have very simple user interfaces that any beginner can learn quickly. For example, Google Analytics essentially presents a more friendly and simplified version of Urchin for mass consumption. Google states on its site that it believes "Web analytics should be simple and sophisticated at the same time." (Sort of like this book!)

At the entry level, you get quite a bit of mileage from your analytics dollar. Free Google Analytics is a massive temptation for marketers who see the possibility of putting budgets currently assigned to tool sets into the advertising market. You can expect a wide spectrum of functions and feature sets among the free tools; at the baseline, though, they all show you metrics, such as hits, pageviews, unique visitors, time on site, and the like.

What not to expect from the freebies

Free tools are great solutions for low-to-moderate traffic sites. When a site grows to higher volumes, though, the solutions might no longer prove effective for anything other than a quick scan of basic metrics. And basic metrics are about all you get with most of the free analytics tools. If you want to engage in complex visitor profiling or ad campaign tracking, don't expect to find that in your freebie tools. Also don't expect to get any type of customer support with most of these tools.

Don't expect to find cutting-edge innovation, either. Sure, some of the programs are *open source,* meaning that developers from all over the world can contribute to the programming to make improvements to the program. Without large development budgets, though, it's unlikely that free Web analytics programs will match costly enterprise-level analytics features and functionality any time soon. Meanwhile, the more expensive solutions just keep getting better.

Although every Web analytics vendor has its own terminology, proprietary tools, and benefits, here is a common denominator among them: They all measure visitor behavior:

- How visitors find your site
- What visitors do when they get there
- How long visitors stay
- Other insightful actions, such as the keywords they typed into search engines to find your site and other sites that referred visitors your way

Be sure to take Web analytics vendors up on their free trial offers and take the software for a test drive before you lay out any cash.

Finding free analytics tools

If you already have a Web site, your likely host offers some sort of free tool on the back end. Read Chapter 3 for step-by-step instructions on how to access your Web analytics tools, take a sneak peak at the data, and start setting some benchmarks.

If your Web host doesn't offer any analytics or if you just want to explore the free landscape, your task is easy. Just go to your search engine of choice and type in **"free Web analytics"**. You'll get a number of results to get you started. Here are a few, however, that have achieved a solid reputation in the freebie market.

Analog

```
http://analog.cx
```

Analog (see Figure 5-1) bills itself as the most popular logfile analyzer in the world. (*Logfiles* are data files that record transactions that occurred on the Web server.) You can learn more about logfiles in Chapter 15. We're not sure about that, but it does offer several advantages. It's scalable, highly configurable — and free. It works on any operating system, and it reports in 32 languages. This free tool offers free support or commercial support. It's very easy to read and offers a quick round up of overall statistics. This software works with any operating system and any browser.

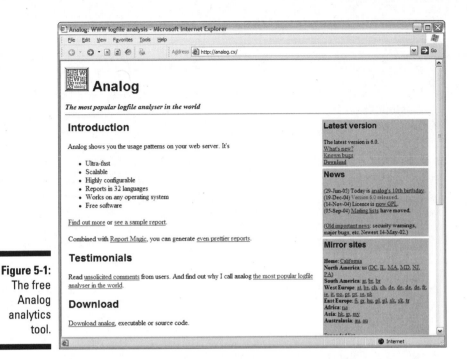

Figure 5-1:
The free
Analog
analytics
tool.

Downside: However, because this is a server-side application, you need root access to your Web server, or you need to ask your hosting company to install this for you.

AWStats

```
www.awstats.org
```

AWStats (see Figure 5-2) generates some fairly robust analytics for a free tool. It analyzes Web, streaming, FTP (File Transfer Protocol), or mail server statistics graphically. It can also analyze logfiles from all major server tools. This open source tool is very easy to read and offers a quick round up of overall statistics. You can even get info on worm attacks with this software. This free tool works with any operating system or browser.

Downside: Because this is a server-side application, you need root access to your Web server, or you need to ask your hosting company to install this for you.

ClickTracks Appetizer

```
http://clicktracks.com/products/appetizer/
```

ClickTracks Appetizer (see Figure 5-3) includes several of ClickTracks' most popular features:

✔ Overlay view

✔ Path view

✔ Page analysis

✔ Basic visitor labeling; tagging visitors based on their use of search engines

✔ Search referrals

✔ Returning visitors

The software is flexible and allows you to select and label visitors who meet criteria important to you. It offers all the usual metrics and more and helps you make comparisons that lead to conversions.

Downside: However, the tool works only with Windows; if you run Mac OS X or Linux, you are out of luck.

ClickTracks also makes for-fee tools that you could upgrade to if you like this vendor's platform. This software is installed directly on your computer and does not utilize your browser.

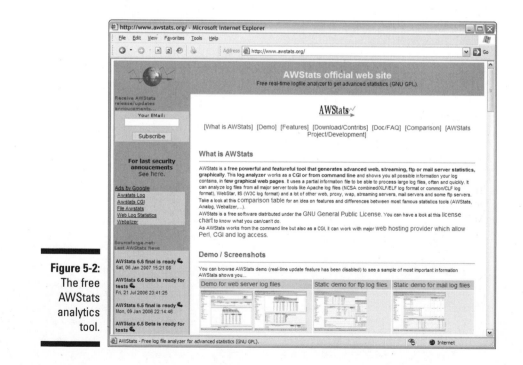

Figure 5-2:
The free AWStats analytics tool.

Figure 5-3:
The free
ClickTracks
Appetizer
analytics
tool.

Google Analytics

www.google.com/analytics

Google's motive with its free analytics tool is to tell you everything you want to know about how visitors found your site and how they interact with it so that you can focus your marketing resources on campaigns and initiatives that deliver a return on your investment. Wow. That's a mouthful!

In short, Google wants to give you a free tool (see Figure 5-4) in hopes you'll spend more on Adwords. If you are a Google Adwords buyer, Google Analytics might be a good choice because it is integrated with the *pay per click* (PPC) platform. Also called *paid search,* this method retrieves listings based on who paid the most money for keywords to appear at the top of the heap. Of course, it also tracks non-Adwords initiatives.

Downside: Google Analytics only updates statistics one time in a 24-hour period. That means you can't get up-to-the-minute stats on a campaign you are running. If that's an important feature, you'll have to choose another tool or use another tool to supplement Google Analytics.

Figure 5-4:
The free
Google
Analytics
tool.

OneStatFree

www.onestatfree.com

OneStatFree (see Figure 5-5) offers free hit counters and Web analytics tools as well as paid options. You can see all the usual *key performance indicators* (KPIs). *KPIs* illustrate how well the site is performing against goals. You can read much more about KPIs in Chapter 11.

What's unique about this tool is that you can see how your site performs compared with other Web sites in the same category or same country, based on the number of *pageviews* (a record of each time a visitor views a Web page on your site). The vendor claims that inclusion in its charts listings boosts traffic to your Web site. This tool works with any platform or any browser.

Downside: The tradeoff is that you have to display a counter/tracker icon on your Web site.

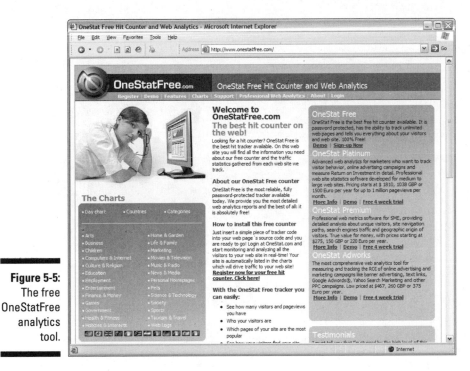

Figure 5-5:
The free
OneStatFree
analytics
tool.

CrazyEgg

`www.crazyegg.com`

CrazyEgg does what no other reputable free tool can claim: visitor visualization. First, CrazyEgg offers a *heat map.* Sort of like an infrared camera, this software literally shows you what's hot on your Web site with red, orange, and blue areas imposed over your site. (See Figure 5-6.) CrazyEgg also has overlays that show buttons containing information on each element of your site, such as how many clicks it received. You can track up to 5,000 visitors per month for free. Or, you can spend $25 per month to track up to 25,000 visitors or $99 per month for up to 250,000 visitors. This is a hosted solution, so there's no software to install. This tool works with any platform or browser.

Downside: The only potential downsides for Crazy Egg is that you have to paste one line of code to the bottom of each Web page you want to visualize, which can be tedious. Also, by its visual nature, you don't get the depth or breadth of reports you might with traditional freebie tools. What's more, free accounts are only updated every few hours.

These are just a few of the many free tools out there. If you want a quick hit on a few more, check out the Cheat Sheet in the front of the book for our recommendations.

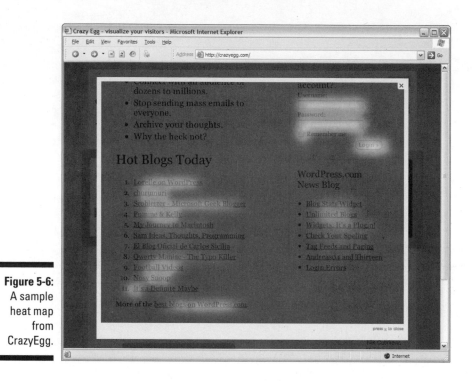

Figure 5-6:
A sample
heat map
from
CrazyEgg.

Low-Cost Solutions, High-End Returns

Free Web analytics solutions are great, but they will take you only so far on your journey to increasing online profits. If you are serious about generating income with your Web site, you probably need to consider using a low-cost solution at some point to calculate metrics that the freebie tools won't even list. The next step on the ladder is an entry-level package. Inexpensive tools such as Unica NetTracker, VisiStat, ClickTracks, nextStat, and IndexTools offer some valuable capabilities at lower price points.

You can subscribe to entry-level hosted solutions for $60 per month or even less. (Some are as little as $15 per month.) For this price, you have more control over the metrics you measure because you can customize the dashboard and use filtering technologies. You can set permissions so that certain users can only see certain data. Some even offer live reporting capabilities. Finally, you get customer support that is often lacking in free tools.

Valuable capabilities for the value-conscious consumers

When you outgrow the freebie tools but can't quite justify spending a fortune on Web analytics at this stage in your business game, don't despair. Plenty of affordable solutions with valuable capabilities are available for value-conscious customers like you. Most low-cost vendors do everything that the freebie tools do and more. At this level, your analytics applications are capable of advanced visitor profiling, high-level ad campaign tracking, and in-depth click fraud detection. Unless you are a Fortune 1000 company, these low-cost tools will likely offer you everything you need to drive value from your measurements.

Getting acquainted with low-cost vendors

No two entry-level Web analytics tools are alike. Some refresh their statistics only a few times a day, and others offer near real-time tracking. Still others allow you to click an Update Now tool when you want the latest stats.

Too, you'll find that some entry-level tools are extremely user-friendly while others are quite complicated. Usually, the more complicated tools pack more metrics into the analysis. Low-cost vendors target small- to mid-sized businesses. Here are a few of the most popular choices to give you an idea of what to expect.

Unica NetTracker

```
http://unica.com
```

Unica NetTracker (see Figure 5-7) is designed to help you optimize your Web programs, such as PPC advertising, e-mail campaigns, search engine optimization, and affiliate marketing. It also targets intranet owners who want to measure the effectiveness of their online knowledgebase and community. NetTracker lets you slice and dice the data in a variety of ways to make important comparisons. You can see clickstream paths, online product interests, Web trends, visitor conversion patterns, and Web content quality and visitor retention rates, among other metrics. You can use page tags, logfiles, or a hybrid of both. (*Page tags* are snippets of code that need to be inserted in your Web pages in order for many hosted applications to gather your data.)

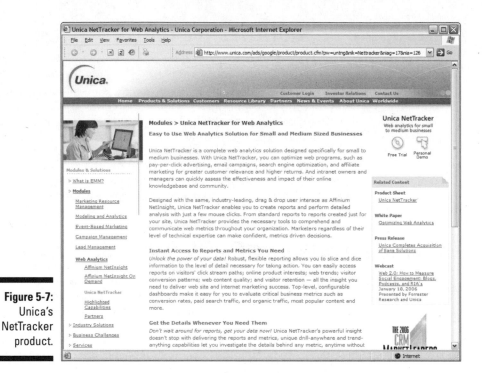

Figure 5-7:
Unica's
NetTracker
product.

VisiStat

www.visistat.com

VisiStat (see Figure 5-8) offers an attractive competitive advantage: live reporting. That means you can see live site visitors, what pages they are viewing, and how they navigate through the site while these events happen. You can also chart pay per click results, track demographic interests, or focus marketing by location. This program helps you identify areas of interest on your site so you can distribute important content to high traffic pages and identify navigational errors. It also offers a laundry list of technical stats, such as report resolution and color depth. You can get this solution for as little as $19.99 per month. This tool works with any operating system or browser.

ClickTracks

www.clicktracks.com

ClickTracks (see Figure 5-9) offers free tools, enterprise tools, and entry-level tools. At the entry level, this vendor offers its Analyzer. This program offers visitor labeling and actually superimposes the data on your Web site so you can see and understand visitor behavior firsthand rather than using charts and pie graphs, rows of numbers, and percentages. You can even select "goal" pages that help you identify which pages lead to conversions. You can get this solution for as little as $25 per month. This tool works with any operating system or browser.

Figure 5-8:
VisiStat
analytics
tool.

Figure 5-9:
ClickTracks
Analyzer
analytics
software.

nextStat

www.nextstat.com

nextStat (see Figure 5-10) is one of the easiest to use among the entry-level tools, but it's also among the least sophisticated. You won't find the level of in-depth analysis with this tool that others in its class have to offer. You can create some solid reports, though. For example, you might choose to see all visitors who browsed a minimum of six pages on the site and then responded to the call to action. This tool also offers the unique feature of being able to click an icon next to each page to see a display of the path analysis for visitors on that page. If it's ease of use you are after, this might be the perfect tool for you. You'll pay more than you do for the others, though, at $59.95 per month. This tool works with any operating system or browser.

Downside: NextStat will only track pages that you tag.

IndexTools

www.indextools.com

IndexTools (see Figure 5-11) offers real-time reporting and a user-friendly interface. You can customize your dashboard for quick access to the reports you need in a hurry. This tool offers some interesting segmentations. If you have a sale on toothpaste in June, for example, you can set goals and quickly determine whether you met your objectives. You can also get an instant snapshot of whether a visitor made a purchase and how much he spent. The program offers a variety of filters that allow you to drill down into visitor segments that interest you the most. You'll pay $49.95 per month for this program, with the option of adding a host of plug-ins for another $30 per month. This tool works with any operating system or browser.

Reviewing vendor pricing models

As the Web analytics space gets more competitive, that trend translates into better deals for Web site operators. One key factor to look at is vendors' pricing models. Some charge a flat fee, and the software is yours to keep. Others charge a flat fee per month. Still others charge according to the number of pageviews that your site registers. Those upfront fees might be only part of the equation, though. You should also ask the vendor whether it makes its money on pageview volume, maintenance and upgrade fees, or add-ons. Judge that cost against your business needs today as well as what you are likely to need in the future. Sometimes the upfront cost can look great, but getting what you really need over time can become very costly if you don't choose wisely from the outset.

HitBox Professional

`www.websidestory.com`

WebSideStory offers an attractive entry-level tool called HitBox Professional (see Figure 5-12). It's aimed toward small- to mid-sized businesses that want to optimize their Web sites, improve customer satisfaction, and optimize online marketing. This is a solid program. It does a lot of the necessary comparisons for you, such as comparing search engine traffic counts and identifying top performing promotions. This can help you focus your resources where the returns are. You can also see what pages your customers looked at — and in what order — so you can identify compelling content and increase visitor satisfaction. This is a bottom-line tool that only costs $34.95 per month. This tool works with any operating system or browser.

MetriServe

`www.metriserve.com`

MetriServe (see Figure 5-13) offers up-to-the minute Web analytics with no logfiles or servers. The firm collects Web metrics directly from the visitor's browser and stores them on its servers. More than 50 real-time reports are provided in MetriServe's online reporting tools, which are searchable and customizable over any date range. You can also export reports as PDF files or as raw data. This program helps you find hidden patterns in how visitors use your Web site as it aims to uncover relationships between pages on your site that you wouldn't otherwise know existed. This is a European vendor that charges by pageviews. It costs about $18 per month for 10,000 pageviews or $600 for 10 million pageviews. This tool works with any operating system or browser.

ecommStats

`www.ecommstats.com`

This program (see Figure 5-14) is heavy into tracking conversions and what caused those conversions. You can quickly see your return on investment (ROI) for your spending on search engine advertising and analyze how your visitors navigate through your site. And as a nice bonus, you can manage an unlimited number of Web sites from a single account. As its name suggests, this Web analytics program is targeted to folks who sell widgets on their site, with features, such as revenue generated by referrer. The program is Secure Sockets Layer (SSL) compatible, so you don't have to worry about techie issues associated with tracking e-commerce sites. ecommStats charges by pageviews. You can choose a plan that runs $25 for 50,000 pageviews up to 200,000 pageviews for $85, with special pricing for higher volumes.

Figure 5-12:
HitBox
Professional
analytics
tool.

Figure 5-13:
MetriServe
analytics
tool.

Figure 5-14:
ecommStats
analytics
tool.

Enterprise Analytics for the Data Hungry

If you have an insatiable appetite for Web metrics — and a real need for deep insights — enterprise-level products might be the only software that will make you content. Enterprise-level tools do everything the freebies and mid-level applications do — and much more. Because they target larger companies, enterprise-level tools are heavily focused on metrics that demonstrate ROI.

Often, these sophisticated vendors offer specialized packages for marketing, commerce, or some other special need. Enterprise-level products are critical in developing custom reports that lighter versions of this software typically can't accommodate. These programs allow you to get details on unique users at a deeper level, which is particularly important in higher price-point sales or higher lifetime value situations in which you might have fewer shoppers and need to make the most of every visit.

The more sophisticated your business, the more sophisticated the software needs.

Enterprise solutions are not for companies with shallow pockets. The price tags on these powerful solutions start around $15,000 per year. With such a hefty investment in analytics, many businesses that operate at this level have one person dedicated to analyzing and parsing all this data. Such analysis can get pretty complex, and training someone who is uninitiated can be a costly proposition. The future will likely see Chief Analytics Officers and Directors of Web Analytics who have a prominent position and considerable salaries.

If you want to run with the big dogs, you'll want to take a look at vendors such as WebTrends, Omniture, WebSideStory, and Coremetrics. These solutions all have their proprietary bells and whistles, but generally speaking, they tell you more about your visitors than entry-level and midrange solutions ever could. They also have some interesting features. Here are a few standouts from some of the leading enterprise vendors.

WebTrends Web Analytics 8

`www.webtrends.com`

This software (see Figure 5-15) lets you benchmark KPIs and explore what-if scenarios to identify where to focus your budgets. It gives you a complete view into which campaigns are successful and which aren't, from e-mail and online advertising to affiliate and partner programs. You can monitor search engine optimization and PPC results, drill down into your Web site stats by search engine and phrase, and integrate your PPC cost data with your Web site stats for a complete marketing ROI breakdown. You can even optimize conversion rates for each page, path, and conversion scenario.

Creating customized reports

No two businesses are alike. That's why enterprise-level tools offer customizable reports, which combat information overload and offer quick insights into enhancing online revenue opportunities. You can tailor these reports to your specific online business objectives that are most relevant to your bottom line. You can find out what the marketing ROI of your marketing initiatives is, what visitor segments are likely to convert into customers; where the bottlenecks are in your purchase path; what content, products and services visitors prefer; and much more. WebTrends' custom report engine is both flexible and advanced, allowing you to measure users across a buy cycle, and then deduce and update their status accurately. WebSideStory's HBX lets you integrate external cost data. Coremetrics has a strong focus on merchandising as well as lifetime profiling. These powerful analytics engines allow you to blend elements that are most important to you with just a few clicks.

Figure 5-15:
WebTrends
Web
Analytics 8.

Omniture Site Catalyst 13

www.omniture.com

This program (see Figure 5-16) includes Web 2.0 Business Optimizations for Web site owners struggling to measure this new technology. *Web 2.0* is part of the ongoing transition of the World Wide Web from a collection of Web sites to a comprehensive computing platform that serves up Web applications to end users. Some believe that Web 2.0 will eventually replace desktop applications. Omniture is on the cutting edge with its software, which offers the standard enterprise-level analytics. In addition, you can find special measurement tools for social networking sites, blogs, rich Internet applications, dynamic site search, and visitor interaction profiling.

WebSideStory HBX

www.websidestory.com

HBX (see Figure 5-17) is a powerful tool that offers features such as Web site navigation analysis, robust e-commerce analysis, campaign analytics, and custom reports in executive dashboards. However, this program also offers some over-the-top functions, such as internal search tracking, detailed content analysis, and an active segmentation model that lets you combine any number of visitor session characteristics in order to create segments on the fly. Cross-channel integration is another interesting feature, correlating Web site behavior with offline sales conversions through technology integration with Salesforce.com.

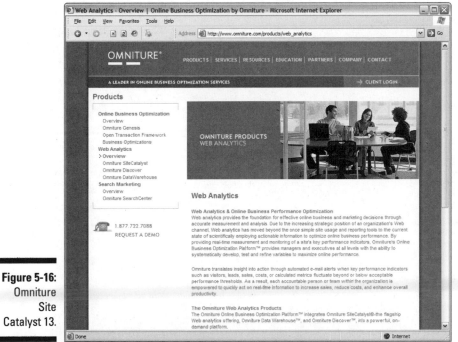

Figure 5-16:
Omniture
Site
Catalyst 13.

Coremetrics Online Analytics

www.coremetrics.com

Coremetrics Online Analytics (see Figure 5-18) aims to serve as a single resource for planning, measuring, and testing integrated marketing efforts. The vendor brags about its visualization tools and targeted business solutions that allow you to uncover value and take action. Coremetrics offers an interesting feature — LIVE Profiles — that delivers information on actual customer behaviors. This vendor takes a cross-channel approach that incorporates offline and call center activities with Web stats. The software also enables profile mining to allow you to maximize lifetime customer value by identifying high-value visitors and understanding product affinities.

Figure 5-17:
WebSide
Story's HBX
analytics
tool.

Figure 5-18:
Coremetrics
Online
Analytics.

Chapter 6

Discovering Niche Solutions

*W*eb analytics tools used to be one-size-fits-all, relatively speaking. In other words, you wouldn't find much difference between what each vendor could measure. From the genesis of Web analytics — when Web counters tracked nothing more than how many eyeballs viewed your home page — the market is beginning to see waves of niche products designed to track everything from blogs (or *Weblog;* a frequently updated online journal, usually for public viewing) to *Really Simple Syndication* (RSS) feeds (a new way to distribute content over the Internet) to industry-specific metrics.

Indeed, Web analytics was once described as a niche industry with mass market products. Now, it's becoming just the opposite: a mass market industry with niche products. Indeed, because no two companies — or no two Web sites — are alike, Web analytics has matured to offer niche products that fill needs that have emerged as the Internet has matured.

If you're wondering whether you can't just analyze all this information with a regular Web analytics program, the short answer is simple: sure. The better answer is that you can certainly measure *some* of it. However, these special tools zero in on metrics that intend to help you make the most of your niche, typically offering some takes that you can't get with mass market analytics. Read on to discover what you can do with some of these targeted tools. You'll find that many of these niche analytics programs offer similar feature sets. As you review them, consider your budget, which operating systems the software works with, and the features that are most important to you. If you need help understanding what might be important to you, read Chapter 11 for insights on key performance indicators.

Web Analytics: A Boon for Bloggers

According to Technorati (a recognized authority on tracking a monitoring blog usage), about 63.2 million blogs were up and running in 2006. Of course, not all bloggers attempt to generate income through leads, advertising, or affiliate marketing, but many do — enough, indeed, for Web analytics vendors to develop tools targeted at this group of diverse self-publishers. Bloggers range from the casual (diarists, families blogging together, teens blogging in social networks) to topical bloggers (commenting on daily news events in various categories) to technology, political, and self-promoting bloggers (such as attorneys and other service firms hoping to generate leads by positioning themselves as experts).

Blog analytics developers have an advantage: They don't typically need to worry about tracking e-commerce functions. Their goal is to keep a pulse on who is reading what, how often, and when. What's different about blog analytics is that they keep things simple and talk in terms that bloggers understand. Instead of looking at a Most Requested Pages report, you can simply review your Top Posts. Many of these applications also have ways to track comments and RSS feeds, both of which are options that aren't regularly available in mainstream analytics applications.

The blogger who wants to build readership — say, to build credibility for a consultant or other professional attempting to establish expert status in a field — might choose to take the golden nuggets of information the analytics yield and guide the subject matter of his posts. Bloggers could also use the tools to validate traffic statistics in order to turn the heads of potential advertisers or to track links to see who sends traffic.

Here are a few solid tools you can use as well as some good news: Most blog analytics tools are easy to install. Specific instructions for your platform of choice are offered.

Mint

www.haveamint.com

As the first widely known analytics application-targeting bloggers, Mint (see Figure 6-1) took a fresh approach to measurement. This tool is also popular because it blocks referrer spam and comment spam, which is a major battle for bloggers. For a one time flat-fee of $30, you can license this analytics tool that breaks down site referrers by newest unique, most recent, and repeat referrers from a customizable time frame. You can also measure visits, browsers, and platforms; find search terms in popular search engines; and illuminate your most popular pages and most recently accessed content. You can even bookmark or watch individual pages.

Mint may not run on your server, though. It has been developed and beta tested on various Linux servers running Apache with a MySQL database (3.x and up), and PHP scripting (4.2.3 and up). You should check with your host if you aren't sure about those requirements. The developer offers a compatibility test that you can take to find out in a flash.

In order to view Mint, you need a modern browser. Mint recommends Safari or Firefox and only has partial support for Internet Explorer (IE). IE for Mac is not supported at all. In order to record hits, be sure to enable JavaScript on your browser of choice.

Measure Map

`www.measuremap.com`

Measure Map (acquired by Google in February 2006) helps you understand what people do at your blog, how many readers you influence on your virtual soapbox, and how many people respond to your pontifications. Measure Map (see Figure 6-2) presents the information in a compelling way. It not only tells you not how many visitors you had today, but it also immediately tells you, "That's 15 more than you had on an average day." It offers up the same quick assessment for links, comments, and posts. In essence, it does the heavy analytical lifting for you with this snapshot.

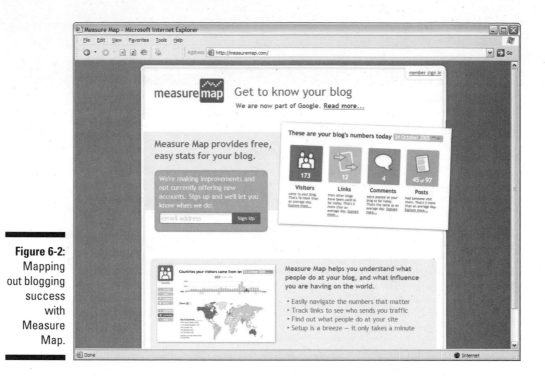

Figure 6-2:
Mapping
out blogging
success
with
Measure
Map.

Bloglet

www.bloglet.com

Bloglet (see Figure 6-3) offers an e-mail subscription service for your blog. The goal is to keep readers coming back by keeping them up to date on recent posts to their favorite blogs. Bloglet offers daily stats on total new subscribers, so you can watch your audience grow. You can also receive stats on how many sites link to you as well as a list of the Top 10, as tabulated by Google. This is a free tool, but unfortunately, it works only with Blogger or Moveable Type, which are two popular, free blog hosts.

Technorati

www.technorati.com

Technorati is recognized as the authority on what's happening on the Web. As of the time of this writing, the firm tracks 63.2 million blogs — and counting. Technorati searches, surfaces, and organizes blogs and other forms of independent, user-generated content. Technorati takes a bit of a different approach to analytics. It doesn't provide you with navigational paths; rather, it offers your ranking in

- ✔ the blogosphere
- ✔ the number of links pointing to your blog in the last 180 days
- ✔ the number of distinct blogs pointing to your blog in the last 180 days
- ✔ the total number of links it found pointing to your blog

This is a good way to compare your blog with the rest of the blogs in the blogosphere. However, you first have to "claim" your blog. Just visit www. technorati.com, scroll down to the bottom left of the page, and click Claim Your Blog. You'll be in the system in no time.

Figure 6-3:
Bloglet, a multipurpose tool.

103bees.com

www.103bees.com

103bees.com (see Figure 6-4) isn't a hive of stinging creatures: It's a free, real-time online tool for Webmasters and bloggers that is highly focused on natural search engine traffic analysis. It offers tons of detailed statistics and in-depth information on search terms that drive visitors to your blog. If you want to search engine optimize your blog, this is the tool for you. If you want to measure your Internet marketing initiatives, this tool is right up your alley — and it's free. 103bees.com helps you discover the *long tail* — all the keyword combinations that work for your Web pages. This is valuable because you can unlock hiding opportunities beyond the Top 10, such as new blogging content ideas that attract readers. Instead of paying for ads, you can merely mine your long tail of search and use those keywords to drive more traffic.

Read more about long tail referencing in Chapter 12.

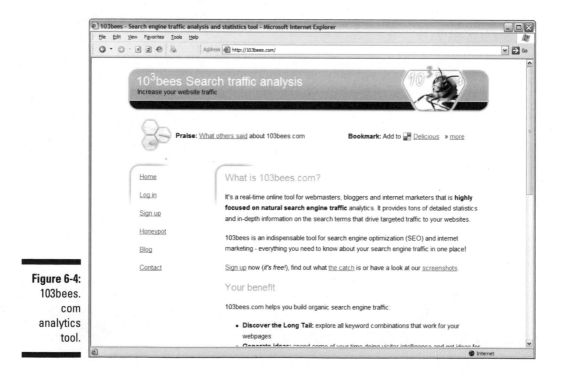

Figure 6-4:
103bees.
com
analytics
tool.

Battling blog spam

Blog spam, also called *comment spam,* is much like its annoying e-mail counterpart. These are unsolicited messages that usually advertise something that nobody wants. These bogus commenters aren't adding value to your blog. Instead, they attempt to use your blog to promote their products and services. These leeches know that if they can use comments, pings, or trackbacks to get a link from your blog, it will boost their search engine ratings. (A *trackback* is an automated comment that is added to one blog when another blog references it.) You can't complain to the perpetrator because you probably can't find him. It probably wouldn't do a bit of good, anyway. No, you've got to put on your combat gear and battle back.

Blogger (www.blogger.com) has an interesting approach to this. The Google property requires the poster to solve a captcha puzzle before posting. *Captcha* is an acronym for Completely Automated Public Turing Test to Tell Computers and Humans Apart. You've probably seen one before. It sort of distorts the letters so they look like a reflection in one of those mirrors you find at the county fair. The poster has to type in what the letters say. This verifies that a human being, rather than a spambot, is on the other side of the connection because computer programs can't read captchas. Alternatively, you can use a spam filter that comes with your blog. WordPress (www.wordpress.org) uses a program called Akismet to catch spam automatically. Or, you can choose to manually approve each comment, but that can be a pain to maintain, especially if your blog is getting a lot of comments, for good or bad.

Read All about It: RSS Analytics

RSS (Really Simply Syndication) is just that: a simple way to syndicate content online. It's a content delivery channel for publishers and bloggers who want to push their words out to the masses rather than waiting for the readers to come to them. According to Nielsen/NetRatings, RSS is riding on the blogging phenomenon to a large extent, but major online newspapers and magazines are also coming aboard. Research firms predict dramatic growth in RSS, and literally millions of feeds already exist.

RSS offers benefits to the reader and the sender. For the reader, RSS keeps the e-mail box free of newsletters. For the sender, RSS can boost search engine rankings. Your Web site link will show up on many RSS readers and increase your link popularity, which is one of the factors that search engines consider when determining your ranking. Setting up an RSS feed is easy, but the challenge is similar to blogging in that you have to continually provide new content. That's why RSS and blogs are often tied together. Bloggers use the tool as a way to let readers subscribe and pull the content in.

Like blogs and podcasts, RSS offers advertising opportunities. We're talking multiplied millions of dollars of ads getting pushed out to content readers through RSS feeder advertising networks, such as FeedBurner and Pheedo.

RSS ad spending is projected to reach $129.6 million by 2010, according to PQ Media. Wherever ad money funnels in, is a need for measurement tools. The promise of RSS riches, then, has spawned some niche analytics tools designed specifically to measure the impact of these feeds. These tools allow you to measure RSS specific metrics like the number of subscribers, clickthroughs from feeds, RSS usage patterns, and site usage patterns for RSS traffic.

FeedBurner

www.feedburner.com/fb/a/home

A testimony to the growth of blog analytics, Nielsen//NetRatings reports that FeedBurner (see Figure 6-5) is growing faster than Web 2.0 champions MySpace, a free online social networking community, and Digg, a user-driven content Web site. FeedBurner, a feed management provider, offers Web-based services designed to help bloggers, podcasters, and commercial publishers promote, deliver, and profit from their content on the Web. FeedBurner also offers the largest advertising network for feeds that brings together content aggregated from leading media companies, A-list bloggers (influential bloggers, with many other bloggers and Web sites linking to their blogs), blog networks, and individual publishers.

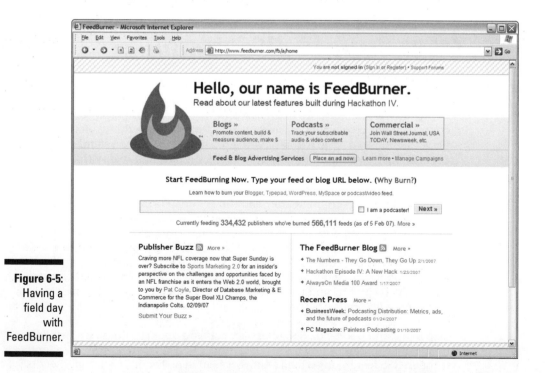

Figure 6-5:
Having a field day with FeedBurner.

With so much content flying around, FeedBurner has made heavy investments in analytics to capture subscriber statistics. Designed for the serious content producer, FeedBurner offers core statistics with detailed visibility into specific item statistics as well as an easy user interface. FeedBurner's *StandardStats* — its free service — leverages the critical mass of feed readers, bots, search engines, news filters, and other common feed sources. You can find out where your content is referenced as well as measure how many subscribers versus nonsubscribers access your productions. It even tracks the number of downloads of rich media files, such as audio and video podcasts.

TotalStats, the FeedBurner premium service, tells bloggers what percentage of the total subscriber base is actively reading and clicking individual items within a feed. Like newspapers and magazines, a certain percentage of readers subscribe while a certain percentage actively open and act on content. The Reach metric offers insight into the second group. TotalStats also offers Item Popularity stats, which offers a more thorough drill-down through the popularity of individual items in a feed. This gives you insights about specific posts on specific days as well as a history of activity.

FeedFoundry

`http://www.feedburner.com/fb/a/publishers/feedfoundry`

For larger publishers, FeedBurner offers a tool called FeedFoundry (see Figure 6-6). It's designed to let you manage large sets of feeds across multiple properties. You can track circulation and ad performance in aggregate and make real-time adjustments to improve the reach and profitability of your syndicated content. This is the RSS analytics equivalent to enterprise Web analytics tools. If you just publish a simple blog, you probably don't need this much power — and it may even confound you. This is high-level insight, guys, with a mega-dashboard, customizable reports, and security features. Pricing includes a monthly subscription that is based on several factors including number of subscribers.

Pheedo

`www.pheedo.com`

The Pheedo RSS Analytics toolset is turning plenty of heads and getting lots of *ink* (journalist talk for media exposure) with its RSS advertising solutions for publishers. Pheedo (see Figure 6-7) is going head to head with FeedBurner with tools that offer the same sort of measurements e-mail campaigners enjoy, such as how many people open a feed and how many clickthrough and read an article. Although this is not a pure analytics tool — you can't adopt it unless you are part of the ad network — if you hope to *monetize* (generate revenue) your RSS feeds, this is a strong tool.

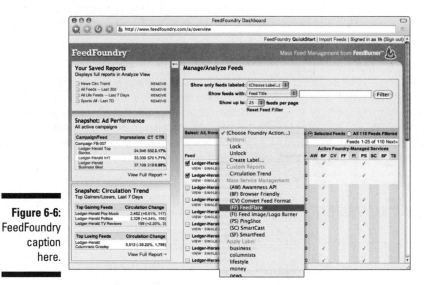

Figure 6-6: FeedFoundry caption here.

SimpleFeed

www.simplefeed.com

SimpleFeed is Pheedo's pure publishing and analytics partner. SimpleFeed (see Figure 6-8) offers more comprehensive RSS analytics. Each subscriber has his own URL, so you can measure RSS subscribe and unsubscribe rates as well as individual content interests. Using SimpleFeed in conjunction with Pheedo offers some interesting analytical benefits, such as better ad rotation, personalization and *frequency capping,* which allows you to limit the maximum number of impressions/views of an add a visitor can see within a defined period of time. SimpleFeed is available in three flavors, Basic $99/mo., Pro $199/mo., and Entrprise (which requires you to contact the company for pricing).

Figure 6-7:
Feeding on
Pheedo.

Figure 6-8:
SimpleFeed
caption
here.

Analytics in a Pod

Are you podcasting? Millions of others do. In fact, researchers at the Diffusion Group predict that the U.S. podcast audience will climb from 840,000 in 2004 to 56 million by 2010. More optimistic measurements approach the 70-million mark. Three-quarters of all people who own iPods or some other MP3 player will be listening to podcasts by that time. It's all part of the user-generated content phenomenon. (For more information on podcasting, check out Wiley's *Podcasting For Dummies* (Tee Morris and Evo Terra).

Sounds like a good venue for (yes, that's right) more advertising. PQ Media figures that podcast advertising will climb to $3.1 million by 2010. That's some serious money for people with a compelling voice and something interesting to say. Like other forms of advertising, advertisers want measurements. Anticipating the promise of the just-around-the-corner future, podcasting analytics tools are already starting to spring up on the market.

Tracking with PodTractor

www.podgarden.oneupweb.com/tracking/podtractor.htm

PodGarden, a podcast production company, launched the PodTractor podcast analytics tool, which is billed as the industry's first comprehensive, hosted podcast tracking system. We're not sure whether it's the first, but we can vouch for the comprehensive part. You don't have to rely on your gut feelings when you use this tool. It lets you know right where you stand without having to weed through server logfiles or asking listeners to install software on their mobile players. PodTractor (see Figure 6-9) tells you what your most popular series and episodes are, which domains listeners visited and what each of them downloaded, and your top podcast referrer. It also separates subscribers from nonsubscribers, shows you your top converting keywords, reveals partial versus completed downloads, and lots of other cool stuff. You have to contact PodGarden for pricing.

Just like regular Web analytics, podcasting analytics hits can fool you into thinking you are the next greatest broadcasting star when you really have only a handful of people listening to your ramblings. The number of hits to a file will undoubtedly be greater than the number of folks who actually download your podcast. By the same token, the number of folks who download your podcast will probably be greater than the number of people who actually listen to it from the opening music to the "until next time."

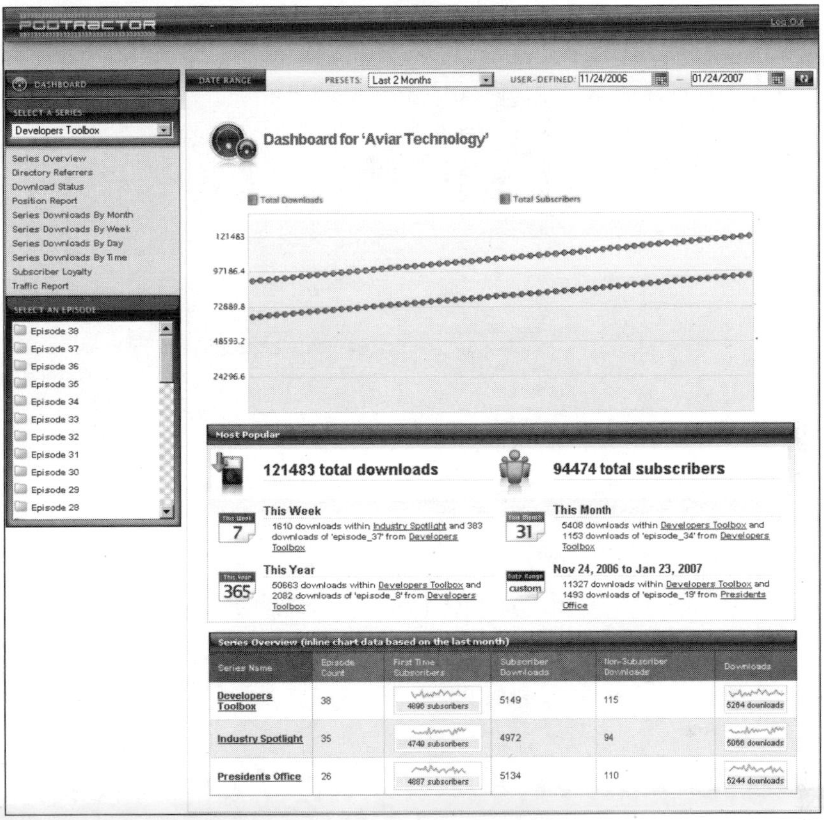

Figure 6-9:
Tracking
with
PodTracker.

RadioTail Ripple

www.radiotail.com/ripple

RadioTail (see Figure 6-10) is a podcast advertising network, advanced metrics, and dynamic ad serving technology. The company's aim is to make sure advertising in podcasts reaches the right audience and delivers a solid return on investment (ROI). The analytics tool is RadioTail Ripple. It's a free control panel that lets you analyze stats on your podcast and build a trusted profile with verified visitor statistics that advertisers demand. Ripple also lets you monitor offers from advertisers and track your account balance from one location in real-time. This control panel offers plenty of snazzy pie charts to display info on users by geography, user agent, and operating system.

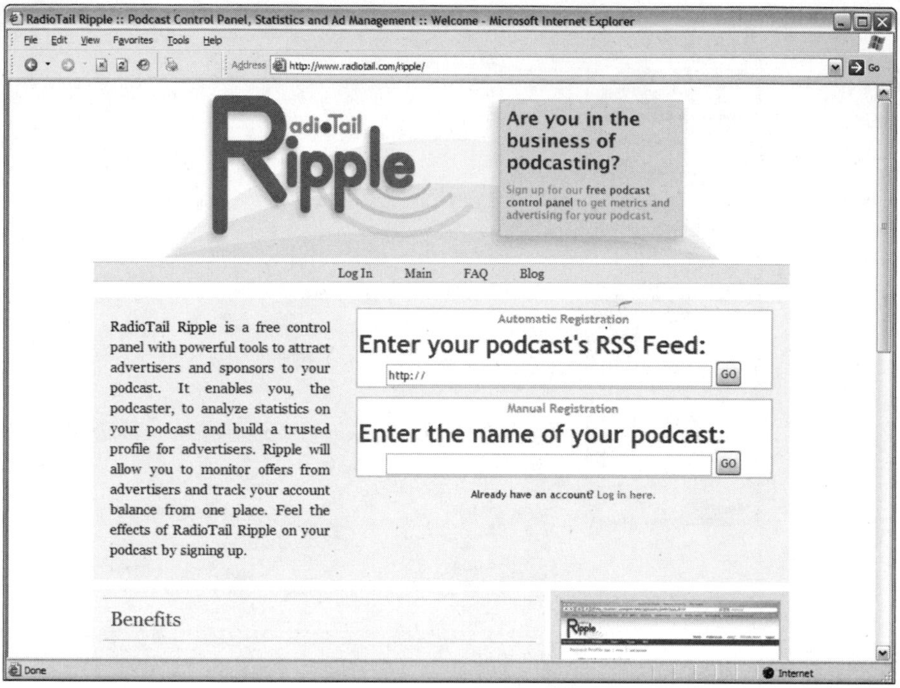

Figure 6-10:
Reading
stats with
RadioTail.

Because You Are Paying Per Click

Online ad revenues just keep climbing higher and higher. According to the Interactive Advertising Bureau Internet, advertising revenues for the first half of 2006 totaled a mind boggling $7.9 billion. That was a record, folks. It was also a 37-percent increase over the first half of 2005. But here's the rub (and a very sad rub, at that): Not all those ad dollars reaped a return. There's no telling how much of that money went down the dot-com drain — unless you use Web analytics to calculate it.

Don't be fooled. Pay per click (also called PPC — these are search engine listings where advertisers pay per click for placement) can run up a tab that you can't afford to pay in a heartbeat. We're talking thousands of dollars here. If you're going to play the PPC game, you must get into the Web analytics game. No ifs, ands, or buts. Not only do you need to monitor your Web analytics, but you might also need to invest in some PPC optimization analytics for the serious online marketer. These tools tell you exactly where your money is going as well as what kind of return those dollars are bringing in so that you can make changes to your campaigns for better performance.

CampaignTracker 2.0

www.semphonic.com

Semphonic publishes CampaignTracker 2.0 (see Figure 6-11). It provides PPC and competitive reporting about search engine marketing (SEM) campaigns. You can make engine-to-engine comparisons, track groups of keywords, track position performance, and much more. This software breaks down keywords in every possible way that you can imagine and also scans the Web to find out how your competitors are using keywords. This is business intelligence at its finest. A single-user license for this software costs $499.

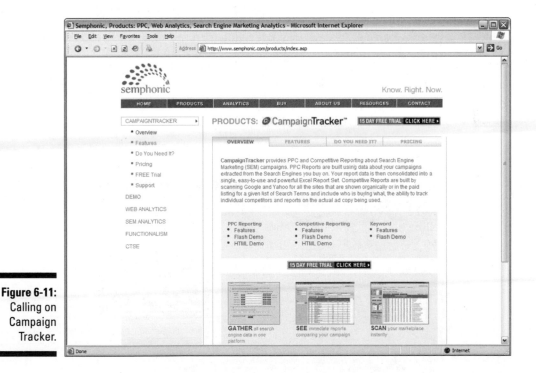

Figure 6-11: Calling on Campaign Tracker.

Beware of products and services that guarantee results through bid management or PPC optimization services that they run for you. Bid management tools might have tracking systems, but it's not the same as analytics. Vendors who promise high-traffic volumes for pennies on the dollar are usually scams. Sure, they might send you hits, but that might make you feel like hitting them back after you get the bill and realize that the traffic was purely junk. If the traffic isn't *targeted* — that is, if the folks who come to the site have no interest in what you have to offer — it probably won't convert. If it doesn't convert, you just threw your money out the window with the junk traffic. Get your own analytics tools and find out for yourself what works.

BlackTrack

www.blacktrackanalytics.com

BlackTrack Analytics (see Figure 6-12) is unique in that it offers a live cost analysis. That's right — you can view live information from the leading PPC search engines and compare that with the revenue earned on your site. You can measure your search ROI for each keyword with the latest up-to-date information and increase your revenue with the same ad spend. Sounds pretty good, doesn't it? This is a great tool for on-the-fly optimization because you can see what keywords aren't performing right away. Why wait? You can buy the entry-level package for $79.95.

Figure 6-12: BlackTrack brings campaigns to life.

When clickers are cons

Click fraud occurs when someone purposely clicks ad listings with no intention to buy from the advertiser. Here are at least a couple of motives for this scam, depending on who is committing it: A competitor might click your PPC ads repeatedly to exhaust your advertising budget so that he can benefit from the traffic. Or, an affiliate marketer might click through on links from his site to drum up revenue. If you see repeat visitors from the same IP address, you could be the target of click fraud. Other suspicious signs are one-page visitors, clicks at unusual hours, visitors who do not accept cookies, and short time spans onsite. Of course, any of these metrics could be legitimate, but they could be costly in combination. Niche Web analytics tools have emerged to help you reign victorious against these Internet con artists, such as ClickLab, ClickSentinel, and ClickForensics. These are strong tools that automatically detect and isolate potential click fraud activity. Some of them will even help you get your money back from paid search providers. If you are sinking with the click fraud ship, you might want to consider one of these strategic analytical weapons. To find out more about these tools, read Chapter 14.

People Watch with Live Analytics Tools

What if we told you that you could watch an individual visitor clickthrough your site, enter keywords into your internal search engine, stop to read a specific product description, place the item in his shopping cart, and repeat the process? Perhaps you have to see it to believe it. Live analytics tools let you do just that. Live analytics tools are a special subset in the Web analytics market. These tools are usually tied to live visitor chat programs.

It only makes sense. This virtual customer service agent can watch the visitor's every move. If a visitor seems to be struggling to find something — as evidenced by typing in various or similar keywords into the internal search engine — a live chat rep can pop up with a message asking whether the visitor needs any help (just like in a brick-and-mortar store). If the visitor seems to be having a hard time getting through the checkout process, once again, your live chat rep can sweep in and serve as the hero, saving the sale from shopping cart abandonment oblivion. Live chat helps build trust for your site, too, because visitors know that help is only a click away. No 24-hour waits for e-mail customer service.

Live stats also help you get a handle on PPC campaigns and click fraud. The overall goal of live stats is to help you close more sales more efficiently. These tools are especially valuable for e-commerce vendors who want to understand how their site is working and what improvements they can make to the navigation and other elements. Live analytics take the guesswork out of what the visitor did because you can watch the action blow by blow and take the appropriate actions before it's too late.

Lots of Web analytics vendors will claim real-time. Thus, you should understand the difference between real-time and live-time.

- ✔ *Real-time* means that your analytics program allows you to refresh the stats at any time to get the latest counts.
- ✔ *Live-time,* by contrast, means you can actually watch what your visitors are doing right now, second by second.

This is an important distinction. Don't be fooled.

WhosOn

www.whoson.com

WhosOn? (see Figure 6-13) lets you watch visitor activity on your Web site as it happens and interact with your visitors as they browse. You can watch them walk through the door, holding their PPC or natural search keywords, and move from page to page. You can see where they are in the world and how they found you. You can detect and deter click fraud. And you can chat with them in real-time to guide visitors to the correct part of your site. This can lead to cross-selling and up-selling opportunities as you proactively engage your visitors in a one-on-one relationship. On top of all this, this program records histories and other analytics that are standard practice in the industry. You can choose a client-side, or installable version ($365) or a hosted version ($35 per month) of this tool. The installable version requires Windows 2000, XP, Vista or 2003.

VistorVille

www.visitorville.com

VisitorVille (see Figure 6-14) applies video game principles to help you visualize your Web site traffic statistics. This is cool stuff. Here's how it works: Each building represents a Web page. Each bus is a search engine. Each animated character is a real-life visitor on your site. All you have to do is paste a tracking code into your Web pages and launch the program. You'll enjoy the visual metaphors, and your visitors will enjoy the integrated live chat feature. You can even keep tabs on competing companies visiting your Web site. Let us put it to you this way: Would you rather read a report that said Overture sent you a visitor, or would you rather see the Overture bus drop the visitor at your virtual doorstep? If you chose the latter, VisitorVille is for you. The program offers all the usual stats and more for as little as $14.99 per month.

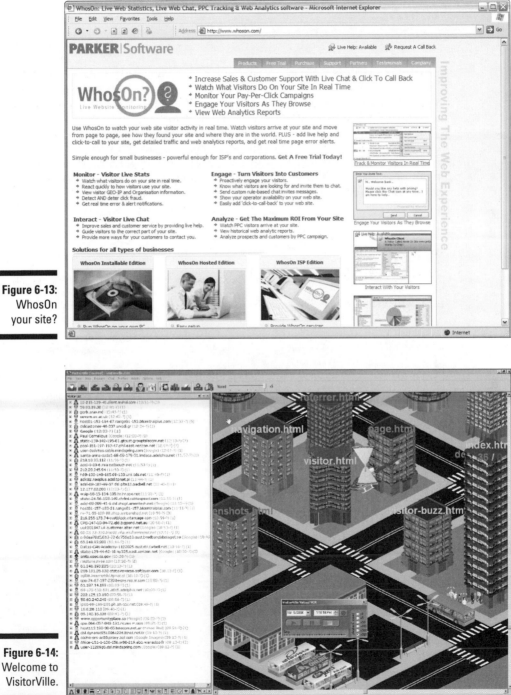

Figure 6-13:
WhosOn
your site?

Figure 6-14:
Welcome to
VisitorVille.

VisiStat

www.visistat.com

VisiStat (see Figure 6-15) is a pioneer of what it calls *statcasting technology* that streams live data into your reports. You see your Web site pageviews at the very second when a visitor clicks your pages. The StatCaster displays the current visitor's geographic location. In real-time, VisiStat interprets your Web site traffic and builds dynamic reports for trend and marketing analysis. You can get some helpful ad-on modules with this software, too, like AdCaM (which tracks all your campaigns) and PageAlarm (which monitors your Web site 24/7/365 and lets you know whether the site goes down for any reason). You can get started with this program for $19.95 per month.

Figure 6-15:
VisiStat live statcasting.

Exploring A/B and Multivariate Testing Software

If you truly are ready to optimize your site, consider exploring some A/B and multivariate testing software. These tools help you take the guesswork out of site changes. Who wants to pay a Web designer big bucks to redesign your whole site when maybe you just need to tweak some of your landing pages? No dummy we know.

Also called split testing, *A/B testing* allows you to compare different versions of your site and measure the impact they make on conversions. *Multivariate testing* goes a step further to let you test multiple versions of the same Web site. You could literally test hundreds of different variations in the placement of Buy Now buttons, product images, copyrighting, and the like to figure out which site variations do the best job persuading visitors to take action. To read more about how to optimize your site, read Chapter 15.

Just like you would with any software vendor, be sure that the costs are crystal clear, review the types of reports you will receive, ask for an estimate on ROI (that's always a hard question to answer, but you should ask it), and by all means ask for references. Lots of scammers are out there who attempt to take advantage of good folks who are trying to make a go of it online. Check for BBB Online seals and other industry affiliations that lend credibility to their services.

Chances are that if Microsoft, Amazon, and other Fortune 1000 companies are using the firm, you are in good hands. A few reputable firms include

- **Offermatica:** www.offermatica.com
- **SiteSpect:** www.sitespect.com
- **Optimost:** www.optimost.com
- **SplitAnalyzer:** www.splitanalyzer.com
- **Lunametrics:** www.lunametrics.com

Most of these tools allow you create variations of dynamic and static content without changing the actual code on your site, launch tests in hours without any IT or technical expertise, run tests on visitors and track behavior across multiple visits, analyze results in real-time, and target testing efforts more effectively through visitor segmentation.

Part III
Searching for Statistical Treasure

The 5th Wave   By Rich Tennant

Don't worry, this time I'm playing the odds. Statistically speaking, two good luck charms should double my chances of winning.

In this part . . .

Searching for statistical treasure is the glory of Web analytics. Your job is to define what you are looking for so that you'll recognize it when you see it. After all, there is plenty of data that just really doesn't matter, like non-human users and referrer spam. Once you get rid of this analytics "trash" it's easier to find those precious gems of information.

In this part, we'll show you how to take out that trash and understand your Key Performance Indicators (the data that matters most). You'll discover how to put metrics like average time on site, average number of *pageviews* (a record of each time a visitor views a Web page on your site), and shopping cart abandonment rates into perspective. We'll also teach you how to wrap your head around what's called the conversion funnel and revisit your conversion rate. (Don't worry. You don't need to be a mathematical genius to calculate conversion rates.)

What you'll soon find is that your Web analytics represent two different groups of friends: site referrers and visitors. You'll discover how to pinpoint which site referrers — such as search engines, content partners, and link exchanges — are sending traffic your way. You'll also learn how to glean valuable insights about visitor behavior based on where they came from, what they did while they were there, and even what country they are surfing from and what browsers they used. It's not about being a nosy snoop. It's about gathering data that unlocks greater profits.

Finally, we'll teach you how to zero in on your most popular pages. We like to call them VIPs (Very Important Pages) because this is where your bread is buttered. In other words, certain pages drive most of your outside traffic and certain pages may convert more visitors than others. Knowing which pages are doing the heavy lifting makes your load a little lighter.

Chapter 7

Taking Out the Trash

In This Chapter

▶ Eliminating nonhuman users

▶ Fighting referrer spam

▶ Ignoring non–mission-critical stats

*I*f you depended on weekly chores to earn a few extra bucks in your childhood years, you're probably familiar with these four words: "Take out the trash!" In fact, in all likelihood, Mom probably had to repeat those words more than once before you got around to taking that Hefty bag down to the curb. Mom was persistent — not because she was giving you a $5-per-week allowance but because she understood the stinky consequences of not taking out the trash. Now that you are all grown up and building your Internet empire, don't forsake Mom's advice: Take out the trash!

Consider Web analytics trash as the metrics that don't really matter. In fact, not only do they not matter, but they can actually stink up your data if you don't weed them out. Trash could be nonhuman users, like *robots.* Also known as *Web crawlers*, *bots,* or *spiders,* a robot is an automated script or program that browses the Web. Nonhuman users could also be *hosting monitoring services* (services that visit Web sites looking for outages) or *e-mail harvesters* (bots that collect e-mail addresses displayed on your pages) or even notification services that tell various search engines that you updated your blog.

If those nonhuman users weren't enough to keep you on your toes, referrer spam can also give you fits. *Referrer spam* occurs when unscrupulous Web site operators use technology to fake sending traffic to your site so that you will see their URL in your site referrer list and visit them. *Site referrers,* or *referring pages,* are the URLs of the previous Web page from which a link was followed. Not only do you want to refrain from measuring it, but you want to fight against it. We'll show you how. Finally, there is other data that just doesn't matter. In other words, you don't want to waste your time with non–mission-critical stats. Those stats will be different for different Web sites. In this chapter, we'll help you determine how to eat the hay and spit out the sticks so you don't choke on irrelevant stats.

You'll also discover that not all traffic is good traffic. We show you how to tell the difference between what matters to you, what doesn't matter at all, and how to wage war against sinister plots that could cause trouble for your site. So put on some gloves and get ready to take out some analytics trash.

Classifying Nonhuman Users

Nonhuman users are just what they sound like: nonhuman users. A *nonhuman user* is any visitor that is not an actual person who uses a browser to navigate your site. The challenge is that nonhuman users can indeed look like living, breathing visitors and be counted as such. Your job, if you choose to accept it, is to eliminate these imposters.

Several different types of nonhuman users exist. You need to be aware of them and classify them so you know what to look for when it's time to eliminate them. You also need to understand the motivation of these nonhuman users so you can decide whether to spend your time trying to shut them out of your online kingdom. Here are a few of the most common types of nonhuman users and some tips on how to respond to them.

Robots, spiders, and Web crawlers

Robots, spiders, and Web crawlers are virtually synonymous. Good bots (which typically come from major search engines like Google and Yahoo!) are on a mission to index your Web site — and that's a good thing. Bad bots, on the other hand, disguise themselves under the cloak of unique visitors with the intent of gathering data from your Web site to use for their ominous purposes. (Read more about e-mail harvesters later in this chapter.)

Of course, not all unidentified bots are necessarily bandits. Some small search engines just don't properly identify themselves. Or, it could be that your site was visited by some college experimenters. (Sometimes university students develop new search engines as part of their curriculum.) In both cases, you can track these bots back to their rightful owner by their associated *Internet protocol* (IP) addresses (a unique numeric code assigned by the user's Internet service provider) or hostname. Just do a search for **IP address lookup** or **hostname lookup** on Google for various tools to help accomplish this.

Some analytics applications provide links to IP address lookups directly from the application. If you use Urchin as your analytics application of choice, you can just click the IP address in the top IP Addresses report (see Figure 7-1) to see what network it belongs to.

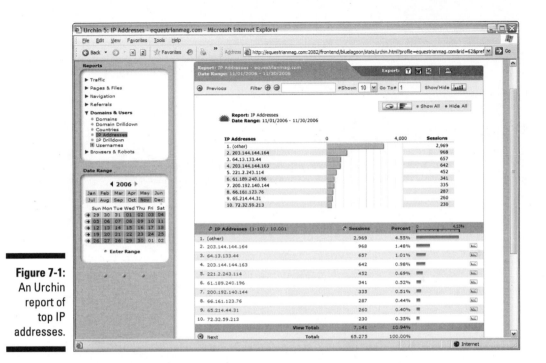

Figure 7-1:
An Urchin
report of
top IP
addresses.

The evil of e-mail harvesters

Some bots are nothing more than e-mail harvesters, also known as *spambots*.
Spambots look for any string of text that appears to be an e-mail address.
They gather these into a database and sell lists to spammers who blast out
unsolicited e-mail with product offers. Spambots are also a method employed
by *phishers,* those nefarious folk who get their list of potential victims by
tricking people into giving them confidential information or doing something
else they normally wouldn't do, typically through spam messages (see Figure
7-2) that appear legitimate (like a bogus bank communication or some message supposedly from eBay or PayPal). E-mail harvesters are one of the evils
of the Internet. If your e-mail address is displayed on your Web page, it's a
target for e-mail harvesters.

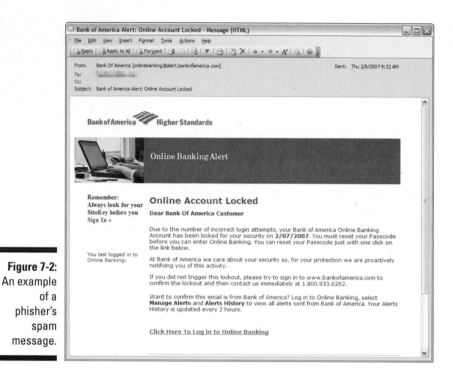

Figure 7-2:
An example
of a
phisher's
spam
message.

Uptime hosting monitoring services

Uptime companies, also known as *hosting monitoring services,* can also visit your site. There are many different services. Some of the most popular are

- ✔ **Hosttracker:** www.hosttracker.com
- ✔ **Alertra:** www.alertra.com
- ✔ **Netcraft:** www.netcraft.com

Uptime monitoring services detect outages in Web servers, e-mail servers, DNS servers, and routers. They *ping:* that is, use a program to test whether a particular network destination is online by sending a request to and waiting for a response from your Web site to make sure it's up and running. If it isn't, this automated software tool notifies the customer via e-mail or text messages to your mobile phone. Large companies can use it. Web hosts can use it. However, anyone who is interested in tracking the uptime of your Web site, for any reason, can arrange for a hosting monitoring service to visit your site. (Sort of makes you feel like Big Brother is watching you, eh?) In the high-stakes world of online business, site downtime can mean hours of lost sales, and that can make the average cost of services like this, often less than $20 a month, well worth it.

Battling spambots

You are not powerless against *spambots,* those automated software programs that collect e-mail addresses for the express purpose of selling address lists to spammers. You can battle spambots in several ways. Of course, each method has its pros and cons.

✔ **Spell out your address.** Instead of using an e-mail link, you could simply spell out the address so that harvesters can't readily recognize it. *Con:* This quick-and-easy solution forces legitimate e-mailers to type out your address by hand — and if they aren't good typists, qualified leads might not find you in time.

✔ **Display your address as an image.** You could also display your e-mail address as an image file so that harvesters can't see it. *Con:* Again, you are forcing legit users to type it in manually.

✔ **Password-protect the address page.** You could put password protection on the page containing your e-mail address. *Con:* This is realistic only for private Web sites and intranets.

✔ **Encode the address.** You could encode the e-mail addresses with JavaScript so that harvesters are blinded. *Con:* If your legit users don't enable JavaScript, they may not be able to see it, either.

✔ **Use a special form.** You could even set up a special contact form that users have to fill out. *Con:* You might need to get a developer to do the coding.

At the end of the day, you need to decide whether this is a battle worth fighting.

Gotta love link checkers and validators

Link checkers and *validators* are nonhuman users that analyze Web sites for broken and problem links. These aren't malicious users at all. You might have even invited them in by subscribing to a link-checking service, such as Link Checker Pro (www.linkcheckerpro.com) or Web Link Validator (www.rel-software.com). Or you might get a report (see Figure 7-3) from a company like InternetSeer that offers you data on your broken links in hopes that you'll subscribe to its link management services. Link checkers can be important because search engines penalize sites with broken links — and, in some cases, won't list sites with lots of broken links. You can also read your Web analytics report's section on broken links. For more information on broken links, read Chapter 10.

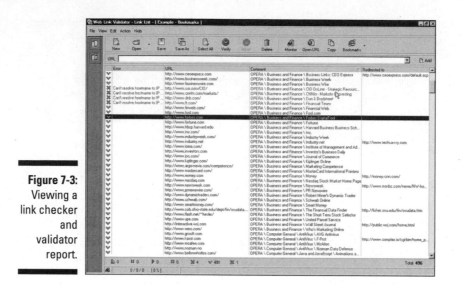

Figure 7-3:
Viewing a
link checker
and
validator
report.

Recognizing RSS feed readers

RSS, Really Simple Syndication, is a method for syndicating content on a Web site. Major newspapers use this method as well as bloggers and others who want to push content out to the masses rather than waiting on the masses to visit their site. *RSS feed readers,* also called *aggregators,* are software applications or remotely hosted services that collect syndicated content from various Web sites into one program for easy viewing. Popular RSS feed readers include FeedBurner, Syndirella, and NetNewsWire. The URL of the referrer contains the name of the reader. You'll find evidence of these readers in your list of site referrers. For more information on RSS analytics, read Chapter 5, which covers niche solutions.

Blog-monitoring services

Nonhuman users can be blog search services or pinging services. In the context of blogging, a *pinging service* tells search engines that you updated your blog. Blog search services allow users to search through a catalog of blogs to discover posts on topics of their choice. Perhaps the most comprehensive blog search and monitoring service is Technorati, which is also a pinging service. Another popular pinging service is Pingomatic. You might see these or other services, such as NewsGator, Feedster, or Blogdigger, listed in your site referrer report. From a blogger's standpoint, this is helpful to determine how many people are searching for topics posted in your blog. But you can just as well look at the pageviews to see which blog topics drove the most traffic. For more information on blogging analytics, read Chapter 5.

Why Eliminate Nonhuman Users?

Because you can't convert nonhuman users to a sale, subscriber, member or anything else, you shouldn't let these stats influence your Web decisions. Imagine quickly glancing at your Web analytics report and determining that Fridays see the most traffic. You confidently decide to launch a special promotion on that day. What you didn't know was that nonhuman users have erroneously inflated your visitor counts. Your highest human visitor counts are actually on Sunday evenings. You just blew your chance to convert the highest possible number of visitors with your special promotion. The point is that you can't make solid business decisions based on bad information.

When you eliminate nonhuman users, don't throw the robot report out the window. You should keep your eyes on your robot visitors on occasion to make sure the Big Three search engines — Google, Yahoo!, and Microsoft — are crawling your site. If these engines aren't crawling your site periodically, you could be losing relevant traffic. Also, keep an occasional eye on your robots report so you can see whether any particular engine is suddenly sending you large volumes of visitors. If you discover that a smaller, niche search engine is sending visitors your way, consider launching a PPC to generate an even greater buzz on with those targeted users. The good news is that good bots aren't registered as human activity, so you don't have to eliminate them from your visitor counts.

Knowing that nonhuman users are traveling across your site is one thing, but knowing how to identify them is another — and it's the first step toward eliminating them from your decision making process. Consider the following steps for identifying nonhuman users:

- ✔ **Review your reports.** Review your Web analytics report each month to look for any user agent names that you don't recognize. Specifically, look at your site referrer list and your Robot report. You should be relatively familiar with your usual site referrers and standard robots. If there is a site referrer you don't recognize, click the link to see who it is. It could be a new ally, but it could be an undercover enemy with malicious intent. The same goes for the Robot report. Some robots don't identify themselves for malicious reasons. Those are your suspects.

- ✔ **Monitor agent behavior.** Robots can be identified by their behavior while on your site (see Figure 7-4). Do some visitors generate pageviews that number 10, or even 100 times the number of pages that your average visitor looks at? If a bot queries you 20 or 30 times per hour, it's probably up to no good. Check with your hosting company or server administrator for ways to block them at the Web server level, stopping them dead in their tracks.

Is the user agent a legitimate spider that appears to be doing its duties? Or does a particular unknown spider use up large chunks of your bandwidth allotment? (*Bandwidth* is the amount of data that can be transferred to and from a Web site in a given period of time. This is usually expressed as bits per second [bps] or higher units like Mbps [megabits per second].) If you see an unknown spider gobbling up bandwidth at rates higher than the Big Three, be suspicious — be very suspicious. These non-human users could be out to extract data from your pages, like e-mail addresses.

- **Exclude the bad apples.** You need to put your user agent data into context to determine whether you should really count the visitor. Wisdom speaks against counting unique visitors who stay less than ten seconds. You don't want to gear your Web decisions around folks who weren't interested in what you had to offer or nonhuman users that were just validating uptime or pursuing click fraud activities. (*Click fraud* involves sending fraudulent clicks to PPC advertisers.) When you eliminate the visitors who stay less than ten seconds, you might eliminate a few valid users with them, but make no mistake: You will be hurt more by including nonhuman users than by eliminating a few human visitors who just didn't buy into your concept.

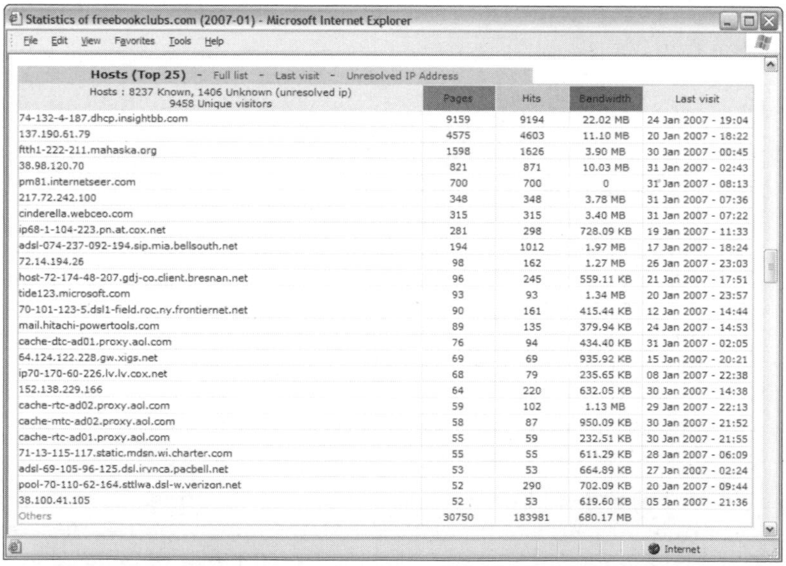

Hosts (Top 25) - Full list - Last visit - Unresolved IP Address Hosts : 8237 Known, 1406 Unknown (unresolved ip) 9458 Unique visitors	Pages	Hits	Bandwidth	Last visit
74-132-4-187.dhcp.insightbb.com	9159	9194	22.02 MB	24 Jan 2007 - 19:04
137.190.61.79	4575	4603	11.10 MB	20 Jan 2007 - 18:22
ftth1-222-211.mahaska.org	1598	1626	3.90 MB	30 Jan 2007 - 00:45
38.98.120.70	821	871	10.03 MB	31 Jan 2007 - 02:43
pm81.internetseer.com	700	700	0	31 Jan 2007 - 08:13
217.72.242.100	348	348	3.78 MB	31 Jan 2007 - 07:36
cinderella.webceo.com	315	315	3.40 MB	31 Jan 2007 - 07:22
ip68-1-104-223.pn.at.cox.net	281	298	728.09 KB	19 Jan 2007 - 11:33
adsl-074-237-092-194.sip.mia.bellsouth.net	194	1012	1.97 MB	17 Jan 2007 - 18:24
72.14.194.26	98	162	1.27 MB	26 Jan 2007 - 23:03
host-72-174-48-207.gdj-co.client.bresnan.net	96	245	559.11 KB	21 Jan 2007 - 17:51
tide123.microsoft.com	93	93	1.34 MB	20 Jan 2007 - 23:57
70-101-123-5.dsl1-field.roc.ny.frontiernet.net	90	161	415.44 KB	12 Jan 2007 - 14:44
mail.hitachi-powertools.com	89	135	379.94 KB	24 Jan 2007 - 14:53
cache-dtc-ad01.proxy.aol.com	76	94	434.40 KB	31 Jan 2007 - 02:05
64.124.122.228.gw.xigs.net	69	69	935.92 KB	15 Jan 2007 - 20:21
ip70-170-60-226.lv.lv.cox.net	68	79	235.65 KB	08 Jan 2007 - 22:38
152.138.229.166	64	220	632.05 KB	30 Jan 2007 - 14:38
cache-rtc-ad02.proxy.aol.com	59	102	1.13 MB	29 Jan 2007 - 22:13
cache-mtc-ad02.proxy.aol.com	58	87	950.09 KB	30 Jan 2007 - 21:52
cache-rtc-ad01.proxy.aol.com	55	59	232.51 KB	30 Jan 2007 - 21:55
71-13-115-117.static.mdsn.wi.charter.com	55	55	611.29 KB	28 Jan 2007 - 06:09
adsl-69-105-96-125.dsl.irvnca.pacbell.net	53	53	664.89 KB	27 Jan 2007 - 02:24
pool-70-110-62-164.sttlwa.dsl-w.verizon.net	52	290	702.09 KB	20 Jan 2007 - 09:44
38.100.41.105	52	53	619.60 KB	05 Jan 2007 - 21:36
Others	30750	183981	680.17 MB	

Figure 7-4: Hosts report from AWStats.

The Danger of Referrer Spam

If you have ever used e-mail, you are overly familiar with *spam,* that unsolicited e-mail with offers for everything from discounted Rolex watches to fake offers from bogus estate holders promising you millions of dollars. These annoying salesmen have wormed their way into many Web sites, too, through referrer spam. Also known as *spamdexing,* perpetrators of referrer log spamming make repeated requests to your Web site using a fake URL that points to a spam-advertised site.

Referrer spam can be inconvenient, muddying up your site referrer report, or it can be deadly, wasting away your bandwidth and causing one of two unwanted problems:

- Excess bandwidth charges
- The inability to serve pages to legitimate traffic because your site is overloaded

Thus, keeping your eye on your Referral report is vital. If you get only an occasional referrer spam, it might not be worth your time to deal with it. If you are getting spamdexed to death, though, it's time to fight back.

The referral spam technique is clever because sites that publicize their referrer statistics, such as blogs, will also link to the spammer's site by default. That link boosts the spammer's ranking in the search engine and gives them a batter chance of getting visitors through natural search. Curious Web site owners (like you) might also decide to click a link that you don't recognize to find the spam-advertised site. That can be potentially dangerous as well because malicious hackers can secretly install spyware or other viruses and bugs onto your computer without you ever knowing it.

Recognizing referrer spam

How do you recognize referrer spam? Some common referrer spam URLs often include words like *casino, poker,* and *texasholdem,* or adult-oriented content. You can also recognize referrer spam by typos in the URL. The referrer spam might also have the name of the product the spammer is selling, like Prozac, Vicodin, or some other prescription drug they claim to peddle at discount rates.

To give you a better idea of what this might look like in your site referrer report, here is a list of referrer spam URLs:

```
http://www.texasholdemcentral.com
http://www.favorite-casino/blackjack.html
http://www.online-casino.blest-casino.com
http://www.fistfulofeuros.net
http://www.poker-4all.com/poker-rooms.html
```

As you can see, if your site doesn't offer poker tips, there is no reason for these sites to send you traffic. So after you identify that you're getting referrer spam, what can you do about it? Fight back!

Fighting Referrer Spam

You can't fight against what you can't see, but what you can't see could be harming you. Referrer spam is like an undetected cancer on your site referrer report. It's eating away at your time because you have to eliminate these non-human users to get to the heart of who is sending legitimate traffic to your site. After you recognize referrer spam as your enemy, you can fight against it. Unfortunately, there is no silver bullet that will stop referrer spam once and for all. Here are, however, some counter tactics that you can deploy against these deceptive foes. Some are technical; others just cost a few bucks.

Blacklist the spammers

You can fight referrer spam with a hand-edited blacklist of known spammers. It might not be the quickest solution, but it works well. If your site is running on an Apache server, the most popular Web server software, and your Web host has enabled the feature, you can use a configuration file called .htaccess to block users or sites that come from a particular domain or IP address.

To implement this fix, you'll either need to find someone who's familiar with htaccess commands, or you'll need to take some online tutorials to bring your htaccess writing skills up to par. What's more, with the speed at which spammers are creating new URLs, it can be difficult — and time consuming — to keep up with this manual remedy.

Use the rel = "no follow" solution

An HTML attribute designed to combat comment spam on blogs, which also works well for referral spam, is `rel = "no follow"`. This fix is easy. You just tag any outgoing link with `rel = "no follow"` attribute to prevent the spammer from enjoying a boost in a search engine's rank. Because the spammers aren't benefiting from spamming your site, they might decide to focus their efforts elsewhere. Here's an example of some code utilizing the `rel="no follow"` attribute:

```
<a href="http://www.dummies.com" rel="nofollow">Visit
        Dummies.com</a>
```

Rely on your analytics tools

For a one-time flat-fee of $30, you can license an analytics tool called Mint. Mint specifically ignores referrer spam. The developer bills it as referrer-spam–proof. Referrers are broken down by newest unique, most recent, and repeat referrers from a customizable timeframe. You can also measure visits, browsers, and platforms; find search terms in popular search engines, and illuminate your most popular pages and most recently accessed content. You can even bookmark or watch individual pages. Mint might not run on your server, though. The developer offers a compatibility test that you can take to find out in a flash. You can visit it at `www.haveamint.com`.

Whatever method you choose, remember these two caveats:

- ✔ **Be sure to review the filters to make sure you aren't getting any false positives.** The last thing you want to do is block legitimate referrers.

- ✔ **Avoid slower performance.** Typically, if you enable methods to combat referrer spam, your Web server logfile is checked against every line in the blacklist file. That means it could wind up taking you much longer to run your reports.

Ultimately, you have to decide what's worse: the pain of fighting referrer spam, or the pain of weeding through it in your referrer report.

Ignoring Non–Mission-Critical Stats

Some data just doesn't matter to most people. It's not critical to your mission. With so many KPIs, it's helpful to ignore the non–mission-critical stats, or at least not spend much time analyzing them. You'll find that your mission critical stats might change over time as your Web site's goals change. Well, you can always change your analyzing strategy later, but your goal with Web analytics is always the same: to use the best data, the best way, to get the best possible results on your site. The following sections discuss some data that might just not matter.

Who needs hit counts?

We'll say it before, and we'll say it again (and again and again): Hits are the most deceptive stat of them all. A *hit* registers each time a file is requested from your site. Each page on your Web site can include photographs, text, graphics, sound files, PDFs, or some other file type. Thus, a request for a page with 10 images would count as 11 hits. Thirty-thousand visitors would easily rack up 1 million hits in a hurry on a catalog-style site that serves up 30 or 40 photos per page.

Don't even pay attention to your hits. It isn't a realistic assessment of how your Web site is performing. It could be that most of your visitors all went to the pages that contained the largest number of files last month but visited the pages with the fewest number of files this month. The data, then, would be far and away skewed. If you track hits, you could swing back and forth from an elated mood to a panic-stricken frame of mind from day to day and month to month. Who needs it?

Do you have the time?

Do you really have the time to keep up with the times of day visitors come to your site? If you take a look at the hour during which your visitors came knocking, you'll probably find that they are navigating your Web site at each and every hour of the day. That's not surprising because there are plenty of different time zones around the world. When it's noon in the United States, it's 5 p.m. in the United Kingdom. When it's midnight in some other parts of the world, it's noon somewhere else. So, knowing whether a visitor came at 2 a.m. or 2 p.m. won't make much difference to most Web site owners. Unless you're trying to measure the effectiveness of your special midnight sales, you probably don't need to sweat these statistics.

Basking in your international appeal

If your site has been up and running for any length of time — and if the spiders are crawling it — the list of countries that your visitors represent is probably lengthy. It can be cool to see all the different flags; see Figure 7-5. (Who would have thought three people from Latvia would ever visit your site?) Unless you are specifically targeting users in certain countries, though, this list just doesn't matter.

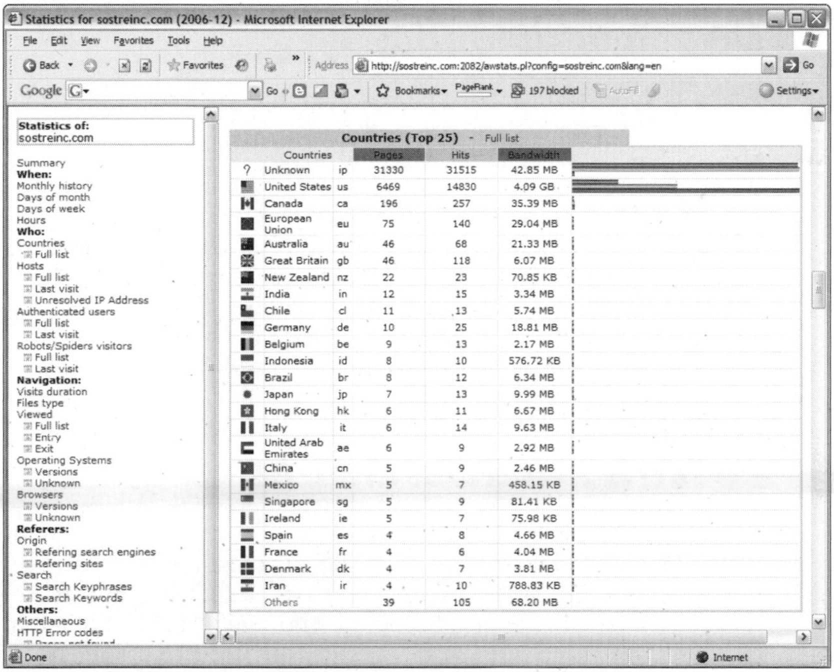

Figure 7-5: An AWStats Top Countries report.

Who's hosting my visitors?

Your Hosts report will offer all the IP addresses your visitors used. It's likely that the host that rang up the most pages is your very own. The host of your visitors won't usually matter unless you are trying to root out abusers. Perhaps a certain visitor from a certain IP address is using most of your bandwidth. This is suspicious activity that needs to be investigated. However, beyond a quick scan, most of this data just doesn't matter.

Authenticated users and anonymous users

Your Authenticated Users report won't matter much unless you are tracking visits to a Member's Only portion of your Web site. In that case, you might want to calculate the difference in traffic between non-registered and registered users to see who comes to the site most often. However, most sites don't even have member's only sites. If that's you, you can ignore these stats, which will merely report 0.

Downloadable files

Your site is probably made up of all different types of files, such as images, static HTML or XML static pages, dynamic HTML pages, Cascading Style Sheet (CSS) files, JavaScript files, and so on. These are the file types that your developer used to create your site, and you can basically ignore those stats. The only time that the Files Type report might matter to you is if you are trying to tack how many times visitors downloaded a PDF or other specific file format. Of course, if you have lots of those types of files, this report won't tell you which particular files were downloaded. You will need to check your Most Popular Files report for that data. At the end of the day, this statistic just isn't terribly valuable to most Web site owners.

Favorites and bookmarks

Your Web analytics program might tell you how many people bookmarked your site or added you to their favorite sites list. First of all, there's no accurate way for a Web analytics program to track that sort of stat. Even the best programs are just guessing. Secondly, who really cares? It might make you smile to think that x number of your visitors liked your site enough to bookmark it. Just because they bookmarked it doesn't mean that they'll ever come back, though. Think about it — how many different sites have you bookmarked, never to return? Case in point.

Miscellaneous miscellany

Your Web analytics program might have a chart for Miscellaneous. Here you'll probably find just that: miscellany. You'll find stats on browsers, such as how many visitors used browsers with support for Java, Macromedia Director, Flash, Real Audio, or some other type of plug-in. If you don't have any of those fancy-schmancy elements on your site — or if you aren't planning to incorporate them — it just doesn't matter.

Chapter 8

Reviewing Site Referrers

· ·

· ·

Marketing gurus suggest asking new customers this question: "How did you hear about us," figuring that the answer to that six-word query will help unravel the mystery of measuring promotional efforts. The only problem is that those same marketing gurus admit that the answers are skewed. In fact, they figure that you're lucky if 25 percent of the responses you get are accurate.

The truth is most people don't remember exactly where they heard about some new retail boutique on Main Street. Maybe they saw an advertisement promising *10% Off* in the newspaper, heard a radio announcement hyping the grand opening celebration, or had lunch with a co-worker who raved about the trendy selection.

The beauty of the World Wide Web, however, is that you can indeed know exactly who referred visitor to your site. Even the simplest Web analytics tools record each and every site referrer. The *site referrer,* or *referring page,* is the URL of the previous Web page from which a link was followed. Whether your visitor is introduced to your site through a search engine, a link building campaign, or some other strategy, you'll be sure to know it.

This chapter covers how to use your site referrer stats in your Web analytics study. We cover how to get the information, what it means, and then how to use it to improve your site's traffic.

Revving Up for Referrers

We use AWStats as our Web analytics tool for the examples in this chapter because it's a free program that many Web hosting firms include as part of your package. And because AWStats is written in Perl, it can work on all operating systems. It's also chock full of features to satiate the data hungry.

If your host offers the cPanel control panel to administer your Web site, you probably have AWStats already installed. If AWStats isn't installed on your Web server, you can ask your host to install it for you.

If you have the right permissions for your server, you can download AWStats from `http://awstats.sourceforge.net` and install it yourself. AWStats can work with all Web servers able to write log file with a combined log format (XLF/ELF) such as Apache, a common log format (CLF) such as Apache or Squid, a W3C log format such as IIS 5.0 or higher, or any other log format that contains all information AWStats expect to find. It also works with most Web/Wap/Proxy/Streaming servers, and some FTP, Syslog, or Mail log files.

Discovering Your Traffic Partners

As you embark on your quest to generate more traffic to your Web site, you'll need your site referrer report to show you the way. *Referrers,* also known as *traffic partners,* are the URLs listed in your site referrer report and are allies in the battle for more online traffic.

This powerful collection of *metrics* — data used to assess and monitor activity on a Web site — unlocks the mysteries of driving more successful marketing campaigns by revealing the names and impact of your site referrers. So what are you waiting for? Gather your referral information and discover your traffic partners so you can make educated decisions about where you spend your marketing time and dollars.

To start using your analytics to direct your marketing efforts, follow these steps:

1. **Gather your referral information.**

   Access your Web analytics tool and look for a section labeled *Referrers.* This is the area within the tool that collects detailed information about your traffic partners. In AWStats, the Referers section can be found about three-quarters of the page down in the left side, below the Navigation section (see Figure 8-1).

The Referers section

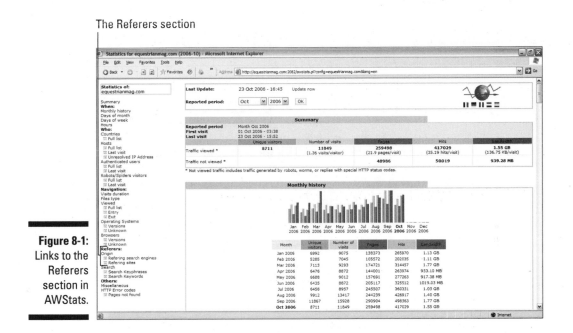

Figure 8-1:
Links to the
Referers
section in
AWStats.

2. Review sources of your Web traffic.

Referrer information is usually grouped into various categories, such as traffic from bookmarks, newsgroups, search engines, and external Web sites. Monitoring repeat visits from users who have bookmarked your site can be exciting, but measuring traffic from bookmarks is difficult at best — and largely unreliable. Web analytics software merely makes an educated guess. Once a powerful way to generate traffic, the use of newsgroups are declining in the face of social networking sites such as MySpace.com and Del.icio.us.

In today's Web analytics economy, traffic patterns generated through search engines and external Web sites are the most vital metrics. The referring search engines section can help you measure and compare *natural search* — traffic that comes from unpaid search engine listings — and *paid search* campaigns, such as Google's Adwords program. Meanwhile, a list of external Web sites that have pushed traffic your way can help you guide your link building strategies.

3. Make educated decisions about your campaigns.

Your referrer report offers much of the data that you need to make educated decisions about your marketing campaigns. Armed with indisputable information about where traffic is coming from, you can compare search engine with search engine and link partner with link partner to determine which marketing wells deserve more investment, where to prime the pump, and when to shut off the faucet.

The following sections discuss how to gather referral information and review sources of Web traffic in more detail. For more information on making educated decisions about your campaign, see Part IV.

Identifying your referrers

When it comes to displaying where your Web site visitors are coming from, each Web analytics tool presents information in a slightly different way.

Most Web analytics tools are commonly found in the Web-based, hosting control panel, and AWStats is no exception. When you sign up for your Web hosting service, your hosting company should provide you with information about how to access your control panel. For more information on how to locate and log in to your stats application, see Chapter 3.

After logging in, you see AWStats available under the Web/FTP Stats heading. Figure 8-2 shows the main page from AWStats.

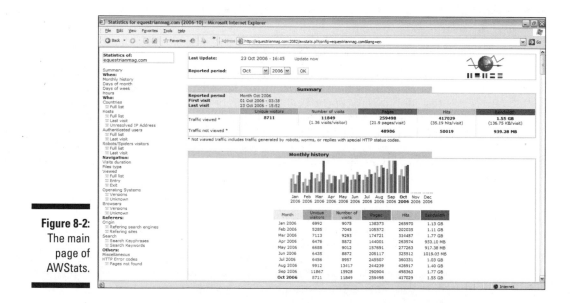

Figure 8-2: The main page of AWStats.

Look for the AWStats Referers section in the lower-left side of the page. This is where you can find all the relevant data you need to make decisions about your online traffic building strategies.

When you click the Origin link, you see the referrers' origin summary section (see Figure 8-3). The information in this section is divided into five categories to indicate the type of source that referred the visitor:

✔ Direct address/Bookmarks

✔ Links from a NewsGroup

✔ Links from an Internet Search Engine

✔ Links from an external page (other Web sites except search engines)

✔ Visits of an unknown origin

Unknown origins are largely such — unknown. Referrers are determined by *reverse DNS look-ups* — that is, translating IP numbers to domain names to uncode the true referrer. Many numerical addresses are of unknown origin. In fact, when you review your site referrers, you might be disgruntled by the percentage of hits that seem to wear the cloak of anonymity. Even the best analytics programs are stumped, it seems, although this is clear: If you see a high level of use from an unresolved IP number, it could be *spiders*. Also known as Web crawlers or robots, a spider is a program or automated script that browsers the Web. You may occasionally hear spiders referred to as ants, automatic indexers, bots, or worms. Search engines use spiders to gather up-to-date data as they index the Web.

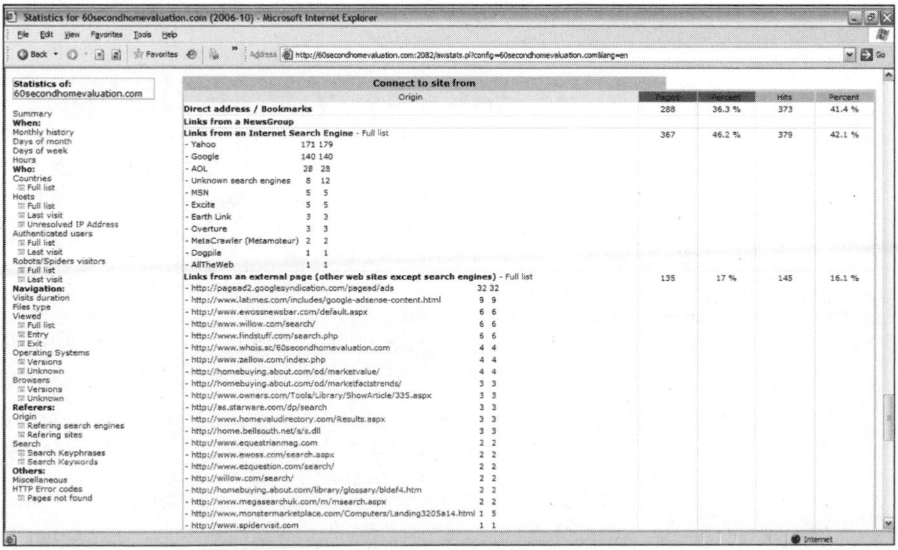

Figure 8-3: Referrers Origin summary in AWStats.

Who's trying to find out who I am?

If you run across a site referrer that looks something like: `www.whois.sc/yourdomain.com` (where `yourdomain.com` is replaced with your actual domain name), someone tapped into the Whois Lookup database to find out who you are. Why do they care? Here are several reasons:

✔ **To find out who the registered owner for the domain is:** Maybe someone wants to partner with you. Maybe a competitor is conducting some business intelligence. Maybe it's an old friend who's looking for your number. We call these folks *Curious Georges*.

✔ **To find out when a domain name is going to expire:** These seekers are people who want your domain and hope to snatch it out from under your feet when it expires. Services from Internet registrars like GoDaddy.com offer automatic renewals so this can't happen.

✔ **To place a bid on a URL that you're selling or just not using:** You might own a couple dozen (or more) URLs as you take dominion on the World Wide Web. It's your right to sell them to the highest bidder.

✔ **To find out where a domain is hosted:** Who would want to know that, you ask? A Web developer who needs to look up technical details, like your IP address, the DNS servers, or your Web host to make changes to the location of your Web site.

If you don't like the idea of total strangers visiting your site, getting your address and phone number, and waiting to snatch up your domain, you can opt for a private listing. Just like the phone company, you can keep your information hidden for a small fee.

Typically, when you register your domain name you can opt to keep it private during the sign up process. If you did not initially choose to keep your information private, you can return to your Domain Name provider and opt to pay for the privilege later. Simply log in to your account, look for the domain manager, and select the privacy feature. This typically costs about $5 a year.

Classifying sources of Web traffic

The first step toward making the most of your Web site traffic is getting acquainted with the various referrers and recognizing who's who in the referrer list. The following list discusses some of the more popular sources for Web site traffic:

✔ **Search engines:** If your traffic is coming directly from Google, MSN, Yahoo!, or some other search engine, your analytics tool can break down the metrics by the search engine's name and how many hits it sent your way.

✔ **Web ring partners:** *Web rings* are a way to interlink related sites so that people can visit many similar Web pages simply by clicking a traditional Next link, often located at the bottom of the page. You can identify other Web sites from your Web ring by visiting the URL and looking for a mention of the Web ring on their Web sites.

✔ **Link partners:** Trading links with business partners, friends, and colleagues is old-fashioned networking at its best. If you keep a list of Web sites that you've exchanged links with, you can recognize these allied URLs by cross-referencing that list with the list of external referring sites.

✔ **Affiliate marketers:** If you have an affiliate program in place that pays Web site owners for each lead or sale they send your way, you can compare your list of external referrers with your list of affiliate marketers to find out which affiliate marketers are sending traffic.

✔ **E-mail campaigns:** If you put a link to your site in an e-mail marketing campaign, you might see referrals from Web mail services such as Hotmail and Yahoo!.

This works, however, only with e-mails sent to recipients who have Web-based mail.

As you wade through the mountains of relevant data Web analytics software generates, take some time to comb through your list of site referrers, no matter how long or short it is. Site referrer statistics are like latitude and longitude designations on a map: They offer a frame of reference as you explore the world of search engine advertising and link building campaign strategies.

Searching for Statistical Treasure

Scavenger hunts can be fun, but treasure hunts are more profitable. With your site referral stats in hand, you don't have to play guessing games to determine where traffic is coming from. You know exactly what you are looking for — whether it's how many hits you got from your new link partner yesterday or how many visitors Google sent through your virtual doors last month — and you will recognize it when you find it.

Of course, you have to know where you are before you forge ahead with new traffic generation campaigns. Web analytics gives you a point of reference that acts as a yardstick for your traffic building efforts. From there, you can measure the success or failure of your strategies.

This section can help you unlock information to measure the payoff from your current internal search engine optimization efforts, your paid search campaigns, and your various link-building strategies. You might think you get the most traffic from Google, for example, but you could find out that you get the most conversions from the traffic Yahoo! refers. You might even discover that you're missing golden opportunities because you aren't drawing traffic from the hundreds of second-tier search engines (such as www.alltheweb.com and www.altavista.com) that scour the Web for sites like yours.

Which search engines list your site?

Hundreds of search engines are on the Web: shopping search engines and kid search engines, country-specific search engines and multimedia search engines, metasearch engines and pay-per-click search engines. The list goes on. Your Web analytics tool will reveal which engines your site is most likely listed in. Refer to the chart in Figure 8-3 to see the search engine Referers section from the AWStats Web analytics tool. This simple report shows a list of the top (up to ten) search engines, ranked by pageview, along with a link to see the full list. A quick glance at the Links from an Internet Search Engine section shows which search engines send traffic to your Web site. Chances are that if your Web site is listed in a particular search engine, the engine will drive at least some traffic. You can glean several valuable nuggets in this course of our treasure hunt:

- **Hitting the Big Three:** Our sample Web site is listed in Google, MSN, and Yahoo!, which are widely recognized as the Big Three search engines. It's great that your site is on the map, so to speak, but don't pat yourself on the back just yet. These mainstream engines have overactive *Web crawlers,* so they're often quick to find Web sites without much effort from you. (Web crawlers are automated scripts that scour the Web, adding or updating the search engine's database of Web sites. Read more about them in Chapter 2.)

- **Getting to the next level:** The sample Web site isn't getting any traffic from *second-tier search engines,* like Ask Jeeves, AlltheWeb, and Mamma. That could mean one of two things: Either these search engines aren't sending traffic your way, or you aren't registered with those search engines. The latter is the more likely scenario. The good news is the latter is also under your control. Make sure that you're registered with second-tier search engines that could generate traffic galore. Conveniently enough, you can read how in the following section.

- **Finding the niches:** Our example tool, AWStats, recognizes 122 search engines at the time of this writing. The sample Web site is getting traffic from only eight of them. Time to start registering your site with relevant niche search engines and boost that traffic!

Register your Web site with search engines

If you're not getting the search engine action you need, don't throw up your hands in despair. It's easy to register your site with a search engine. Using Google as an example, registration can be accomplished in five easy steps.

1. **Browse to** `Google.com`.

2. **Like most search engines, you'll find an About link on the home page (About Google, in this example). Click that link.**

3. **In the top-right section — For Site Owners — click the Submit Your Content To Google link.**

4. **Click the Add Your URL To Google's Index link and then submit your content.**

5. **Type your URL, any comments you want to add, and then click the Add URL button.**

The registration process is similar with most search engines. If you'd rather not manually enter your registration at the hundreds of online search engines, you can hire a service handle the submissions for you, as we discuss in the next section.

Hiring a service

If you're not the do-it-yourself type, you might want to look at hiring a service to handle your search engine submissions. Many are out there, but we would caution you to avoid the ones that promise you the world. Number 1 rankings for high-traffic keywords aren't easy to come by, despite what search engine optimization company salespeople tell you. A reputable company will explain to you that natural, *or unpaid,* search engine marketing is a process that takes time and offers little guarantees. Look for references and contact information from previous clients — then do your homework and contact those clients to hear about their experience firsthand.

Are you missing out on the search action?

No hard and fast rule exists as to how much traffic search engines should drive to your Web site. Some Web site owners might generate only minimal traffic from search engines because they concentrate their marketing efforts on link exchanges. Other Web site owners might depend exclusively on search engines to let the world know how to find them. To determine whether you're missing out on the action, considering the following factors:

✔ **Is your traffic membership- or loyalty-based?** If your Web site depends on membership- or loyalty-based strategies to woo visitors, you shouldn't be dismayed if search engines are driving only 25 percent of your traffic. Membership-based sites could be forums or online communities to which members must register to gain access to certain portions of your site. Loyalty-based traffic characterizes visitors who bookmark your site. If you already have an established following, a large percentage of your traffic will naturally fall under the Direct address/Bookmarks section of your site referrer report.

✔ **How much unique content do you offer on your site?** Unique content is the food of choice for search engine spiders. If your site offers lots of original, high-quality content on a regular basis, you should expect search engine traffic percentages of 60 percent or more. Blogs are a good example of how the frequent addition of new content drives search engine traffic.

✔ **Are you running search advertising campaigns?** Search engine pay-per-click advertising, such as Google Adwords or Yahoo! Search Marketing, will definitely skew the percentages of search engine traffic. In this case, you might want to evaluate the percentage each engine is driving to your site based on your spending with that particular site (see Figure 8-4). *Pay-per-click* is an advertising pricing model in which advertisers pay agencies a predetermined fee each time a visitor clicks on the promotional link; for more information check out *Pay Per Click Search Engine Optimization For Dummies* by Peter Kent (Wiley Publishing, Inc.).

Figure 8-4:
List of Links
from Search
Engines
from
AWStats.

Which search engines send you traffic?

After you know which search engines have your number, look more closely at which ones visitors are using to dial you up. This metric will reveal where you should be investing your Search Engine Marketing (SEM) dollars. A deeper analysis will even show you which sites are giving you the most bang for your paid search buck.

The mysteries of the unknown

See Unknown Search Engines item in the list in Figure 8-4. AWStats compiles this number from URLs that use a syntax similar to known search engines, like Google and Yahoo!, but that are not predefined as a search engine in the AWStats database. (*Syntax* in this context means the ordering of elements in the URL.) Although you should keep an eye out for major fluctuations in this number, you can generally assume that these unknown engines are not worth their weight in gold.

What engine gets the attention?

Check out Figure 8-4. It's no surprise that Google is atop the list because Google gets the majority of search engine use. According to Nielsen//NetRatings, Google gets 49 percent of all searches, Yahoo! gets 22 percent, and MSN gets 11 percent. Unless you're investing heavily in paid search campaigns with another search engine, Google will probably be atop your list, too. As you can see in Figure 8-4, MSN is an extremely distant second while AOL and the rest barely made it on the chart. Based on what the sample Web site and what we know about search engine traffic in general, you can conclude that you could generate more traffic from Yahoo! — and probably MSN, too.

Looking to throw some extra attention at one of the main search engines? Consider the following factors before investing your resources:

✔ **Is your target site one of the Big Three?** Investing some energy to beef up your ranking in Google, Yahoo!, and MSN is a smart move. Just remember to measure your efforts to make sure that they're paying off.

✔ **Are you seeing traffic spikes from second-tier engines?** If you begin to notice that you're generating significant traffic from a lesser-known search engine, do some testing to determine how you might benefit by investing in that engine. You might find hidden treasure waiting to be discovered.

✔ **Do you peddle niche products or services?** Unless your products and services appeal to niche surfers, tossing your time and money at obscure search engines doesn't make much sense. If the converse is true, then by all means tap into the specialty searchers and draw as much traffic as possible.

✔ **Want to mingle with meta-data engines?** You could score big with meta-data engines such as Dogpile.com and Metacrawler, which draw resources from multiple search engines at the same time. These sites give you a big bang for your buck by pulling from Google, MSN, Yahoo!, and others. The drawback is that fewer consumers use these engines.

Driving more traffic

You can tell that the sample Web site is listed in Yahoo!'s index because it receives some traffic (however paltry) from the search behemoth. In this example, Yahoo! gets about half of the number of Web searches as Google yet draws only 6 visitors to this site compared with Google's 748. So, you can conclude that there is room to grow referrals from Yahoo!.

You can do this in one of three ways: Increase your paid search spend on Yahoo!, optimize your site design for Yahoo!, or optimize your copywriting by using keywords and phrases in the text that draw the type of traffic you're hoping for. The first option costs money, the second option takes time, and the third option requires some common sense and a perhaps a little creativity.

- **Increase your paid search.** Increasing your paid search is a knee-jerk reaction to driving more traffic, and for good reason — it often works. In order to make wise investment decisions, however, you need to become a master keyword analyzer. You need to know not only what engines are driving traffic, but more specifically, what keywords and key phrases do the trick.

- **Optimize your site design.** Search engine spiders, however complex, are still just computer algorithms that respond in predictable ways when you know what triggers them. You can start optimizing your Web site by learning how to properly use page titles, heading tags, and image alt tags. (*Alt tags,* short for *Alternative Text Tags,* appear in place of images when the browser preferences are set for text only. Alt tags allow visually impaired visitors to use speech synthesizers to read the text aloud.) Adding keywords to these three areas can really get you on track for search engine success.

- **Optimize your copywriting.** Search engine optimization strategies often include posting articles on your Web site that are rich with keywords that you expect visitors to use when searching for what you have to offer. For example, if you sell organic dog food, you might write articles that use the phrase *organic dog food* and *vegetarian dog food* over and over again in the context of the article. Your product descriptions and other content would use the same keyword and key phrase strategy.

Although you can use strategies for optimizing your Web site to appeal to particular search engines, proceed with caution. The changes you make could potentially lower your rankings with a competitive Web site. Be sure to explore and fully understand search engine optimization strategies before giving your site a makeover that could leave your face black with backfire. Also be sure to record your search engine rankings before and after any changes so that you can measure the impact. Alas, that is the subject of an entirely different book. For a complete guide on search engines, pick up a copy of *Search Engine Optimization For Dummies,* Second Edition (Peter Kent; Wiley).

Keyword strategies and tactics

Keywords are critical drivers of both natural and paid search. Savvy Web site owners can write Web site content that makes strategic use of keywords and key phrases that specifically relate to their products and services. A pet products store, for example, should be sure to experiment with keywords and key phrases that relate to their unique products, like personalized leashes or organic dog food.

Web site owners can also execute paid search campaigns through Google, Yahoo!, and other engines. Paid search requires an owner to pay a fee that ranges from a few cents to a few dollars for each visitor who comes to that site through the advertised keywords. Whether you depend on a natural or a paid search, understanding which keywords are driving traffic — and where that traffic originated — is vital to choosing and maintaining keywords that grab the attention of searchers. For more information on keywords and key phrases, see Chapter 12.

Beyond Search Engines: Where Else Is My Traffic Coming From?

Search engines are central to any discussion of online marketing campaigns and rightfully so. This is one of the most effective ways to get the word out about your products and services. However, search engine traffic is not the end all of site referrers. You should also examine other sources of traffic, especially when that traffic is coming in droves. Remember that your Web analytics tool asks each and every visitor, "How did you find out about us?" Now it's your job to take the time to listen to the answer. The URLs offer clues that could help you locate buried treasure that wasn't even on your map.

When in doubt, click. If you don't immediately recognize a referring site listed in your referrer list, just click the URL to find out in a snap. You might discover a new ally, an old friend, or a hostile blogger set on tarnishing your reputation.

When you begin to take a closer look at your site referrers, you will quickly figure out what the top Internet marketing gurus already know: You can't take anything for granted on the World Wide Web. That's why Web analytics firms are springing up to cash in on folks like you who are beginning to realize that more is going on behind the scenes of your Web site than meets the eye. You can determine quite a lot from reviewing your list of non-search engine site referrers, including

✔ **Winning marketing methods:** By taking a look at site referrers, you can determine how much traffic came from your e-mail campaign, how much came from your link partners, how much came from your Web rings, and so on.

✔ **Accidental traffic:** With just a quick glance at your site referrer list, you might discover that visitors are being sent to your domain by folks you've never even heard of. In Figure 8-5, for example, you can see that the sample site has referrers that include the popular online encyclopedia Wikipedia. This is a growing collection of information that includes links to Web sites that are relevant to the subject matter entries. Could your site be among them? Who else is doing you a favor by linking to your site?

✔ **Linkage control:** Much the same as favorable accidental referrers, you might discover some unfavorable referrers. In other words, folks out there might talk negatively about your products and services. They could link to you from a blog or a message board in the midst of a rant. This is not the kind of traffic you want, and such posts should be addressed.

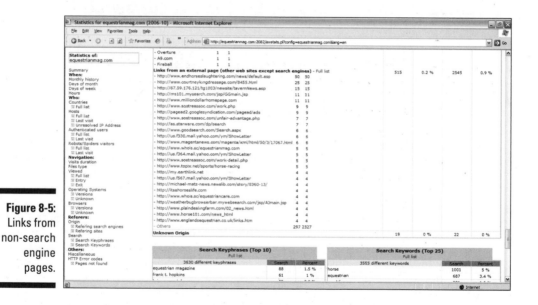

Figure 8-5:
Links from
non-search
engine
pages.

Table 8-1 looks at the pros and cons of some non-search referrers, and the sections that follow discuss them in more depth.

Table 8-1	Non-Search Referrer Pros and Cons
Referrer Type	*Description*
Link-building campaigns	Link-building campaigns are often free, but these initiatives can be extremely time consuming. Web analytics is key to strategic time management because it takes the guesswork out of what's working. Paid link campaigns can be costly, so once again, measurement is key to moving forward.
Web rings	Web rings are free but not always practical. Web rings force you to put a link to the next member in the Web ring, which could ugly up your site. Web rings could also force you to link to a competitor.
E-mail campaigns	E-mail campaigns have the potential to reach several thousands of potential visitors — if you have your e-mail addresses. However, Web analytics tracks only those visitors who came from Web-based e-mail programs.

Measuring the value of link building campaigns

Some Internet marketers consider link building one of the most important strategies for getting direct click-through traffic and improved search engine rankings. *Link building* is simply creating quality inbound links to your Web site. Search engines look at *link popularity* (the number and quality of incoming links pointing to your site) as a factor in Web site rankings. That's one reason why link building has evolved from a friendly practice of "You link to me; I'll link to you" to a strategic business opportunity for link building campaign service providers.

Link-building strategies abound, such as getting listed on partner sites, in e-zines, and in press release syndication. Because link popularity is what gets you into the search engine's elite listings (first-page positioning is where you want to be), you need to understand how your link building campaigns are panning out. Whether you're a do-it-yourself link builder or you outsource to a pro with a track record for success, the results will speak for themselves in your analytics. Once again, it's Web analytics to the rescue.

Looking for some time-tested, link building strategies? At your disposal are literally scores of techniques savvy link builders can use. Here are ten solid strategies for your repertoire:

- ✔ E-mail the Webmaster of a complementary site and ask for a link trade.
- ✔ Incorporate link partnerships with resellers, partners, and vendors.
- ✔ Become a content provider.
- ✔ Issue online press releases.
- ✔ Buy text link ads.
- ✔ Submit articles to syndication sites.
- ✔ Launch an affiliate program.
- ✔ Start a blog and get on other bloggers' blogrolls.
- ✔ Post on discussion forums and include your URL in your signature.
- ✔ Create awards programs for related sites, and place winner logo links on an awards page the winner can link back to.

Keep a list of Web sites with which you have arranged link swaps. Then make a note of any special campaigns, like online press releases. Now scan your Web analytics tool's External Links list for these specific URLs to see which allies and purchased links send the most traffic to your site. The traffic might fluctuate from month to month depending on how much traffic your partner site generates. A review over a 3–6 month period offers the big picture that lets you make long-term decisions.

Look at the AWStats list of referring pages in Figure 8-2. In the sample site, the Endurance.net home page sent about 25 percent of the traffic to Equestrian Mag.com. The site scored those 87 hits by providing content to this leading online resource for endurance and distance riding. A headline on the home page links back to an article on EquestrianMag.com. The rest is Web analytics history. Although you can't expect Endurance.net to send the same number of visitors once the article is bumped from the home page to the archives, you can measure the traffic impact of providing content to this strategic partner.

Are my Web rings really working?

Web rings are an age-old (if there is such an applicable adjective for anything on the Internet) but not forgotten form of link building. *Web rings* are a collection of independently owned Web sites with similar topics that are purposely linked to help generate traffic for the entire group. When a visitor finds one Web site in the ring, he can click a link on the page that sends him to the next site in the group. Web rings have the potential to drive high volumes of traffic, so this aspect of link building deserves special attention in any Web analytics review.

How do you tell whether your Web ring is working? Just record the URL of the Web site before and after yours and look for this domain in your Links from External Sites metric. The resulting traffic might also come from the URL of the actual Web ring or from some other member in the ring. You can discover those referrers by clicking the URL to verify the source. If your analysis consistently shows little to no traffic, or poor quality traffic, you might want to opt-out of your Web ring and rid yourself of the obligation of sending traffic to what could be a competitor.

Counting click-throughs from e-mail campaigns

For opt-in e-mail marketers and e-newsletter publishers, counting click-throughs generated from e-mail distributions is one component of fine-tuning your tactics. Web analytics arms you with the data you need to make decisions. If you consistently get a low response rate, perhaps you're not getting your message to the right target audience, or maybe your messaging needs a stronger call to action. Your Web analytics tools also ante up metrics that draw potential advertisers to your e-mail newsletter. You can figure all that out later. Right now, you just need to get a clear picture of how many subscribers are visiting your Web site as a result of your e-mail campaigns.

Watch out for referrer spam

Referrer spam is spamming aimed at analytics watchers. This dastardly technique involves making Web site requests over and over again by using a fake referrer URL that points to a spam site with an advertisement. These sinister spammers are betting that you'll see their URL on your analytics tool and click through to try to figure out why they're linking to you. The spammers' goal is to build traffic to their sites and try to convert you on one of their (typically shady) offerings. After you identify referrer spam, raise a red flag. You can even use filtering and blocking tools to ban these unwelcome, bogus site referrers. We take a closer look at this issue in Chapter 7.

Before you get too excited, we need to give you a heads up on the limitations of Web analytics for tracking e-mail campaigns. Here's the deal: This data shows only links from Web mail. It will not show how many visitors linked to your site from a desktop e-mail application, such as Microsoft Outlook. Web analytics won't track how many times subscribers open the e-mail you sent them, either. Don't worry, though: You can find services designed to offer detailed e-mail campaign reporting on the market. You can find a list of these in Chapter 6.

So what do site referrers from your e-mail campaigns look like? You can find them quickly by looking for URLs that include the word *email, webmail,* or *mail.* Here are a few examples:

- ✔ http://email.secureserver.net/view.php
- ✔ http://us.f327.mail.yahoo.com/ym/ShowLetter
- ✔ http://by101fd.bay101.hotmail.msn.com/cgi-bin/getmsg
- ✔ http://webmail.bellsouth.net/cgi-bin/gx.cgi/ AppLogic+mobmain
- ✔ http://webmail.tm.net.my/frame.html

This traffic is most often generated by users clicking a link in your newsletter or e-mail promotion via Hotmail, Yahoo! Mail, or some other Web mail service. If you haven't sent newsletters or e-mail campaigns and still see these site referrers, your visitor was probably encouraged to check out your site by a friend or associate who posted a link to your site in her e-mail.

Chapter 9

Getting to Know Your Visitors

· ·

· ·

*Y*ou're probably familiar with the golden rule of real estate. (For those of you who are scratching your heads right about now, here's a hint: location, location, location.) Well, having valuable Internet real estate — also known as a *stellar domain name* — is a good place start, but it's not enough to guarantee success. To win in an ultra-competitive online environment, you also need to exercise the golden rule of customer service: Listen, listen, listen. Online or offline: To succeed in the business world, you need to listen to your customers to find out what they like, what they don't like, what they would like if you offered it, and so on.

We can hear your objections now: "Sure, that's easy for an online customer support center, but what if my visitors never bother to e-mail me? What if I don't have live chat? How am I supposed to know what my visitors are thinking if they don't tell me? I'm not a mindreader!" Never fear, Web analytics is here to serve as your secret agent. Although you won't get a list of physical traits (height, weight, hair color, and so on) in the form of a dossier. The information that Web analytics offers is, in many ways, even more telling.

Web analytics offers the promise of *visitor segmentation,* which groups users based on similar traits or activities. After you segment your visitors, you can compare behavior of one group of visitors with another group of visitors as well as to the broader visitor population. You can segment your visitors into any number of categories, from geographic region to language preference to the age group or even job or income classifications they chose on a registration form. You can explore how first-time visitors behave in the checkout process compared with loyal customers. The ultimate goal is to increase *conversion rates* — that percentage of visitors who take the desired action on your site — of your visitors by making adjustments that better serve their needs.

With that said, read on to discover how to find the data you need to better understand your visitors and serve them at higher levels than your closest competitor, who really is only three clicks away. Because of its unique visitor segmentation features and its affordability, we illustrate our examples with ClickTracks Web analytics software to demonstrate visitor segmentation principles throughout this chapter.

Gleaning from Your Visitors' Past

Through Web analytics, online ventures enjoy customer service advantages that are difficult, if not impossible or at least not affordable, for most to attain in the bricks-and-mortar world. Sure, a suit retailer can ask everyone who walks through the door where he was before he decided to drive over, and the answer could be somewhat helpful. If he came from a fine restaurant, you can deduce he's probably got plenty of money to spend on one of your more expensive suits. If he came from a burger joint, you might come to the opposite conclusion. Of course, even still, you are merely making assumptions (and you know what they say about folks who make assumptions). What's more, the customer might not wish to tell you where he just came from — and possibly get offended if you ask — or maybe even tell you a bold-faced lie.

Using Web analytics, however, takes the guesswork out of your visitors' past and offers reliable insights that could help you convert them at higher rates. Web analytics offers information, such as the URL of the site that the visitor came from. This is also known as the *referring site*. You can also discern the search terms visitors use to find your site as well as what country they came from. Collecting this data forms the foundation of visitor segmentation.

Paying attention to where your visitors came from can tell you plenty about them. For an exhaustive exercise in reviewing your site referrer reports, read Chapter 8. For this section, we focus on how the referrer reports can help you segment your visitors. First, get your list of referring sites from your Web analytics software. In ClickTracks, follow these steps:

1. **Open the ClickTracks application.**

   If the site you want to look at is already open in the ClickTracks dashboard, go to Step 2.

   Otherwise, you need to open the dataset for the specific site you want to review.

   a. Choose File⇨Open Dataset (or press Ctrl+O).

   b. Navigate to your dataset file.

By default, the file is saved in the My Documents⇨ClickTracks Datasets folder, and it usually looks something like *yourwebsite-com.tks*.

2. **Click the Change Dates button in the middle of the home screen to select the dates you want to analyze.**

3. **Click the Site Overview button.**

4. **Scroll down until you find a section titled Top Referrers (see Figure 9-1).**

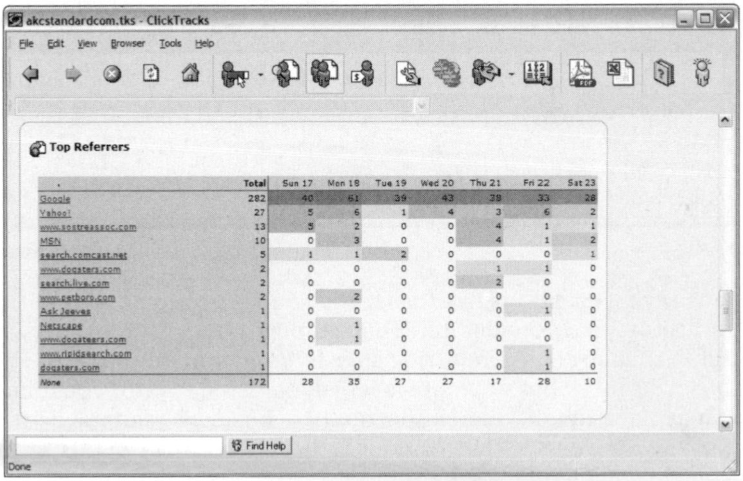

Figure 9-1: The Top Referrers section in ClickTracks.

As you can see in Figure 9-1, ClickTracks does not separate the search engine referrers from non-search engine referrers. If you want to see only the non-search engine referrers, try using AWStats to look at your referrers. You can find detailed instructions for AWStats referrer lookup in Chapter 8.

With your analytics program open, take some time to familiarize yourself with the sites on your site referrer report. You can safely conclude that your visitors trusted the sites that referred them to you enough to click through. Now consider the following questions to glean from your visitors' past:

✔ Are the referring sites targeting consumers, or are they business-to-business–focused?

✔ Does the referring site target a particular gender or nationality in particular?

✔ How tech-savvy do those Web sites require their visitors to be?

✔ Did your visitors enter your site by clicking a link in an e-mail?

✔ Did a separate URL you own and have pointed to your Web site bring them in?

When the cookie crumbles

For all the Web analytics myths and mistakes, misconceptions about cookies are making it more difficult to measure unique visitors. *Cookies* are small files that hold information on times and dates when a user visits your Web site. Examples are log-in or registration information, online shopping cart data, user preferences, and the like. Cookies allows online vendors such as Amazon.com to recognize you, serving you a list of personalized product recommendations. Until you register, Amazon knows very little about you and can't target its marketing efforts to your sweet spots.

Cookies are invaluable to Web site owners and can be convenient for users, but the fear of spyware leads many consumers to rid themselves of the files. In fact, a survey conducted by market research firm JupiterResearch (www.jupiterresearch.com) found that as much as 39 percent of U.S. Web surfers delete cookies from their computers at least once per month, with 17 percent erasing cookies once per week and 10 percent cleaning them out daily. That means the sheer number of your unique visitors could fluctuate dramatically over a 30-day period.

By answering questions like these, you can discover characteristics about your visitors that you might not have thought to consider otherwise. For example, if many of the referring sites to your content portal have a business-to-business focus but your site is largely targeted toward consumer news, you may have an untapped opportunity in business readers. If you operate a travel site but you see that you receive a good number of hits from golf sites, you might want to consider adding a section specifically for golf travel. If you find that many of the referring sites use technology that you previously avoided because you felt it was too "techie" for your users, maybe it's safe to begin implementing some new technology you've been wanting to explore, such as steaming video or downloads.

Searching for Significance

Visitor search terms are perhaps the most intriguing and valuable data that Web analytics produce. Search terms provide a very clear answer to a very clear question: What is your visitor looking for? In a bricks-and-mortar retail store, the very first question you hear from a sales person is often, "Can I help you find something?" Sound familiar?

Every visitor who is referred to your site through a search engine comes in the door with that answer in hand. It's up to you to look at the reports to determine popular search terms; find requests for products, services or information that are related to what you offer on your Web site but don't sell (and could potentially profit from adding); and refer off-the-wall requests to respected partners who might to do the same for you.

Once again, we use ClickTracks in this chapter because it offers a robust view of the reports we are discussing. To find your Web site's top search *keywords* (terms entered into the search box of a search engine) in ClickTracks, just follow these steps:

1. **Open the ClickTracks application.**

   If the site you want to look is already open in the ClickTracks dashboard, go to the next step. Otherwise, you will need to open the dataset for your site.

   a. Choose File⇨Open Dataset (or press Ctrl+O).

   b. Navigate to your dataset file.

   By default, the file is saved in the My Documents⇨ClickTracks Datasets folder, and it usually looks something like *yourwebsite* com.tks.

2. **Click the Change Dates button in the middle of the home screen to select the dates you want to analyze.**

3. **Click the Site Overview button.**

4. **Scroll down until you find a section titled Top Search Keywords (see Figure 9-2).**

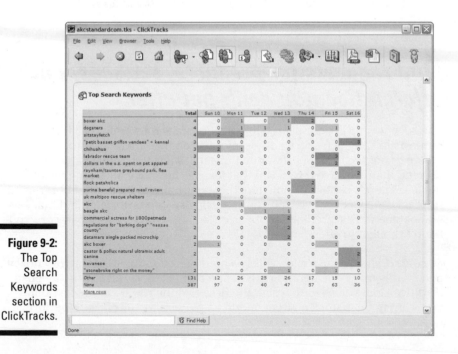

Figure 9-2: The Top Search Keywords section in ClickTracks.

Figure 9-2 shows the Top Search Keywords report for AKCStandard.com for a one-week period. Notice some of the surprising search terms in this report, such as *commercial actress for 1800petmeds,* or the informational requests like *dollars in the U.S. spent on pet apparel* that probably came from a student doing a research report.

Determine popular search terms

The first step in your quest to benefit from referring search terms is to determine popular search terms or phrases that correlate to the products or services you offer. Then you can give more weight to those sections by adding more content or by featuring them more prominently on your site.

For example, if you operate an online bookstore and you see that the number of search queries for a particular author is increasing, consider adding a special section to the site just for that author. If you are a marketing communications firm and you see significant numbers of searches for press release writing, beef up the descriptive content in that section using those keywords. This is one aspect of *search engine optimization* — a method of improving the rankings for relevant keywords in search results by making changes to the content or navigational structure of a Web site. For an in-depth look at this subject, check out *Search Engine Optimization For Dummies* by Peter Kent (Wiley Publishing, Inc.).

Find requests for products, services, and information you don't yet offer

The second step in your search for significant search terms is to find requests for products, services, or information that are related to what you offer on your Web site but that don't qualify as a match made in heaven. Pretend that you have a Web site that focuses narrowly on selling historical books. (There's certainly enough of them out there to fill several libraries.) Now, imagine you've reviewed your referring search terms and find that several people were searching for books on Japanese history — a category you hadn't thought to offer.

Of course, just because a few folks wanted books on Japanese history doesn't necessarily mean you should rush to add that category. Like with any business decision, you need to weigh the risks and the rewards. The last thing you want to do is stock an item or add employees to your firm to perform a service for which there isn't a strong demand. So, while you search for new opportunities in your keywords and *keyphrases* (a collection of terms entered into the search box of a search engine), be sure to put what you find into context. Is it an ongoing trend? Do you get requests for Japanese history books (or what ever you peddle) frequently? Or was it a fluke?

Referring off-the-wall requests

As you review your keywords and keyphrases reports, you are sure to stumble upon at least a few terms that represent requests for products, services, or information that you have no intention of ever offering. Such requests might even be related to your products, services, or content tangentially, but you just have no interest in including them in your repertoire.

When that's the case, you still don't have to waste the opportunity that Web analytics affords you. You could take the chance to build your referrer partner network. If it's possible, add a link to a related resource that you can genuinely recommend. Part of good customer service is being able to help customers solve problems, even when you don't profit from the solution. If you can refer visitors to a site that will help them, it can build brand loyalty for your site and build strong ties with referrer partners who might do the same for you. Think of it as paying it forward: It comes back to you.

Gleaning from Clickstreams and Labeling

Also called navigational paths, *clickstreams* — the recorded path, page by page, of the pages a visitor requested while navigating through a Web site — can speak volumes. If Sally Visitor came in your virtual doors through a Google search for leather handbags, you'll see that. If she went to the shoe section afterward, you'll see that, too. You can tell at what point she entered items into the shopping cart and whether she viewed your return policy. Her entire visit on the site is mapped out, step by step. What's more, you can also see how long Sally spent on each of the pages she visited.

Clickstream analysis helps you make decisions about your site in many ways. For example

✔ **You can get some clues about product affinities that you hadn't discovered.** Maybe you want to offer a few matching pairs of shoes on the handbags page for Sally to consider.

✔ **You can tell you how many customers are concerned about your return policy, and how long they spent reading it.** If they abandoned the site after reading your return policy, you have a clue that they didn't like what they read.

✔ **You can tell which keywords led to the most conversions and which led to the highest sales.**

Putting a magnifying glass on your clickstream can offer you a virtually endless list of combinations, especially when you use Web analytics software that allows you to label visitors and segment them accordingly. Some Web analytics tools incorporate the clickstream analysis to put visitor behavior into context and compare one group of visitors to another.

As we mention earlier, ClickTracks offers some fairly sophisticated tools on a budget price. One of them is Visitor Segmentation. Using the ClickTracks labeling features takes the headache out of grouping users into custom groups and analyzing those visitor segments. Labeling features are conveniently located on the application home page or dashboard in ClickTracks. To access them, just follow these steps:

1. **Open the ClickTracks application.**

   If the site you want to look is already open in the ClickTracks dashboard, go to the next step.

   Otherwise, you will need to open the dataset for your site.

   a. Choose File⇨Open Dataset (or press Ctrl+O).

   b. Navigate to your dataset file.

   By default, the file is saved in the My Documents⇨ClickTracks Datasets folder, and it usually looks something like *yourwebsite-com*.tks.

   In the center column is the Enhance Reports section. That section includes the buttons for Quick Labels and Advanced Labels. (See Figure 9-3.) Quick Labels offers you a simple way to get started with labels.

2. **Click the Quick Labels buttons to open the Label Wizard, as shown in Figure 9-4.**

   This includes such options as Reached Checkout, New vs. Returning Visitor, Compare Search engines, and Short Length Visit. These options will initiate you into the concept of seeing data by custom defined groups.

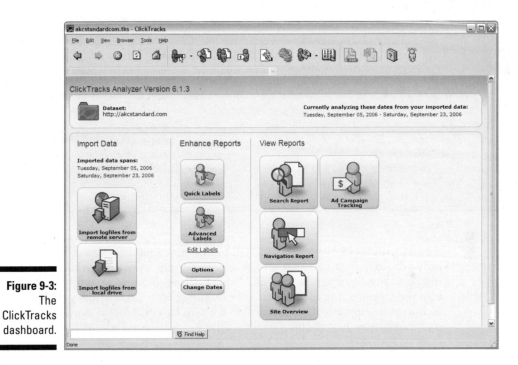

Figure 9-3:
The
ClickTracks
dashboard.

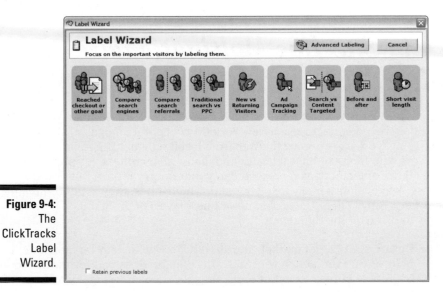

Figure 9-4:
The
ClickTracks
Label
Wizard.

One niche, many segments

Even if your site has an extremely narrow focus (say, horses), you'll probably find many different visitor groups searching through its pages. Sostre & Associates property Equestrianmag.com, for example, serves several different user groups, including children looking for information about horses for a school report, horse owners looking for health care tips for their pets, and professional riders looking for the latest event results. Visitor segmentation is important even within highly targeted sites because it will show you who your biggest fans are. Then you can gear your products, services, and content to the visitors who represent the highest conversions.

As you progress in your Web analytics experience, you should eventually move to Advanced Labeling, which lets you group users by a wide variety of metrics. You can see how groups of users behaved based on which page they entered the site. You can group users by the search engine query they used to find your site. You can even define a group by combinations of these metrics. For example, you could analyze data for only users who came from Google and viewed the About page on your site. The possibilities are virtually endless.

Wow! My Site Has Multinational Appeal!

The World Wide Web isn't called the World Wide Web for nothing. Your Web site has the potential to reach New York City corporate moguls, Asian manufacturing workers browsing the Web from a cell phone, Latin American taxi drivers who frequent Internet cafes and many, many others. It's pretty cool to see all the different flags represented in your country report. But how do these Web analytics really help your site? The truth is, they might or might not help you at all, or they could unlock new levels of profitability. Here's how to discover the difference:

> ✔ **Define your target market.** You should know who your target market is before you ever launch your Web site, of course. As you review the country report in your analytics tools, though, keep your target market in mind.

✔ **What are your multinational visitors doing?** Now, review the click-stream analysis on your site to see what these foreign visitors are doing and how they are behaving. Are they flocking to certain products or services? Or are they just visiting for a few seconds and then leaving? Are visitors from some countries converting at higher rates than others.

✔ **Serve country-specific needs.** If your products and services are available only in the United States but you have considerable numbers of visitors from other countries browsing through them, perhaps you should begin catering to this market with offering international shipping, or even launch a separate site that caters to certain countries specifically, with their culture and language in mind.

✔ **Consider translating your site.** Are you getting droves of customers from Latin America or China? It could be time to consider getting your site's content translated into the native languages for some of your top non–English-speaking countries. Finding translation services online has become easier than ever, a quick Google search for the phrase **Web site translation service** will yield many results for you to choose from.

Betting on Browser Data

If you aren't a Web developer or programmer, tracking the technical details behind your Web site's visitors probably isn't on your list of top ten favorite analytics categories to review. It's true that these aren't the sexiest stats in the log. In fact, sometimes this data is not worth wasting your time on. Of course, there are two sides to every story, and it's also true that you can find some valuable nuggets of information in this miscellaneous data. In fact, in some cases, what you glean from the technical details can have a positive effect on future Web site development and positioning efforts.

Monitoring browser usage

Microsoft's Internet Explorer (IE) is the top dog when it comes to browsers, but with more and more users moving to alternatives such as Firefox, Opera, and others, what does that mean for your site? Web analytics can give you some clues.

Just the facts, ma'am (Or sir)

First, consider the facts. According to an OneStat.com report issued in November 2006, IE accounted for 85 percent of all browser usage around the world. Its next closest competitor, Mozilla's open source Firefox browser, accounted for about 12 percent of global browser usage. Apple's Safari browser trails behind at 1.8 percent, Opera scraped together 1 percent, and the rest are too small to really count. From month to month, those figures don't change all that much and few predict that Microsoft will lose its browser crown, despite alternative browser momentum.

Compare and contrast

Compare the global OneStat.com estimate with what you see in your own Web site statistics. If you use AWStats to gather your Web site's statistical treasures, follow these steps to find browser usage statistics for your visitors:

1. **Point your browser to the control panel.**

   Generally, you can access your cPanel installation by typing in your URL followed by a slash and cpanel. Here's an example:

   ```
   http://www.yoururl.com/cpanel
   ```

   That URL will probably direct you to another URL that corresponds with your Web hosting provider, so don't be alarmed if the URL changes.

   If you know that your hosting company offers cPanel but the preceding instructions above don't take you anywhere, you might need to contact your hosting company to get the URL for your cPanel installation.

2. **Enter your username and password.**

   You are greeted with a pop-up box that instructs you to enter your Name and Password. (See Figure 9-5.) You can choose to select a check box that offers to remember your password so you don't have to enter it in the next time around. (If you've already forgotten your name and password, of if you never knew what they were to begin with, contact your Web hosting provider for details.)

Figure 9-5:
The cPanel login dialog box.

3. **Click Log In to gain access to the control panel.**

4. **Locate the AWStats section.**

   The AWStats section is located in the center column —, the second category, named Web/FTP Stats.

5. **Open AWStats.**

6. **Find Miscellaneous data.**

   Look at the column to the right, towards the bottom, for the Navigation category. Under that, you'll see Browsers.

7. **Click the blue link for Browsers.**

   You're in business.

With your analytics program open, review your browser statistics. If you discover that browser usage for your site is pretty close to the data from the OneStat.com report, you know that you're serving a fair representative group of Web users. On the other hand, if you find that alternative browser usage is much higher, you might want to consider the possibility that your audience is more tech-savvy and then take that into account when deciding what technologies and features to add to your site. You might even want to consider optimizing your site for that browser.

Mulling over miscellaneous browser data

With your AWStats analytics report open, scroll down to the navigational list on the left hand side until you see the Others category. There, you will find what the program dubs Miscellaneous data. As it relates to browsers, this could offer some important insights under certain circumstances.

You'll find stats on browsers, like how many visitors used browsers with support for Java, Macromedia Director, Flash, Real Audio, or some other type of plug-in. If you're thinking about adding some fancy stuff to your Web site, such as streaming videos or Flash components, you might want to review these stats first. If you find that nobody has the plug-ins that would support your high-tech dreams, you likely want to avoid the nightmare of annoying visitors with pop-up messages telling them they can't view your site without special software.

Chapter 10

Identifying Your Most Important Pages

*E*very professional sports team has its all-stars. These Very Important People (VIPs) get paid much more than their teammates because management believes they make a greater impact on the game than the rest of the pack. Although sports fundamentalists may not agree with the inflated salaries, few would leave Dwayne Wade or LeBron James off their NBA Fantasy League rosters. Their productivity stats — rebounds per game, points per game, minutes per game — prove that individual player's worth to the overall team.

Much the same, stats also prove an individual Web page's worth to the overall site. Indeed, every Web site has its VIPs, or Very Important Pages. If you want to look at it in terms of productivity, think of the Pareto Principle, better known as the 80/20 rule. This rule states that in anything, a few (20 percent) are vital, and many (80 percent) are trivial. Twenty percent of the people do 80 percent of the work; 20 percent of your tasks account for 80 percent of your income; and so on.

Using the Pareto Principle as a guideline, it is likely that 20 percent of your pages are generating 80 percent of your revenue, subscribers, or leads. That's okay as long as you learn to identify which pages do the heavy lifting. And that's where Web analytics comes into the game. The software doesn't leave room for opinion: It makes no bones about which pages are most productive and therefore deserve the coveted VIP status.

In this chapter, you discover how to identify which pages bring your visitors back again and again — and which pages keep them there the longest — as well as how to spot pages that might send your visitors running to a competitor's site. Our goal with this chapter is to help you define which pages bring the most value to your Web site so you can try to duplicate the success of those pages in other areas.

It's Not a Popularity Contest — Or Is It?

No doubt about it: Some pages on your Web site are simply more popular than others. Few visitors might actually read an e-commerce vendor's privacy policy, for example, but the return policy page could see heavy traffic during the holiday season. An online news portal might see less traffic to its World News page during the World Series, but the sports section might near bandwidth overload.

Some pages on your Web site are likely to be more popular than others regardless of what big event or seasonal reason people have to visit. A quick scan at your Web analytics dashboard will probably reveal that your home page is one of the most popular, if not the most popular, page on the site because it's the Web address you use in most of your offline advertising initiatives. Face it, though — your home page is only the door. Your primary interest in this popularity contest is landing pages and other pages beyond the home page. A *landing page* is a specific Web page at which a visitor first arrives in response to organic search or paid search initiatives. To discover ways to measure your organic and paid search initiatives, read Chapter 14.

If your Web site markets your services — maybe you are a consultant, dentist, accountant, or attorney — you might discover that your About Us page gets much more traffic than your Contact Us page. That makes sense because prospects want to know more about you before they engage your services. If your bio page is boring or fails to illustrate your expertise (complete with fancy certifications, awards, and the like), you could be losing prospects no matter how strong your homepage is.

Insights like the About Us revelation make judging the Web page popularity contest well worth your time. That's the good news. The even-better news is that it doesn't even have to take much time. Google Analytics, which we discuss at length in Chapter 5, makes it automatic with a report titled Top Content. This report displays your top Web pages based on how many unique views they tallied.(For more on unique views, see Chapter 2.)

If you use Google Analytics to track your Web site statistics, you can access the Google Analytics Top Content report by following these steps:

1. **Open Google Analytics.**

   Because this tool is Web-based, opening the application is as easy as dialing up the URL and logging in. Simply visit `www.google.com/analytics` and log in, using your e-mail address and password (see Figure 10-1). If you don't have a Google Analytics account, see our instructions for registering in Chapter 5.

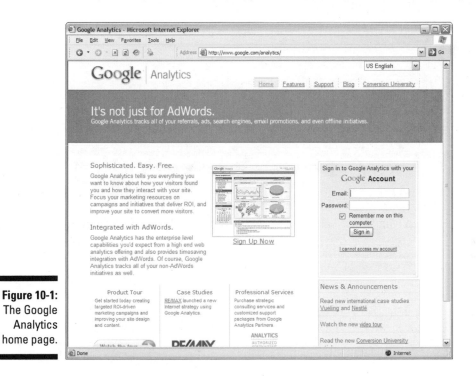

Figure 10-1:
The Google
Analytics
home page.

2. **Opening reports for the domain you want to analyze.**

   When you log in to Google Analytics, you are escorted to your analytics settings page. Whether you are using this freebie tool to track 1 Web site or 20, the list of your sites is displayed in the Website Profiles section. Now find the Web site you want to review.

3. **Click the View Reports link, shown in Figure 10-2.**

   After you click the View Reports link for your Web site, you are sent to the Executive Overview Dashboard.

4. **Click the All Reports heading for the Content Optimization category.**

   When you click this, a list of subcategories drops down. The report you're looking for is beneath the Content Performance subcategory.

5. **Click Content Performance.**

   Voilà! A list of reports appears. The first report on the list is your Top Content report.

6. **Open the Top Content Report.**

   Just click the report name to open it up, and the results of your Web site's popularity contest are revealed. (See Figure 10-3 for an example report.)

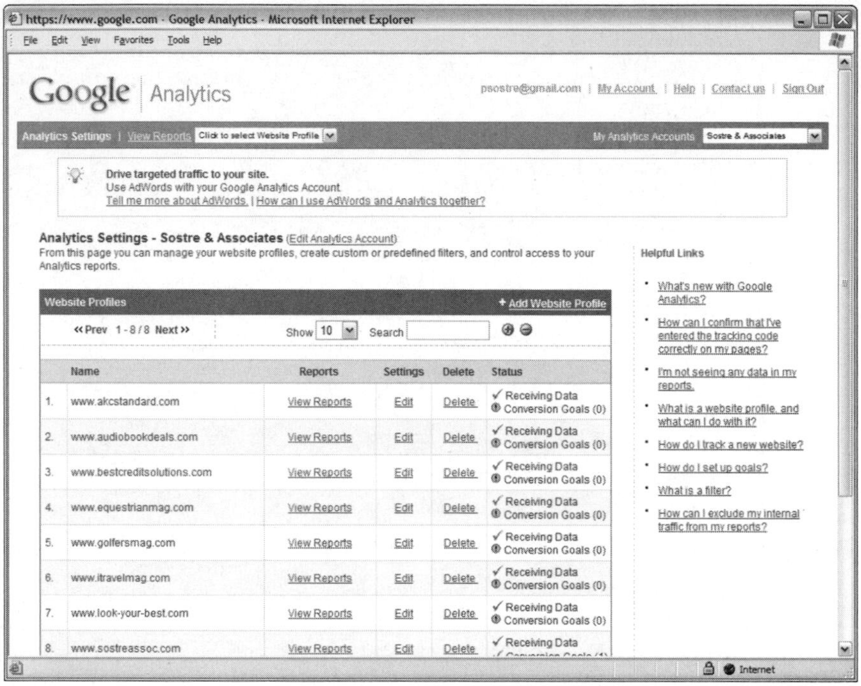

Figure 10-2:
The View
Reports link.

Figure 10-2:
The View
Reports link.

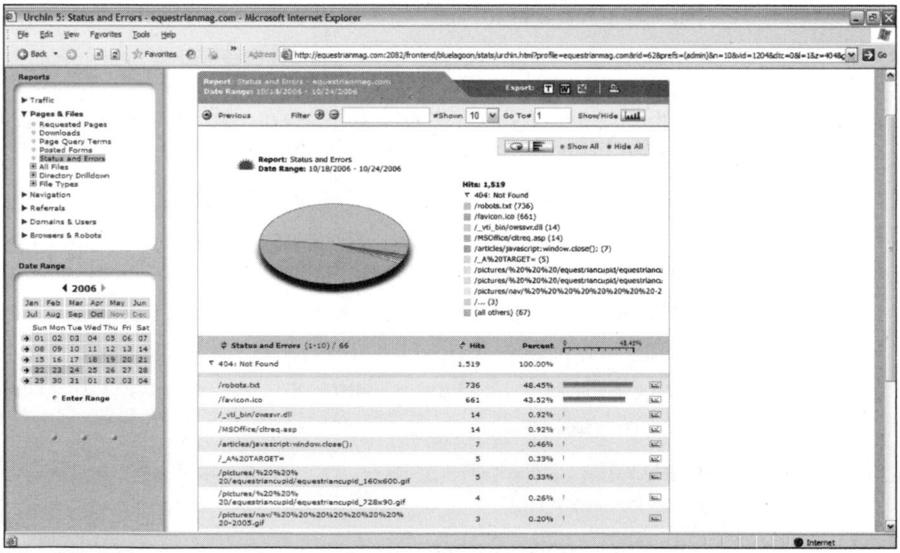

Figure 10-3:
A Google
Analytics
Top Content
report.

You can also choose to sort your Top Content report by *pageviews* (a record of each time a visitor views a Web page on your site), average time on page, or the percent of users who exit at that page. Although the default sort order of unique views is the default for good reason — it clearly defines the most visited pages — you might want to look at the pages from another angle to put the story into context.

Google obliges by letting you view the Top Content sorted by which pages have the highest average time on page and the percent of users who exit the site on these "top" pages. You might discover that one of the so-called top pages in this report has a 95-percent exit rate and really doesn't belong in the winner's circle after all.

Which Pages Drive Your Traffic?

The pages that are most popular and the pages that drive the majority of your traffic could be two entirely different sets of pages. In other words, just because half your visitors browse your sneaker section doesn't mean that they stayed there long. Maybe it took them longer to pick out jackets than shoes. Perhaps your selection of jackets is larger, or maybe you just have picky customers. (Web analytics hasn't figured out how to tell how persnickety your customers are yet, but you as the Web site owner know the breadth of your product selection and can infer some insights from the comparison.)

The pages that drive most of your traffic are probably pages that visitors found while searching for products and services on the Internet rather than by browsing through internal site pages that link to one another. Most visitors probably find your Web site through organic or paid search. *Organic search* is an online search that retrieves results by indexing pages based on content and keyword relevancy. Paid search, or *pay per click,* is a method that retrieves listings based on who paid the most money for keywords to appear at the top of the heap.

Whether you pay for your traffic or depend on high page ranks and well-optimized content to send visitors your way free of charge, you need to know which pages drive most of your traffic. If the wrong pages are generating the greatest visitor counts, you might not wind up converting those visitors. And by the *wrong* pages, we mean pages with your least important content. You aren't hosting traffic just for the heck of it. The name of the game is conversions.

If you discover that your most popular pages aren't converting visitors into customers, consider embarking on a search engine optimization (SEO) campaign. *SEO* is a method of improving the rankings for relevant keywords in search results by making changes to the content or navigational structure of a Web site. Pick up Wiley's *Search Engine Optimization For Dummies* to read more about this hot topic.

Of course, generating traffic is only part of the equation. *Bounce rates* — a metric that shows the percentage of entrances on any individual page that resulted in the visitor's immediate exit from the site — also play a role in your popularity contest. In order to earn the title VIP, your most-popular pages should not only attract lots of traffic but also entice visitors to surf the site for a while. The longer they stay on your site, the better chance you have of converting them. Web analytics offers a clear view of the big picture, so you can be a just judge.

To avoid losing visitors to high bounce rates, you need to view a Web analytics report that clearly depicts your strong traffic-generating pages, alongside their bounce rates. You can access the Google Analytics Entrance Bounce Rates report by following these steps:

1. **Open Google Analytics.**

   Go to www.google.com/analytics and log in, using your e-mail address and password. If you don't have a Google Analytics account, see our instructions for registering in Chapter 5.

2. **Select your Web site.**

   When you log in to Google Analytics, you are escorted to your analytics settings page. As we said before, it doesn't matter how many sites you are tracking. Just select the Web site you need statistics for from the Web Site Profiles section.

3. **Click the View Reports link.**

   After you click the View Reports link for your Web site, you are taken to the Executive Overview Dashboard.

4. **Click the Content Optimization category under the All Reports header.**

   A list of subcategories drops down. The report you are looking for falls under the Navigational Analysis subcategory.

5. **Click Navigational Analysis.**

   A list of reports appears. The first report on the list is your Entrance Bounce Rates report.

6. **Open the Entrance Bounce Rates report.**

   Just click the report name to open the report. (See Figure 10-4 for an example report.)

Figure 10-4:
The Google
Analytics
Entrance
Bounce
Rates
report.

To Err Is Human, to Fix Is Divine

When a customer sees a broken image, stumbles onto a `Page Cannot be Found` error, or clicks a link that is no longer active, your Web site's credibility takes a nose dive. Put yourself in the visitor's shoes: You've been scouring the Web for the perfect venue (to buy shoes, to read about something, or to find a consultant who can help you launch your new product). You finally find a Web site that looks promising only to be met with error messages. Wouldn't you be frustrated, too? You are lucky if those visitors try again later.

Web analytics programs are designed to help you avoid these potentially costly *faux pas* by alerting you to these errors. You can discover them in a section of your Web analytics software, named something like HTTP Error Codes or Error Log. We recommend becoming acquainted with this report and to look at it at least once a month. Finding the errors is not enough, though. You also need to know what the codes mean so you can fix them in a hurry.

Deciphering error codes

If you've ever heard someone say she received a *404 code* and wondered what she meant, you are about to find out — and you need to know because it could happen to you.

Are you using the right tools?

Just like a doctor needs the right tools to diagnose a patient, you need the right tools to diagnose your Web site. In this chapter, we use Google Analytics to check the pulse of top-performing pages. However, this freebie tool remains relatively silent when it comes to error pages because it's a hosted analytics tool. Hosted tools rely on snippets of code placed on your Web site pages to record individual visits.

Because broken images and missing pages cannot be tagged, hosted applications tend to leave you in the lurch. If you rely solely on a hosted Web analytics tool, you might not find out about errors on your site unless you stumble upon them yourself — or unless a frustrated customer e-mails you in the midnight hour. For a full review of the pros and cons for the different types of analytics tools, see Chapter 4.

When a visitor requests a file, the Web server records an *HTTP response code*. Some response codes are good, some are bad, and some are downright ugly. The server goes through this process every single time a visitor requests a file. Most Web analytics applications make reference to Web site errors by their designated HTTP response code. Because these are common and because even well-maintained sites are liable to throw errors from time to time, wisdom dictates getting familiar with the errors you are likely to encounter on the road to Web success.

Seeking success codes

Some people use the phrases *response code* and *error codes* interchangeably, and these numerical distinctions don't always bring bad news. Although these success codes are reported in many Web analytics applications, the user doesn't generally see response codes that don't indicate an error. They occur behind the scenes while your browser continues to take you to the requested file. Here is a list of non-error response codes, however, that you might come across:

- **200 OK:** The page was served successfully. No additional work required. Congrats!

- **206 Partial Content:** The page was loaded, but some of the content might not have loaded properly. One common reason happens when a user clicks the Stop button on his browser, which stops the server from downloading the files in midstream. In most cases, the user might not even realize that parts of the page didn't load. This is an error you can ignore. If you see this error occurring frequently, however, consider optimizing your pages or contacting the person responsible for managing your Web server. (That's usually your hosting company or IT department.)

✔ **301 Moved Permanently/302 Moved Temporarily:** Sometimes, you need to redirect users from one page to another automatically. This can happen if you have an old URL that still receives traffic, but you want to automatically direct those users to your newer products. In these cases, the server logs this response code while it automatically redirects the user to another page. This usually requires no interaction from the visitor.

✔ **304 Not Modified:** The file being requested has not changed since it was last accessed or cached. This code might be generated by bots (Web crawlers) looking for new content or browsers that try to optimize user downloads by checking whether a page has changed before updating their cache. (Read more about Web crawlers in Chapter 3.)

Deciphering error codes

Success codes are mostly good but sometimes a little bit bad. Comparatively, error codes are often bad and can even be ugly. If you see any of the codes described below, ***something went wrong.*** You should investigate any URLs that display the following response codes — and fast.

✔ **401 Unauthorized:** A visitor attempted to access a password-protected page, such as a members-only area of the site. In general, users who don't have a username and password won't bother attempting to gain entry into these areas of the site. Some might have forgotten their username or password. However, it could be that the page in question has been password-protected by mistake. When that's the case, you need to unlock that page so all can freely partake of its contents.

✔ **403 Forbidden:** The most common reason for this error code is when a user tried to *browse a directory* (view all the files within a particular sub folder) when directory browsing is not allowed. Directory browsing is disallowed when server administrators don't want nosy people snooping around their directories, opening files. However, if you don't mind users browsing directories and accessing photos, documents, old Web pages, and other file types posted on your site, just leave directory browsing enabled, and you'll never see this code.

✔ **404 Not Found:** The file in question does not exist. This is the most commonly seen error code and can often be identified by the tell-tale `Page Cannot be Found` message on the visitor's end. Your job when you see one of these errors in your error log is to either create the page or image that is supposed to be there, or to make note of the referring URLs for those missing files and update the links on those pages so that they point to a file that does exist.

✔ **500 Server Error:** These errors are often seen when a Web application, such as a CGI (common gateway interface) script, is configured in a way that conflicts with the server configuration. This is the most technical of the errors and generally requires a programmer to correct.

Common files in the 404 report

Two files that almost always appear in the 404 error report: `favicon.ico` and `robots.txt`.

✔ **`favicon.ico`:** This is a file requested by Web browsers. Browsers use it to display a custom icon for your Web site in the address bar and bookmark lists. Most Web sites do not have this file; if you don't, it's really no big deal.

✔ **`robots.txt`:** Search engine spiders look at this file prior to accessing your site. `robots.txt` tells spiders which pages they can and cannot access on your site. If you don't need to restrict search engines spiders from any areas of your site, you don't need a `robots.txt` file.

Read about spiders in Chapter 3.

Unearthing unsightly errors

You could spend half your day browsing every single one of your Web pages and links looking for broken pages and images. Or, you could get smart and employ the right Web analytics tools to make unearthing unsightly errors, such as missing pages and files, easier than pulling weeds. Several of the popular and free server-side analytics tools, including AWStats (`www.awstats.sourceforge.net`) and Urchin (`www.google.com/analytics/urchin_software.html`), report on error codes. If you use Urchin for your Web analytics, follow these steps to explore your Web site's HTTP request codes:

1. **Open your Urchin analytics page.**

   This usually involves visiting a specific URL provided by your hosting company or navigating to the system through a Web-based control panel, such as cPanel. If you don't know how to access your Urchin analytics account, ask your hosting company for specific instructions.

   When you access Urchin analytics, you see a pane in the upper-left side of the page labeled Reports. The first option in that list is Traffic, which might already be open by default. The second bold option in the list should be labeled Pages & Files.

2. **Click Pages & Files.**

   You see a drop-down list of related reports, one of which will be Status and Errors.

3. **Click the Status and Errors report to open it.**

   The results appear in the main section of the screen.

4. **View files resulting in `Page Cannot be Found` errors for users.**

   After the report is open, it shows a list of Status and Error codes, some of which will have an arrow next to them that you can click for more detail.

5. **Look for the line that reads** `404:Not Found`, **under the Status and Error column header.**

6. **Click the arrow to the left of that row.**

   The report refreshes with a list of URLs that are generating this error for users. (See Figure 10-5 for an example report.)

After you have a list of files that are generating 404 errors, you can proceed to clean up the mess before any more of your users encounter the broken files and before your site loses any more credibility.

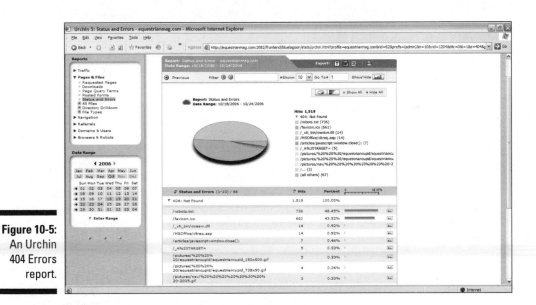

Figure 10-5:
An Urchin
404 Errors
report.

Working with Dynamic Pages

HTML (HyperText Markup Language) will always play a role in Web design, but new programming languages are offering more dynamic experiences for visitors and easier management for the Web site owner. In fact, there is a mass movement from static HTML-only pages to sites that leverage databases, and the server-side programming languages like PHP, ASP (Active Server Pages), and ColdFusion for those very reasons. With these new languages, you can create *dynamic pages* (with changing content). It's important to note that not all Web analytics programs provide accurate reporting for dynamic pages. Unfortunately, the challenges involved in tracking dynamic pages are inherent in the benefits of dynamic pages.

Tricking your Web analytics software

If you consider yourself tech savvy, or you know someone who is, you can pull a trick from your sleeve that will fool the world and offer a loophole to the dynamic page-tracking dilemma. *Dynamic pages* are pages that are generated by programming languages ASP, PHP, or ColdFusion. The secret is to use a common tool developed by *Apache,* which is a popular Web server software. The `mod_rewrite`. `Mod_rewrite` tool lets you define rules that tell the server to interpret specifically formatted, static-looking URLs as their dynamic counterparts. When you use a `mod_rewrite`, it effectively hides the fact that you are using dynamic pages from users, Web analytics applications, and search engine spiders. Taking this path has two benefits. First, it allows your Web analytics tools — even the ones that don't work well with dynamic URLs — to track your dynamic pages properly. Next, it tricks search engine spiders into thinking that your site is composed of many static pages instead of one dynamic page. Some search engines will even rank your site higher because of this. Visit `http://httpd.apache.org/docs/1.3/mod/mod_rewrite.html` to discover more about this technique.

Dynamic pages are just that — *dynamic.* They change. Practically speaking, an online magazine could create a single page and use a language like PHP to pull thousands of articles. If the developer used HTML, he would have to create 1,000 different HTML pages. Here's how it works: The page programmed with PHP pulls all the articles from the e-zine's database in accordance with the parameters, or variables, that the publisher configured. So the Webmaster would make a call to `article.php?id=325` to display article number `325` in the database. This means that just by changing the variable at the end of the URL to a different ID — say, `article.php?id=722` — you can get a page with entirely different content.

The tricky part is that many Web analytics tools tend to ignore the variable that makes your pages different. So even though `article.php?id=100` serves a story about international travel and `article.php?id=750` serves a story about getting the best deal on car rentals, your Web analytics application regards them the same and displays statistics for both, as though they were the same page, `article.php`. That makes it difficult to determine the visitor's navigational path through your site as well as the time spent on each page or even the exit page.

Here's the bottom line: If your site uses dynamic pages, you'll want to make sure that your Web analytics applications can still deliver the information you need. That means investing some research time up front so you choose the right Web analytics vendor. You can read more about how to select a vendor in Chapter 5. What you'll soon discover is that some analytics applications just aren't as good at handling dynamic pages as others are. In particular, Google Analytics and ClickTracks do a good job reporting on dynamic pages individually, whereas AWStats and Webalizer ignore the accompanying parameters and report on dynamic pages as one page.

Chapter 11

Key Performance Indicators Insights

*I*magine driving your vehicle down an interstate on a rainy day. You're on your way to an important business meeting, and you have a long journey ahead of you. The road is slick, visibility is dim, and the traffic is heavy. If you navigate these unexpected highway challenges successfully and make it there on time, you'll stand a strong chance to close a lucrative business deal. If you get lost or arrive late, though, you could blow the show.

The reality is that even if you can have the best driving skills in the world, if you don't monitor your dashboard along the way, you could end up in trouble. You've got to keep your eye on the speedometer because if you drive too fast, you may get pulled over by the police. If you drive too slowly, you're sure to be late. And if you run out of gas, well, the story is over. You'll be walking to your business meeting in the rain — and it's a long, long way.

In terms of Web analytics, think of your Web site as that vehicle you're driving down the Information Superhighway. On the way to online success, you will certainly face challenges in the form of competition, poor product mixes, and even stalled sales. Just like you keep an eye on your car's dashboard to monitor how the vehicle is performing, you need to keep your eye on your Web analytics *dashboard* — the area that displays important information about your site — to understand how your Web site is performing.

This online analytics dashboard displays *key performance indicators* (KPIs), which are metrics that illustrate how well your site performs against goals. Also known as key success indicators (KSIs), offline businesses have been using these metrics for decades as a sort of report card for their business. A manufacturing plant, for example, might use KPIs to assess production or quality (average number of units produced per hour). A fast food chain, by contrast, might choose to use KPIs to measure customer service (average time that a customer waits in the drive-thru line).

In this chapter, we take you on a stroll down KPI Lane and show you everything you need to know about these qualitative metrics. If you're launching a brand new Web site, you might discover that you have more KPIs than you do visitors. Or if you have a well-established site, you might discover that you've been measuring the wrong metrics entirely. We segment these KPIs into categories and narrow down a long list to help you drill down into your metrics until you hit a gusher.

KPIs: When Not Just Any Data Will Do

Web analytics software gathers mountains of raw data. It could take you hours to climb to the top and get that bird's-eye view of your site — that is, unless you focus on KPIs. There are scads of KPIs, from how many users visited the site to where they came from to what pages they visited and so on. You can easily get caught up in the thrill of reviewing these metrics, but it's your KPIs that hold the keys to improving your Web site's performance.

KPIs can obviously differ from site to site because each site has unique goals. If you're trying to build traffic so that you can sell online advertisements to big name brands, the sheer volume of your unique visitor counts in combination with the average time spent on site are critical. However, if you're trying to generate leads, the quality of the visitor is more important than the mere quantity. And if you're trying to sell widgets, the top ten keywords or keyphrases might be key.

Much like how selectively reading one sentence out of an epic novel can offer an altogether incorrect understanding of the book's theme, pulling any one metric from your Web analytics reports and making decisions can lead you into error. KPIs put your raw data into the appropriate context so you can get the full meaning of your Web site's story. Allow us to illustrate:

- 50,000 visitors came to your site in March. That's neither good nor bad in and of itself. It's a neutral observation unless it's in context:

- If 500,000 visitors came to your site in February, a quick comparison of last month's traffic with the current numbers tells you that something is terribly wrong. You just lost 450,000 visitors. Run for the fire extinguisher!

- If only 5,000 visitors came to your site in February, congratulations! You gained 45,000 visitors. Now figure out what you did right and do more of it. Mining data, such as search keywords and site referrers, can give you a clue. (A *site referrer*, or *referring page*, is the URL of the previous Web page from which a link was followed.)

As you can see, raw numbers are relative and must be put into the context of KPIs before they can really communicate meaningful insights that can help you take giant leaps toward your goals.

Calculating basics: Percentages and rates; averages; and ratios

Taking columns and columns of raw numbers and putting them into context means understanding percentages and rates; averages; and ratios. Sometimes Web analytics programs will calculate these arithmetic puzzles for you, but sometimes they don't. If you're concerned about having to do this yourself, be sure to ask your vendor whether its software offers this capability. You can read more about how to choose the right Web analytics software in Chapter 5.

Assuming that you have to do the math, we want to equip you to avoid potentially costly errors. Don't zone out on us now. Writers don't like numbers any better than the average reader. We're here to help. (For those of you who didn't believe you'd ever need the stuff you learned in math class, we're here to say on behalf of your 8th grade teacher, "I told you so.") Now, for the quick refresher course.

Practicing percentages

According to Wikipedia, "A percentage is a way of expressing a proportion, a ratio or a fraction as a whole number, by using 100 as the denominator. A number such as '45%' ('45 percent' or '45 per cent') is shorthand for the fraction $\frac{45}{100}$ or 0.45."

Still confused? Fair enough. Try this: To calculate a percentage, take the number that represents a part of the total and divide it by the total. Here is a good, old-fashioned word problem that will take you back in time and tell you a lot about your Web site:

> If you have 12,289 total visitors and 7,844 of them came from search engines, what percentage of your visitors came from search engines?

To solve the problem, take the number of visitors that came from search engines and divide it by the total number of visitors:

> 7844 / 12289 = .6382944

Then move the decimal to the right two places, and you have your answer:

> 63.82944 percent

You could then round up the number (because the first number after the decimal is greater than five) to get a simple 64 percent.

Rates

Rates are expressed as percentages. When you discover that your Web site has a conversion rate of 6 percent, it just means that on average, 6 of every 100 visitors to your Web site will convert to a sale.

All about averages

When you look at an average, you're trying to approximate the most common or the middle number in a set of data. In reality, the three types of averages in mathematics are the mean, the median, and the mode. The most common method, and the one generally referred to simply as the average, is the arithmetic mean.

You can calculate the arithmetic mean by adding up a group of numbers and then dividing that by the number of elements in the group. For example, if you want to calculate the average number of *pageviews* (a record of each time a visitor views a Web page on your site) per user and your data looks like this:

> User A: 3 pages
> User B: 1 page
> User C: 2 pages
> User D: 6 pages
> User E: 1 page

You simply add the number of pages for each user:

> 3 + 1 + 2 + 6 + 1 = 13

And then divide that result by the total number of users in the sampling:

> 13 / 5 = 2.6

You could then say that the average pageviews per user for your sample set of 5 users was 2.6 pages.

Ratios

Ratios are another way to compare and contrast data. They are generally expressed in this context: the ratio of visitors to buyers is 10:1 (read that as "ten to one"). That simply means that for every 10 visitors, you have 1 buyer.

Keeping up with common KPIs

A shoe seller's KPIs might be much different than a media portal's KPIs, and a media portal's KPIs will surely be altogether different than a lead generator's KPIs. Each type of business has different goals. The shoe seller is about increasing sales. The media portal is about getting new subscribers and advertisers. The lead generator wants targeted traffic that yields qualified leads. However, every Web site owner should keep up with some common KPIs. Consider the following basic KPIs as a bird's-eye view of your Web site's performance.

Average number of pageviews per user

The average number of pageviews per user statistic is a common metric found in many Web analytics applications. This metric is also called Depth of Visit in some applications. Doubtless, the average number of pageviews per user will vary, based in part on the type of Web site you're operating.

Nonetheless, you need to know where you stand. If your average number of pageviews is low, it could mean a couple of things:

- ✔ The user expected something different than what he found on your Web site.
- ✔ What the user found failed to keep his attention or meet his needs.

In most cases, a low average number of pageviews is a sign that you should address your Web site design or your content in a way that will encourage users to stay around a bit longer.

As in other chapters of this book, we use AWStats as our sample Web analytics application. For more about AWStats, see our overview in Chapter 5. Finding your average number of pageviews per user in AWStats is a cinch. Just follow these steps:

1. **Point your browser to the URL for your AWStats application.**

   You can either do this by typing in a defined URL (such as `http://www.`*`yourdomain.`*`com/stats/awstats.pl`) or through a Web-based control panel like cPanel. If you don't know how to access your statistics application, see our tips in Chapter 3.

2. **Look for the Summary section.**

   AWStats displays the Summary section near the top of the right pane.

3. **Find the Pages heading.**

   In the middle of the Summary section is a blue header labeled Pages. Under that label, you see a number that indicates total page views, and under that number, you will find a line that reads something like `##.## pages/visit`. (See Figure 11-1.) That number is your average number of pageviews per user.

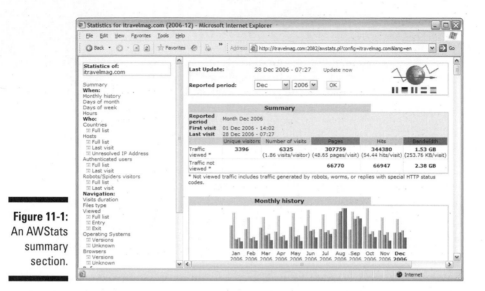

Figure 11-1:
An AWStats
summary
section.

Notice that our example site boasts a hefty 48-plus pages per visitor metric. That's enough to send you doing cartwheels in the backyard, but before you do, take a reality check. Unfortunately, although having a number that high would be great, it might not be accurate.

One downfall to AWStats as well as many other *server-side* Web analytics applications (software installed on the Web site's server) is that if a site uses server-side includes, it often counts each included page as one pageview.

A *server-side include* is code that displays other pages within one page, and is commonly used to simplify Web site management. For example, you could have a single file that contains the HTML code for your Web site navigation and include that one file on all the other pages of your site. If you later needed to change your navigation, you would need to update only one file, as opposed to updating every page on your site. But, as you can see, this method could wreak havoc on some of your statistics. *Hosted analytics* — Web analytics applications hosted by a service provider on its server — avoid this pitfall. For more about hosted analytics applications, read Chapter 4.

Average amount of time users spend on the site

The average amount of time users spend on your site can give you a clear indication of both your Web site's first impression and also the quality of your content overall. First impressions are critical. It's been said that it takes seven consecutive good impressions to make up for a poor first impression. The only problem is that visitor might not come back those seven times if he didn't like what he saw the first time. That means that the time, effort, and perhaps cold hard cash you spent to get that visitor there is in a virtual wasteland. The average amount of time users spend on the site, then, is a KPI that every Web site owner should keep a close eye on.

Generally, the longer visitors stay on your site, the better — with one exception. If you're an affiliate marketer hoping that the traffic you captured will clickthrough to the companies for which you are advertising, you want them to clickthrough so you can cash in. An affiliate marketer is a Web site owner who advertises another company's products or services on his venue through banner ads or text links. In that case, it doesn't really matter whether a visitor stays on your site for 15 seconds, as long as he ultimately clicks through to the affiliate site.

The concept of sticky content is often misappropriated in the context of this KPI. When the Web was young, having *sticky content* came to mean that the longer you could keep users on your site, the better your content was. However, we've since learned that is not always the case. Remember, the idea behind KPIs and Web analytics in general is not just to gather the numbers but rather to try to understand the meaning behind the numbers. For example, if you have an e-commerce site and you discover that hundreds of visitors stay on your site for a long time, that's not necessarily a good thing. It could just mean that they are having a hard time finding the information or products they're looking for. On the other hand, if your Web site is content-based, it's safe to say that a higher average amount of time is better.

Many Web statistics programs also commonly calculate this KPI, including AWStats, our example application for this chapter. To find the average amount of time users spend on your site, follow these steps:

1. **Go to the URL for your AWStats application.**

   This can either be done through a specifically defined URL (such as http://www.*yourdomain.com*/stats/awstats.pl) or through a Web-based control panel like cPanel. If you don't know how to access your statistics application, see our tips in Chapter 3.

2. **Find the Visits Duration link.**

   AWStats houses all the main navigation on the left side of the page. In the third section down, under the title Navigation, the first link is Visits Duration. Click that link.

3. **Find the average time on site.**

   After clicking the Visits Duration link in the left navigation, you see the Visits Duration box in the upper-middle part of the page. Just under the title, you will find what were looking for. (See Figure 11-2.)

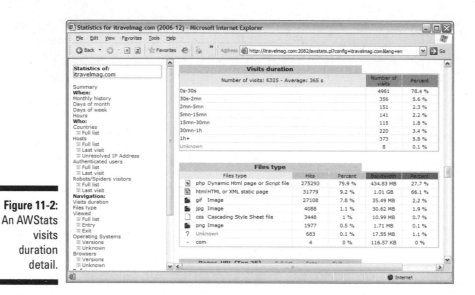

Tabbed browsing and average time on site

Mozilla introduced tabbed browsing to the masses with its popular open source browser, Firefox. Tabs allow users to view multiple sites in a single browser window and easily switch from one site to another. Visitors doing a little comparison shopping and product research can bounce back and forth.

For example, Jack is looking for a new set of golf clubs, so he opens a browser to his favorite comparison shopping search engine and scans the options for the brand name he's looking for. He finds three vendors that look like a bargain, clicks those links, and winds up with three tabs open. When he opened those sites, the server registered a pageview and started the clock ticking to measure how long he stayed on the site. The only problem is that he hasn't actually viewed all the sites yet because they are hidden behind one tab. He can view only one site at a time.

Talk began in the Web analytics community about the potentially serious effects this new functionality could have on the software's ability to accurately calculate statistics because it

falsely — and dramatically — increases the average time onsite across the board. Jack might open a dozen or more links in his search for the perfect set of golf clubs and the accessories that go along with them. However, he might never actually view the contents of some of those tabs if he is satisfied with the vendor under tab 5 in his sequential review.

When Firefox was the only popular browser to use tabbed browsing, this was not a major concern. However, all that changed when Microsoft introduced the tabbed browsing for Internet Explorer 7, which is the dominant browser on the market as of October 2006. The full effects of tabbed browsing are not yet fully understood, but we do know this: It can have major implications in terms of cookies, a visitor's pathway through the site, Web browsing behaviors, time on site, and even paid search. Be sure to ask your Web analytics vendor its strategy for dealing with tabbed browsing.

Shopping cart abandonment rate

You might say the shopping cart abandonment percentage is the inverse of the conversion rate. Instead of telling you how many visitors became customers, this metric tells you how many almost became customers but ditched the cart in aisle number nine.

To put it another way, the *shopping cart abandonment rate* tells you how frequently a visitor adds products to their shopping cart but then for one reason or another, does not complete the purchase. In order to make this statistic more widely valuable, we call it the *conversion process abandonment percentage*. Although this number might not be applicable to strictly content sites, it does have value for support sites, lead generators, and (of course) e-commerce sites.

An online sale has many opportunities to break down. For straight shopping cart abandonment, you can simply take the number of completed purchases and divide it by the number of users who added items to their shopping cart. The result is your shopping cart abandonment percentage. Here's an example of 120 users who converted to 18 sales:

18 (sales) / 120 (users who added products to shopping cart) = .15

Now calculate the difference between conversions and 100 percent:

1.00 − .15 = .85

Convert .85 to a percent, and you can see that your

Shopping cart abandonment rate = 85 percent

Support ticket abandonment rate

For support sites, you might want to use a variation on the shopping cart abandonment rate. Take the number of visitors who submitted a support ticket and divide that by the number of visitors who started the support ticket submission process. If your support system offers easy access to frequently asked questions (FAQs) or suggests answers based on the question the user has entered, this is a good way to see how effective those tools are.

Again, you need to make sure that you take some time to dig deeper than just the bare numbers. If you find that only 30 percent of the users who started the process to submit a ticket actually did submit a ticket, you need to ask what happened to the other 70 percent. Did they abandon the process because they found the answers they needed? Or was it because they couldn't figure out how to submit a ticket and thus left in frustration? Remember that getting the numbers is just the beginning. The real work starts as you strive to understand the meaning behind the numbers.

This means that 85 percent of the people who add items to their shopping cart ultimately decide not to purchase from your store. Why is that? Are your shipping charges too high? Is your shipping process too slow? Is pricing different than they expected? The possibilities are just short of endless, but we'll help you resolve some of the more common shopping cart abandonment causes in Chapter 16.

Conversion rate

If you own a lead generation site, try dividing the number of leads by the number of people who visited the lead generation form. Say that you get 433 leads from 3624 visits to the lead generation form:

433 (leads) / 3624 (visits to the lead generation form) = .119

Calculate the difference between conversions and 100 percent:

1.00 – .119 = .881

Convert .881 to a percent, and you can see that your

Conversion process abandonment rate = 88.1 percent

Wow! Over 88 percent of the visitors to your lead generation form are leaving without submitting a lead! Could the form be improved? Do users have a reason not to trust that their information will be safe? See Chapter 15 for tips and tricks on how to lower your conversion page abandonment rate.

The Granddaddy List of KPIs

As you've probably already figured out, you could choose to calculate dozens of KPIs. This section features a list of some potential KPIs for you to consider for your Web site.

User and traffic growth KPIs

Tracking your Web site's traffic growth — unique visitor growth, in particular — can tell you a lot about how much effect your site is making. Use the following KPIs to keep an eye on these numbers:

- ✔ **Percent of User Growth This Period:** This is the total number of users in this reporting period, divided by the total number of users in the preceding reporting period. (Periods are usually measured in months or years.)

  This metric provides a snapshot view of your user growth. This KPI is the best way to track how well your site is performing when it comes to attracting new visitors. If this number remains stagnant for months or even weeks, you might need to start thinking of new ways to attract new users.

✔ **Percent of Traffic Growth This Period:** This is the total number of visits this period, divided by the total number of visits in the preceding period. (Periods usually measured in months or years.)

This KPI lets you see how much your traffic has grown since the last period. It is different from Percent of User Growth in that it counts each time someone visited your site, as opposed to only counting new visitors. That means if someone visits your site 15 times this period, it counts all 15 times; the former metric counts only one visit per user. New or repeat users could generate traffic growth.

✔ **Percent of Traffic from Search Engines:** This is the number of visits that were referred from search engines divided by the total number of visits. Keeping an eye on this stat can help you decide whether your current search engine marketing (SEM) campaigns are doing their job to increase traffic. *SEM* is a method that seeks to increase the ranking and visibility of a Web site in search engine results pages. SEM includes paid search campaigns.

✔ **Percent New Visitors:** This is the number of new users divided by the total number of users. Getting return visits is great, but it's also important to make sure your site is being exposed to new visitors on a regular basis.

Content-effectiveness KPIs

After users get to your site, your content needs to keep them there. Having lots of users visit your site but leave immediately after arriving does not bode well for the future of your Web site. Make sure that the following KPIs are kept in check.

✔ **Average Page Views Per Visit:** This is the average number of pages that a visitor views while on your Web site. In most cases, if a majority of visitors leave after seeing only one or two pages, you might need to do more to entice them delve deeper into the content your site has to offer. You might need better headlines, photographs, or other article teasers.

✔ **Average Visits Per Visitor:** This is the average number of times that a visitor views your Web site within a given period of time. If the same visitors come back to you time and time again, congratulations. You created a site with compelling content that your users just can't get enough of. If they don't come back again and again, maybe start thinking of ways to encourage them to do so. Maybe you need to offer more regularly updated content or some downloads that they can keep on their desktop so they won't forget you.

✔ **Percent of Returning Visitors:** This is the number of returning users divided by the total number of users. Although a high percentage of new visitors tells you that you're doing a good job marketing your site, a high percentage of returning visitors tells you that you're doing a great job developing Web site tools or content that keeps users coming back. Here's one more thing to consider when you have a high percentage of returning visitors: These people have already seen your site, so you can feel safe designing a site that offers less introductory content and more new content. In other words, you don't have to do a lot of explaining about who you are and why they should keep coming back. You've gained their trust.

✔ **Ratio of New to Returning Visitors:** The number of new visitors compared to the number of returning visitors. Do your visitors know about you already, or should your Web site talk to them as if they have never heard of you before? Determining the voice for your Web site is essential to a successful marketing campaign. If your ratio of new to returning visitors is 20:1, you need to start with the basics and offer introductory information on your Web site. If that number is reversed, however, and you're seeing 1 new visitor for every 20 returning visitors, you're probably safe skipping the introductions and just immediately making way for the content they're looking for.

✔ **Percent Low/Medium/High Time Spent Visits:** This is the percentage of visitors who stay on your Web site for under 30 seconds (low), between 30 seconds and 2 minutes (medium), or longer than 2 minutes (high). Knowing how long a visitor was at your site can be an important piece of the puzzle to show you how effective your site really is. For content-based sites, such as a news portal or a blog, long stays at your Web site generally mean your content is doing a good job at capturing your visitor's interest. Comparatively, a high percentage of short visits can indicate the opposite.

✔ **Percent Low/Medium/High Click Depth Visits:** This metric breaks down visitors into groups based on how many pages they visited on your site. *Click depth* is also referred to as pageviews. Expressed as a percentage, this metric is also effective for determining how well your content appeals to your visitors and how effective your individual pages are at getting users to visit other pages on your site. Content-based sites should track this metric regularly.

✔ **Percent Low/Medium/High Frequency Visitors:** This percentage illustrates know how often visitors are coming back to your site. Low frequency visitors come to the site once; high frequency visitors just can't get enough of the site and visit all the time. If one of the goals of your site is to keep users coming back, a high percentage of high-frequency visitors indicates that you're doing plenty right. Otherwise, maybe you need to include more calls to bookmark the site or some other verbiage that encourages users to come back often, such as teasers about upcoming content specials.

✔ **Page Bounce Rate:** This is the percent of users who leave immediately after viewing the page. If many users leave your site immediately after getting there, that could indicate that either something about your Web site — design, content, and so on — is turning them off. Or, the source of your traffic is sending lots of untargeted traffic. This is a good metric to watch when you want to see whether a particular campaign is reaching the right audience or if you suspect high levels of click fraud on a pay per click (PPC) campaign. *Click fraud* is when a person or robot purposely clicks ad listings without any intention of buying from the advertiser — and it's becoming a big problem online.

Internal search effectiveness

If your site boasts an internal search function, you need to keep tabs on its performance. The ability to track these statistics isn't common in the free or lower-end analytics applications, so you might need to shop around if you determine that this data is vital to the success of your Web site.

- **Percent Visitors Using Search:** This is the percentage of visitors who use the search function on your site. Is an internal search vital to your site? One of the ways to determine the answer to that question is to keep tabs on what percentage of your site visitors are actually using it. If the number is high, you'd better make sure that your search function works well and delivers the results they're looking for. Otherwise, if your internal search doesn't see much action, you can leave well enough alone and focus your efforts on other aspects of the site. (For more insights into internal search, read Chapter 12 for more on sifting through search data.)

- **Average Searches per Visit:** This is the average amount of times that a user uses the search function on your Web site. If users have to embark on four or five searches per visit and your site isn't a search engine, you need to ask yourself why. Why aren't users finding what they want on the first search? Having to do multiple searches to find something almost always leaves visitors frustrated, and frustrated users are bad for business. Of course, perhaps they were searching for four different items. That's good news because it means the visitor is interested in building a relationship with you at some level.

- **Percent "Zero Result" Searches:** This is the percentage of searches that yield no results. If your visitors frequently see no results for the terms they're searching for, you probably need to do some digging into the search terms they use. Should your site offer content for those keywords? If many of your users are searching for them while on your site, the answer is a resounding "yes."

- **Percent "Zero Yield" Searches:** This is the percentage of searches in which the user doesn't click any of the results. What good is providing search results if users don't click them? If your site generates lots of searches but users don't click the results, possibly your search engine is identifying bad search matches. If that's the case, you should consider upgrading your search function to one that provides more relevant results.

Let your visitors tell you what they want

Keep an eye on the search terms that your site visitors use on your internal site search (if you have one). The ones that yield zero results can offer important clues in your quest to better serve your site's visitors. Put on your customer-colored glasses for a moment. Something about your site made them think that you offered what they were searching for. It could have been a word in a promotional blurb on your site that was inconsequential to the actual product. It could have been a sentence in your blog that was taken out of context by a search engine. Who knows? The point is your visitor probably left disappointed when he discovered that you did not have what he was looking for. Whether it was your fault or not, you can use this data to discover what areas or product or service offerings you should develop next.

Marketing-effectiveness KPIs

How well is your marketing campaign performing? Watch these KPIs if you want to keep tabs on your online marketing efforts. *Note:* Because many of these stats need to be taken in context, you will see metrics side by side in this format: for example, KPI-1 vs KPI-2. This simply indicates that you need to look at both numbers in relation to each other in order for them to carry any real meaning.

- **Average Cost per Visitor vs Average Revenue per Visitor:** The average cost to acquire a visitor compared to the average dollar amount that visitor spends on your site. *Average cost per visitor* is the amount of money spent driving traffic to the site divided by the number of visitors. *Average revenue per visitor* is the amount of revenue generated divided by the number of visitors. In conjunction, these metrics help you determine how successful your current marketing strategy is. If the average revenue is much more than your average cost per visitor, you can pour more money into the current marketing strategy. On the other hand, if your cost per visitor is more than your average revenue per visitor, maybe it's time to tighten the purse strings and explore other marketing options or perhaps make some site optimization to increase conversions.

- **Percent Revenue from New Visitors vs Returning Visitors:** This is the amount of revenue generated by new visitors divided by the total amount of revenue generated and the amount of revenue generated by returning visitors divided by the total amount of revenue generated, respectively. This metric is essential in determining whether new or return visitors drive your revenue. Determining who pays you is one of the first steps in determining where to spend your marketing efforts.

✔ **Percent Revenue from First-Time Customers vs Repeat Customers:** This metric is similar to the previous one except that in this KPI, you track where the bulk of your revenue is coming from:

- *First-time customers:* People who have never made a purchase from you before
- *Existing customers:* People who have made purchases from you in the past

Coming to terms with this metric can give you insight into whether your time is better spent selling to existing clients or finding new ones.

✔ **Percent Orders from New Visitors vs Returning Visitors:** This is the percentage of orders from users seeing your site for the first time compared with the percentage of orders from users who have been to your site. Do most people buy your product on their first visit, or do they have to come back several times before they make the decision to purchase? Tracking this metric can enlighten you to your customer's buying process. For example, if your average customer needs to see your site four times before he makes a purchase, what can you do to make sure that he comes back four times?

✔ **Percent Orders from First-Time Customers vs Repeat Customers:** This is the number of orders from first-time customers divided by the total number of orders and the number of orders from repeat customers divided by the total number of orders, respectively. Are the bulk of your orders being generated by people who have ordered from you before, or is it from visitors ordering from you for the first time? Track this metric to find out.

✔ **Average Items per Cart Completed:** This is the average number of items in each completed purchase. Everyone who has eaten at a fast food restaurant has probably heard the phrase, "Do you want fries with that?" That's because those restaurant owners understand the power of cross-selling. If you sell products that can easily be cross-sold, this number can tell you whether you are doing a good job. If the number is low, make sure that your Web site is doing everything it can to cross-sell related items before your visitor clicks the Checkout button. That might mean installing software that makes recommendations automatically or perhaps bundling related items in internal search results.

✔ **Average Order Value vs Average Cost per Conversion:** The *average order value* is the amount of revenue generated divided by the number of orders. Your *average cost per conversion* is the amount of money spent driving traffic to the site divided by the number of conversions (sales, leads, newsletter subscriptions, and so on). This is your bottom line. How much is each sale worth, compared with how much you paid to get it? As long as you're paying less to get the sale than your business makes from it, your business should hum along smoothly. The alternative is a business that loses money as well as lots of headaches.

Remembering lifetime value

When you assess the value of your customers, be sure to look beyond the here and now to the lifetime value. Customer *lifetime value* (also known as *long-term value,* or LTV), which is one of the greatest assessments of customer loyalty. This metric is used to describe the value an individual customer has over the life of her relationship with your Web site. You can use this metric as the basis for developing special offers, such as private sales and other discounts and benefits that show your appreciation. You could calculate this in several ways: total dollar amount for each visitor, frequency of visits, or a combination of both. Keep in mind the X-factor: subscription models.

Many businesses are built around subscription models. That means the customer continues paying even after the initial sale. For example, if you sell a subscription for a digital download of the week for $15 per month but you also offer other digital downloads that the visitor can purchase at-will, the potential lifetime value of the customer has to be viewed in that light. The point is, KPIs are not always cut and dried. You have to continually put the numbers in context and even consider some what-if scenarios. Enterprise-level Web analytics programs often offer what-if and other predictive tools that allow you to see into the future.

Conversion KPIs

At the end of the day, your business probably exists to make sales, and your conversion KPIs are where you find out how well your Web site is performing in your never-ending goal to gain conversions.

- **Average Visits Prior to Conversion:** This is the average number of times that a visitor views the site before making a making a purchase, joining a newsletter, requesting more information, and so on. If the number is extremely high, perhaps you need to work harder to build trust. Copywriting or security seals can help. If that number is very low, you are probably executing your branding efforts well.

- **Conversion Rate:** This is the number of conversions divided by the total number of visitors. Converting visitors into buyers, members, or subscribers is the name of the game. This is the core metric around which everything else ultimately revolves. If this number is poor, you could go out of business. If this number is healthy, you could get rich quick. Okay, so those are the extremes. The point is that this is a number you must keep your eye on continually.

- **New Visitor Conversion Rate:** This is the number of conversions divided by the total number of new visitors. Are new visitors converting immediately? Or are they running in the other direction? If you convert visitors on the first visit, congratulations. You've hit on some winning search engine, branding, merchandising, or copywriting strategies (or all the above).

✔ **Returning Visitor Conversion Rate:** This is the number of conversions divided by the total number of returning visitors. As a general rule, repeat visitors are coveted online because it takes less marketing dollars to get the sale. If you can spend less to get them there in the first place — and convert them, to boot — you are ahead of the game.

✔ **Conversion Rate for Campaign "X":** This is the number of conversions divided by the total number of visitors generated by a particular campaign. Was it those Yahoo! ads that paid off or the Google ads? Was it the campaign for toothpaste that paid the bills or the campaign for mouthwash? This metric will tell you.

Shopping cart KPIs

Shopping cart effectiveness is often the elephant in the room. Companies will spend thousands on their Web sites only to leave their shopping cart process for an afterthought. This results in unusually high abandonment rates and many lost sales. By watching these shopping cart KPIs, you can head off poor shopping cart performance before it bankrupts your business.

✔ **Shopping Cart Abandonment Rate:** This is the number of users who complete the checkout process divided by the number of users who start the shopping cart process, usually by adding an item to their cart.

✔ **Cart Start Rate:** This is the number of users who start the shopping cart process, usually by adding an item to their cart, divided by the total number of users who visited the site. If this figure is high, you need to investigate why they didn't seal the deal. Were the shipping costs too high? Was there some other barrier to entry? It could just be that the phone rang and they forgot to wrap it up, but there could be a reason that demands your attention. If you get a high cart start rate, you should investigate your buying process to see whether it's too complicated.

✔ **Cart Completion Rate:** This is the number of users who complete the shopping cart process, usually by clicking the Checkout button, divided by the total number of users who started a shopping cart. If this number is high, you've either made it very easy for your visitors to close the sale, or they wanted what you were selling badly enough to jump through pages of hoops to get through the buying process. If this number is low, maybe your buying process is too complex. Try to limit the number of steps to three.

✔ **Checkout Start Rate:** This is the number of users who start the checkout process, usually by clicking a button to check out, divided by the total number of users who visit the site.

✔ **Checkout Completion Rate:** This is the number of users who complete the checkout process, usually by finalizing and paying for an order, divided by the total number of users who start the checkout process.

Which KPIs Are Right for You?

After you get a solid understanding of the basics of KPIs, you might want to know which KPIs you should track for your site. Calculating all 40-plus KPIs listed in this chapter would be too time consuming, not to mention fruitless, for most Web site owners. Each business needs to develop a short list of KPIs to track based on the type of Web site it is operating — and more specifically, for the goals of the organization.

Every organization is different. And because KPIs are largely determined by the goals of your organization, they vary for each organization. We can simplify the KPI selection process, however, based on the type of site that your organization operates. Keep in mind, though, that when it comes to Web sites, there are really only four major categories of sites:

- E-commerce
- Content
- Lead generation
- Customer support

Within those types, we can assume some generally valuable KPIs.

Alright, pay close attention. If you are an e-commerce site, we have narrowed the KPI field for you. If you are a lead generator, we made it easy to understand what to watch for. If you are a content portal, a quick glance will highlight all the KPIs you need. If you are running a customer support site, we've got you covered, too. Now it's up to you to figure out what those numbers really mean and take the appropriate actions to optimize the online channel.

E-commerce sites

E-commerce sites exist to sell products. They are the Amazon.coms, the redenvelope.coms, and the bluenile.coms of the Internet world. The desired flow of an e-commerce site is to get users in, direct them to the items they want, try to up-sell if possible, and finalize the purchase. With that flow in mind, here are some basic KPIs that every e-commerce site operator should be watching:

- Average Cost Per Conversion
- Average Order Value
- Average Items Per Cart Completed
- Conversion Rate
- Conversion Rate for Campaign "X"
- Shopping Cart Abandonment Rate

Content sites

The goal of most content sites, or information sites, is to generate as many new visitors and pageviews as possible. Because these types of sites are often monetized — to generate revenue from a Web site — by selling targeted advertising, the more traffic they generate and the more revenue potential they enjoy. Content sites include news sites, forums, directories, and generally any Web site where visitors come to the site in search of information and not necessarily to purchase a product or service.

Common KPIs for content sites include

- Percent of User Growth This Period
- Percent of Traffic Growth This Period
- Percent of Traffic from Search Engines
- Average Page Views Per Visit
- Average Visits Per Visitor
- Percent Low/Medium/High Time Spent Visits
- Percent Low/Medium/High Click Depth Visits

Lead generation sites

Lead generation sites are essentially sites that sell a service. These can include personal services (such as consulting and legal services) or service comparison systems (such as lendingtree.com or lowermybills.com). These sites make money by when visitors submit their information, and the company closes the lead for personal services or sells the lead to another company that can perform the desired service.

KPIs for lead generation sites include

- Page Bounce Rate
- Average Cost Per Visitor
- Average Cost Per Conversion
- Average Revenue Per Visitor
- Conversion Rate
- Conversion Rate for Campaign "X"

Support sites

Support sites are commonly designed to help users get answers to technical or customer support questions. They help organizations save money by reducing customer turnover rates and eliminating much of the personal interactions required through the use of FAQs and well-organized, searchable information.

Support site KPIs include

- ✔ Percent of User Growth This Period
- ✔ Percent of Traffic Growth This Period
- ✔ Average Page Views Per Visit
- ✔ Average Visits Per Visitor
- ✔ Percent New Visitors
- ✔ Percent Returning Visitors
- ✔ Ratio of New to Returning Visitors
- ✔ Percent Low/Medium/High Time Spent Visits
- ✔ Percent Low/Medium/High Frequency Visitors
- ✔ Percent Visitors Using Search
- ✔ Average Searches Per Visit
- ✔ Percent "Zero Result" Searches
- ✔ Percent "Zero Yield" Searches

Creating Your Own KPIs

As we discuss throughout this chapter, many organizations can benefit by developing a list of KPIs that are relevant to their individual organizational goals. When developing KPIs, keep the following recommendations in mind:

- ✔ **Be specific.** Don't define KPIs that are vague, such as *Develop more incoming links*. Instead, look for more specific metrics, such as *Number of incoming links this period vs last period*.

- ✔ **Make sure that the KPI is quantifiable.** *Get more visitors to like our site* is not a measurable, or quantifiable, goal. Make sure that your KPIs can be measured with data. Something like *Percent of returning visitors* is a KPI that can really be measured.

- ✔ **Work with what you have.** Some analytics programs are more robust than others. You might not be able to measure everything you want to measure within your analytics software budget. So work with what you have, or upgrade to a more sophisticated tool. To read more about the various tools that are available, see Chapter 5.

Part IV
Knowledge Is Power — Making Analytics Work for You

The 5th Wave   By Rich Tennant

"Right here. Analysis shows the well-run small criminal organization should have no more than nine goons, six henchmen, and four stooges. Right now, I think we're goon heavy."

In this part . . .

Making Web analytics work for you isn't rocket science if you've set goals and determined the Key Performance Indicators that measure your progress toward them. Making Web analytics work for you is a matter of taking the pertinent data that you've gathered and putting it in action.

In particular, you must understand where you've been, where you are, and where you want to go before you begin applying this powerful knowledge to your site. This is where chronicling your Web analytics history comes into play. If you do this, you can even use your historical data to see the invisible — and to predict the future. We'll show you how.

In this part, you'll also receive insights into how to find new customers and partners by monitoring your keywords and referrer reports. What you find there may surprise you. You'll also understand why you should not neglect internal site search data while you are combing through site referrals from Google, Yahoo!, and the other major external engines. Internal search results can help you expand your product and service horizons. You can even cash in on common misspellings if you can identify a trend in search reports. Again, we'll show you how.

Of course, with an arsenal of search engine information at hand, you may discover that it's time to change your online advertising strategy. We'll offer hands-on demonstrations of how to use tracking URLs and ferret out ad campaigns that don't work. And since conversions are the name of the game, we'll also show you how to unravel the conversion funnel breakdowns.

All of this falls under the guise of Web site optimization, which we believe is the Holy Grail of Web analytics. You can use your data to guide Web site redesigns, optimize your home page and landing pages, put a stop to shopping cart abandonment, and, finally, measure the impact of your site changes. Just as Web analytics never stops collecting and presenting data, you should never stop measuring your progress towards your goals and making adjustments to get there faster whenever possible.

Chapter 12

Sifting through Search Data

● ●

In This Chapter

▶ Discovering surprise keywords that drive traffic

▶ Spying on internal searches

▶ Maximizing opportunities with misspellings

● ●

*T*he business world holds the generally accepted tenet that retaining an existing customer is far less expensive than acquiring a new one. Just think about all the preapproved credit card offers that the postman delivers to your house on a daily basis offering low introductory rates. The average household receives two credit card offers each week, according to the U.S. Public Interest Research Groups. And although all those mailings cost money, after you sign the dotted line, card vendors can stop sending mailings and start collecting interest.

Web analytics offers unique opportunities to find new customers and even new partners by mining your external and internal search reports and site referrer data. Also called the referrer page, a *site referrer* is the URL of the previous Web page from which a link was followed. Instead of buying a direct mailing list — or, in the case of online marketing, an opt-in e-mail list that can cost thousands of dollars — you can merely review your analytics reports and discover valuable information about your traffic and its origin.

Web analytics allows you to do what even the most targeted advertising campaigns can't offer: to discover exactly who sends visitors to your site and what those visitors expect to find when they gets there. Armed with this information, you can optimize your Web pages, optimize your merchandising scheme, or reach out to your top referrers to form strategic alliances that will send even more traffic your way.

Indeed, if you subscribe to the generally accepted customer-acquisition rule (keeping a customer is easier than getting one), Web analytics offers you the best of both worlds because you can glean insights into what your current customers want as well as what your potential customers want. Either way, you can target your visitors with the most tempting products and services and turn them into customers — or repeat customers, as it were.

This is a much different strategy than merely blasting advertising or marketing campaigns to the masses in the brick-and-mortar world, even if you target masses in a narrowly focused trade journal or via television broadcast. It's different because oftentimes, the target can immediately respond by clicking through to your site and accepting your call to action. Customers don't have to pick up the phone to order or drive to a store near them: Their fingers literally do the walking.

What you discover in this chapter may surprise you. So get ready to delve into your search and referrer reports to

- Find keyphrases you never dreamed were driving traffic.
- See how to monitor your internal site searches for maximum conversions.
- Cash in on common misspellings.
- Plenty more!

If you implement these measures, you not only have the potential to attract new visitors, but you'll also serve your loyal customers more effectively.

Sifting Your Search Terms

Web analytics offers you the opportunity to get inside the heads of your visitors. (Whether you get inside their wallets depends on other factors, such as compelling products, site design, a trusted brand, and so on). In other words, you can discover how your visitors are thinking as well as what they expect to find when they entered your virtual outpost. Reviewing your *keywords* (terms entered into an external search engine) and *keyphrases* (multiple search terms used together) reports is a fascinating exercise, but beware that it can be addictive. Reviewing these reports is more than an exercise in satisfying snoops: It's the first step in driving additional traffic. More traffic equals more opportunity to turn visitors into customers, subscribers, and readers.

Accessing the search data

Practically speaking, most Web site owners should sift through their search terms every month or so to discover what keywords and keyphrases are used on search engines, and then respond accordingly. If you get more than a few thousand visitors per day, we recommend reviewing your data weekly or even daily. Most importantly, don't ignore this opportunity to optimize your site and your online advertising efforts by using this data. It could realistically double or triple your traffic virtually overnight. You decide how much time and money you want to put into traffic-acquisition strategies.

Using AWStats as our example analytics tools, accessing your keywords and keyphrases reports is as simple as one, two, three (and four).

1. **Point your browser to the control panel.**

   Generally, you can access your cPanel installation by entering your URL, followed by a slash and `cpanel`. Here's an example:

   ```
   http://www.yoururl.com/cpanel
   ```

   That URL will probably direct you to another URL that corresponds with your Web hosting provider, so don't be alarmed if the URL changes. If you know that your hosting company offers cPanel but the preceding instructions don't take you anywhere, you might need to contact your hosting company to get the URL for your cPanel installation.

2. **Enter your username and password and click OK to gain access to the control panel.**

   You are greeted with a pop-up box that instructs you to enter your Name and Password. (See Figure 12-1.) You may choose to select a check box that offers to remember your password so you don't have to enter it the next time around. (If you've already forgotten your Name and Password, of if you never knew what it was to begin with, contact your Web hosting provider for details.)

Figure 12-1: cPanel login dialog box.

3. **Locate the Web/FTP Stats section.**

   Note the Web/FTP Stats section in the center column (the second category). Several different links appear in this section, as shown in Figure 12-2, which vary depending on what your Web host has enabled for the server.

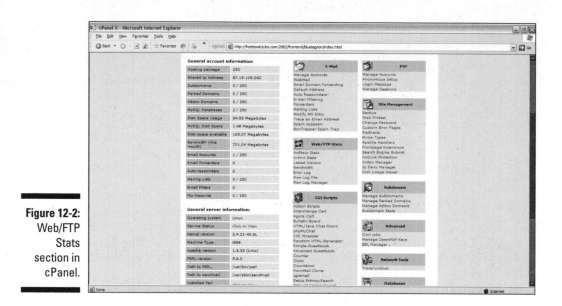

Figure 12-2:
Web/FTP
Stats
section in
cPanel.

4. **Click the software that you would like to use.**

   Voilà! You have access to a world of data.

5. **Locate Search statistics.**

   On the left side of the screen is a list of link options. Toward the bottom is the Referrers section. Under that category, you'll see Search. Click that link.

   Your Search Keyphrases (Top 10) and your Search Keywords (Top 25) reports display. You'll also see a link to Full List under the heading. If you have more than 10 search keyphrases and 25 search keywords, click this link to display each and every one of them.

Reviewing your top search terms

When you review your Search Keyphrases and Search Keywords reports, note how the charts are broken down into three columns. (See Figure 12-3.) In the chart below, for example, are the columns 3,638 Different Keyphrases, Search (lists how many times visitors used those specific terms to find your site), and Percent (tells you what percentage of your visitors who came through an external search engine used those specific terms).

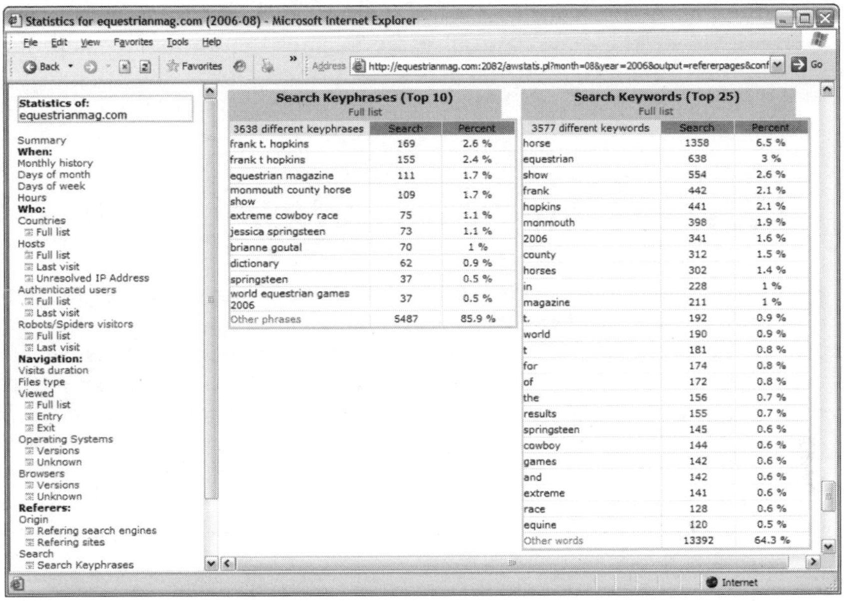

Figure 12-3:
The Search
Keyphrases
and Search
Keywords
reports.

Looking at our example, you can tell that the most popular keyphrase was *Frank T. Hopkins,* followed closely by *Frank T Hopkins* (without the period after the middle initial). In fact, more than 5 percent of the visitors who found this site through an external search engine (such as Google or Yahoo!) used those terms. And what does that have to do with the resulting target, EquestrianMag.com? As you can likely guess, the site features an article about the legendary endurance rider, Frank T. Hopkins. More searchers find Equestrianmag.com by searching for *Hopkins* than they do by searching for *equestrian magazine,* which only garnered 1.7 percent of the searches. That is telling.

So, what do your search reports tell you? What are your most popular keywords and keyphrases? These are the search terms that will probably drive the most traffic through a paid search campaign, so if you want to boost your traffic, that's an option. For more good stuff on online advertising, read Chapter 13.

Sifting through these top keywords and keyphrases is important because what you find can actually be disturbing. Perhaps you discover that the most popular search terms don't relate to the product or service that you're laboring to sell. The search engine terms that your visitors used most could direct them to a product that has low margins or to a service that isn't all that profitable. Don't get us wrong: Getting visitors in the door however you can is great, especially through natural search, which doesn't cost you a penny. However, the same natural search engines that brought less profitable visitors through your virtual doors can bring visitors who are looking for high-margin products and banner services. Why not optimize for that juicier fruit?

My Visitors Are Searching for What?!

When you review your search reports, you might discover that some surprising keyword and keyphrases are opening the door to your site. The Web site This Might Be a Wiki (www.tmbg.net) offers a list of amusing search engine keywords and keyphrases that took visitors to tmbw.net for one reason or another, including *linky dinky, bicycle wrecks, how to become a robot,* and *help me match my clothes.* Get the picture? Some keywords that your visitors use might give you a good chuckle; others may disgust you; and still others can offer you insights into products, services, content, and customer service answers you could be offering. Unfortunately, others could be wasting your Benjamins.

Pleasant surprises

The Holy Grail for many Webmasters is to find their site listing on the first page of the search engine results for his terms of choice. However, using generic keywords rarely does the trick for the average Web site owner. You need to get creative and consider what the competition is doing — think like searchers think. Your Web analytics program can help you do that last part, anyway.

Reviewing your search reports can uncover some surprising and powerful keywords that you can use to generate high volumes of traffic to a specific *landing page,* the specific Web page where a visitor first arrives in response to an organic search or a paid search initiative. Or maybe you'll decide to build landing pages around these surprising keywords so that visitors can enter into the site on the very page that has the products, services, articles, or answers they need. Looking at these surprising keywords can help you come up with names of new products, services, and content categories; or even help you phrase self-service questions and answers in ways that are easier for your customer to understand.

Say you discover that 20 percent of your visitors used the terms *polka dotted pants* to find your Web site. Maybe you need a landing page especially for polka dotted pants. Okay, that's an extreme example, but we're trying to make a point. What search terms are visitors using frequently that you never thought would play up in your copywriting or merchandising schemes? Got it? Now use them to your advantage.

Searching for relevant terms

If you find yourself with keyword block, don't despair. There are plenty of ways to figure out what Web searchers are looking for. For example, Overture (www.overture.com) offers a free Keyword Selector Tools that offer some relief. Hitwise (www.hitwise.com) has a service that shows you the top 1,000 terms in any given industry albeit at a hefty price.

You could skirt both services by doing some undercover searching of your own.

1. **In Google (or your search engine of choice), just enter search terms that are most relevant to your business.**

   You can see the quality of the keyword competition. Pay careful attention to the sponsored links. Those are probably your competitors who bought contextual keywords.

2. **Visit those sites and view the source code to look at the home page's code.**

3. **Look for a list of keywords embedded in their meta tags.**

   You want to see HTML tags that are written into the head section of an HTML page behind the scenes.

Sounds sneaky, we know, but it's not unethical. It's competitive intelligence. You know what they say — imitation is flattery. Besides, their lists might spark even better ideas you can use for your keyword campaigns.

If you need to wrap your mind around this and other HTML issues, pick up a copy of *HTML 4 For Dummies,* 5th Edition, by Ed Tittel and Mary Burmeister (Wiley Publishing, Inc.).

Profit thieves

Although you will surely find some pleasant surprises in your keywords report, you might also find some profit thieves lurking in the wings. We're talking about your *pay per click* (PCC) search campaigns. Also called *paid search,* this method retrieves listings based on who paid the most money for keywords to appear at the top of the heap. What many newbies don't understand is that search engines take a broad approach to keyword traffic. Most engines not only send you traffic based on exactly the search terms you chose, but they also send you traffic that they think relates to the search terms you chose. Search engines can include synonyms, misspellings, hyphenated terms, singular and plural combinations, compound words, or typographical errors related to the words you selected.

Yes, you can direct these engines not to use broad matching when you sign up for your keywords campaign, but if you forget — and even if you do want the broad matches — you might find that these visitors are sucking your PPC ad budget dry without filling up your bank account with sales. Broad match strategies, then, can be a blessing or a curse. You need to keep your eye on broad search terms and take the appropriate action. For example, if the broad matches are a blessing, you can optimize around them. If they are a curse, talk with your paid search provider about shutting the door on these profit thieves — for good.

Cashing In on Common Misspellings

Thank God for spell check. It's made all our lives much easier, hasn't it? Well, there is no spell checker, per se, on the Web. Sure, if you type in *elphant circus* on Google (notice the missing *e*), you will get a red prompt at the top of the search results that reads something like *Did you mean: elephant circus?* And immediately under that you also see links to stories, eBay sellers, movie listings, and gift stores that spelled *elephant* as *elphant*. Buyers do the same thing on your internal site search. They mean *elephant* but type *elphant*. They mean *toilet* but type in the synonym *commode*. They meant one thing, but cultural differences or common misspellings bring up something different — unless you discover how to cash in on these issues.

Names are among the most frequently misspelled words in search engines, as evidenced by the Yahoo! Buzz Log of the Top 20 misspellings for 2006. There, you'll find common misspellings such as Rachel Ray, Louis Vitton, Jimmy Buffet, Brittney Spears, and Anna Nichole Smith. Again, some search engines will attempt to automatically correct the typos, but accounting for the ones that fall through the cracks doesn't hurt.

If you don't see the correlation between the engine and the site, allow us to offer you a real-life example. FreeBookClubs.com (see Figure 12-4) offers some unusual misspellings. After you identify the misspellings (get out your dictionary if you don't spell any better than the average person), you can include those misspellings in your product descriptions so that searchers who aren't quite sure how to spell an unusual author's name or book title can still find what they are looking for. This should be done tactfully and obviously so that users understand why you have misspellings at the bottom of your about page.

Don't go over the top listing misspellings because this tactic can backfire on you big-time. If you have lots of text that is similar or large sections of copy that don't make any sense, search engines might penalize you for what they believe is a slick attempt to get higher rankings and generate more traffic with fluff content. Try to keep your misspellings list to just the most common misspellings, or break it up into different areas on the site. Follow this general rule: If it looks weird or out of place to users, search engines will probably see it the same way.

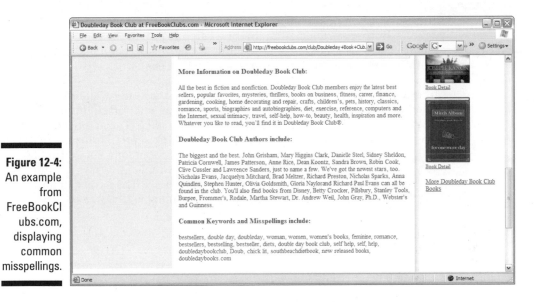

Figure 12-4:
An example from FreeBookClubs.com, displaying common misspellings.

Beyond Traffic to Conversions

Traffic is one thing; conversions are another. Although discovering what search terms drive your traffic is undeniably important, it's equally (if not more) important to discover what search terms convert traffic. After all, you aren't paying a Web host to serve your site to the masses for grins and giggles. Even bloggers are seeking to get subscribers to RSS feeds and on-site advertising these days. And affiliate marketers don't just want traffic: They want visitors who click through to their affiliate partners so they can collect their commissions. Lead generators aren't just bragging about their abilities. They want folks to e-mail them or call them. And customer service operations don't just want visitors to search Q&A databases: They want visitors to find the answers so they won't pick up the phone and call in a nervous tizzy.

Regardless of your conversion goals, Web analytics has you covered with the data you need to demonstrate success (or break the news that you need to change your strategies). We delve into of *search engine marketing* (SEM) — a method that seeks to increase the ranking and visibility of a Web site in search engine results pages — at greater length in Chapter 14, we focus our discussion here on *natural search* (the kind you don't pay for). You'll be pleased to know that several strong search engine optimization (SEO) analytics tools are on the market in various price ranges; they can tell all you need to know about how your search SEO labors are paying off. We've selected a few reputable tools to give you a taste of the market.

If you get out of the shallow end of SEO and venture out into the deep, you'll discover what many online scam artists will never tell you: SEO is not merely about getting first positioning on Google, Yahoo!, and others. It's about conversions. Pop quiz: Would you rather be listed eighth in the rankings and earn $10,000 per month, or be listed first in the rankings and make $200 per month? Don't you wish all pop quizzes were that easy?

Not quite classified as niche programs (because they offer well-rounded analytics packages), software such as TrafficAnalyzer and Portent Interactive are ideal for the wannabe and professional SEO guru alike. These tools offer an in-depth look at keywords so you can decide which search terms are converting and which ones aren't. Although there is still room for a superstar SEO analytics program at the time of this writing, the applications we list here can help you break down your data into actionable steps. Then you can fine-tune your Web site accordingly. (We get to the fine-tuning in Chapter 16.)

TrafficAnalyzer

www.agentinteractive.com

TrafficAnalyzer (see Figure 12-5) is a combined, in-depth keyword tracking and Web analytics solution. This hosted solution is relatively easy to use, and its sole task is to determine the sources of your most profitable TrafficAnalyzer. One of this application's features that turns the heads of SEOs and affiliate marketers is its ability to determine and track unlimited single or multistep conversion points. You can differentiate between sale and non-sale conversions, view new visitor and returning visitor conversions, and identify the best source of conversion-producing traffic. The cost is only $10 per month for up to 1,000 hits.

Portent Interactive

www.portentinteractive.com

Portent Interactive's SEO Analytics (see Figure 12-6) drills down to the bottom line in a hurry. Its program tracks several metrics on every campaign, including nonbranded traffic, percentage of traffic, conversion, and ranking. *Nonbranded traffic* is traffic that you get from terms that don't include your company name. Some call this the truest measure of SEO success. Measuring nonbranded traffic tells you more about how your audience looks for you. This program also tracks the percentage of traffic to your site from major search engines and how many visitors converted.

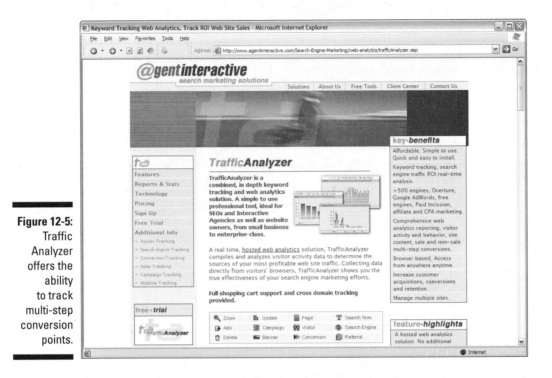

Figure 12-5:
Traffic
Analyzer
offers the
ability
to track
multi-step
conversion
points.

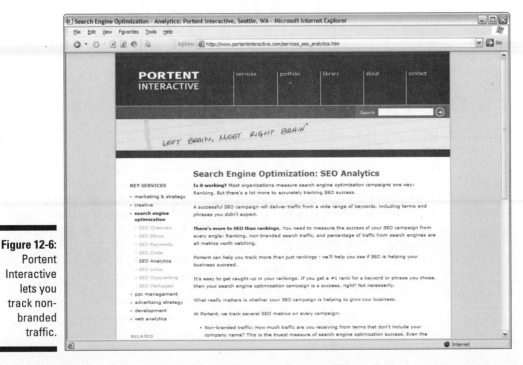

Figure 12-6:
Portent
Interactive
lets you
track non-
branded
traffic.

Don't get sucked into SEO firms that promise to get you number-one rankings on all your keywords. We're not discussing those here because we are talking about Web analytics, which deals with measuring the results of campaigns. But we felt it necessary to warn you that opportunists are on the Web who will promise you the moon and deliver you a large bill that will have you seeing stars. You can do lots to search-engine-optimize your own site; read Wiley's *Search Engine Optimization For Dummies,* 2nd Edition, by Peter Kent for more about that. This book helps you track those efforts. We listed the reputable tools in this section to help you avoid the temptation of the scammers.

103bees.com

www.103bees.com

103bees.com (see Figure 12-7) isn't a hive of stinging creatures. Rather, it's a real-time online tool for Webmasters and bloggers that is highly focused on natural search engine traffic analysis. It offers tons of detailed statistics and in-depth information on search terms that drive visitors to your blog. If you want to search-engine–optimize your blog, this is the tool for you. If you want to measure your Internet marketing initiatives, this tool is right up your alley. Plus, it's free. 103bees.com helps you discover the *long tail* for all the keyword combinations that work for your Web pages. This is valuable because you can unlock hiding opportunities beyond the Top 10, such as new blogging content ideas that attract readers. Instead of paying for ads, you can merely mine your long tail of search terms and use those keywords to drive more traffic.

Flip-Flopping the 80/20 Rule

Many Web site owners are hyperfocused on the Top 10 or Top 25 search keywords and keyphrases. In essence, you might be looking at the top 20 percent of your external search terms and ignoring the remaining 80 percent. Some search marketers flip-flop the 80/20 rule and spend considerably more effort sifting through the latter 80 percent. True, perhaps 20 percent of your search terms drive 80 percent of your traffic today, but there is no reason why the other 80 percent of your search terms couldn't generate enough revenue to put that top 20 percent to shame. (See Figure 12-8.) In our example, the top 10 keywords are responsible for less than 10 percent of all search traffic. Isn't it time to start watching the other 90 percent?

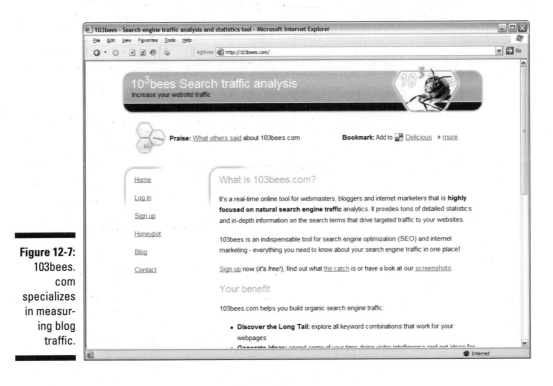

Figure 12-7:
103bees.
com
specializes
in measur-
ing blog
traffic.

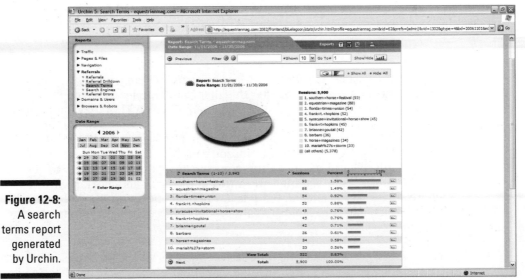

Figure 12-8:
A search
terms report
generated
by Urchin.

This is known as the *long tail principle,* which is a term whose coinage is widely attributed to Chris Anderson, who wrote a book by the same name. The *long tail* (see Figure 12-9) consists of keywords and keyphrases that individually don't account for much traffic but, if maximized, could be potentially powerful tools to enhance revenues, leads, content, or customer self-service opportunities. The long tail, then, helps you uncover product and service niches, no matter how small they are.

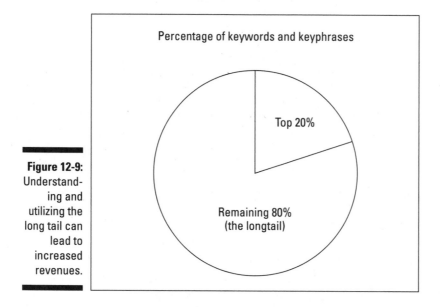

Figure 12-9: Understanding and utilizing the long tail can lead to increased revenues.

You can start using your long tail to swing search circumstances in your favor. But before you do, consider this theory in practice. Amazon.com, for example, might sell 250,000 of its top 20 book titles on Thursday, but it might also sell 1 million book titles that fall under the radar screen of the top 20. By paying attention to the long tail, Amazon can also search for titles it doesn't have that people wanted to buy. Amazon can then stock them on its virtual shelves and begin to sell them, thereby increasing the opportunity to generate revenues. This might not work well in the brick-and-mortar world where shelf space is limited, but it is a winning concept on the Web, where many book publishers can drop-ship products direct to the customer for e-commerce players.

The same concept holds true for customer self-service. Every question that customers type into a search box that isn't answered in your database causes frustration. You can increase customer loyalty by examining the long tail and making sure that you address every customer concern. For content portals and lead generators, the long tail works much the same way. It could be that your firm offers precisely the services the customer is looking for, but the long tail reveals that they use a completely different terminology to describe what they need. Those leads might not have converted simply because you are speaking a different language. Content providers can examine the long tail to discern new opportunities for niche categories of content. So don't limit yourself to the 80/20 rule. Start swinging the long tail in your favor.

Monitoring Internal Site Searches

Internal site search — the search box that should appear on every page of your Web site to help customers find what they are looking for — can help transform a site that suffers from high abandonment rates to one that boasts full carts. It can help extend the one-hit visit into multiple pageviews. It can even take a sad excuse for an online customer support center and give it a makeover that will encourage customer loyalty. That's why you should monitor what some in the industry call *the other search*. Sure, search engine traffic and the keywords that drive it are critical because your visitors might not otherwise find you. However, if they can't find what they are looking for after they get there, they won't stay long.

Stats on site search stats

As you review your site search terms, you'll probably discover that most of them are one or two words. We know this because we keep tabs in industry research, so we can bring you the inside scoop. We turned to WebSideStory (www.websidestory.com) for some stats on visitor site search behavior and came up with some interesting results that serve all types of sites. For the record, WebSideStory studied visitor site search behavior on 42 of its customers sites in May 2006. Fifteen of those sites were e-commerce sites, 14 were media sites, and 13 were lead generators. All in all, the analytics firm analyzed a mind-boggling 34 million site searches to come up with some key findings. Here's what the firm found:

- One- and two-word queries accounted for 83 percent of all site searches.

  That figure was 91 percent on e-commerce sites.

- The top 4 percent of all unique query phrases accounted for half of all site searches.

  For e-commerce sites, 2 percent of all unique query phrases accounted for 50 percent of all sites searches.

- Nearly 12 percent of all sites searches led to 0 results.

- About 0.2 percent of all site searches were, well, blank.

If you have a lead generation site with just a few pages, these might not be the most important pages in the book. However, if you sell widgets (and lots of different colors, sizes, and shapes of them) or if you run a customer service center online, pay very close attention to what we are about to share with you because it could change the face of your business forever. (You can thank us later.) What you are about to discover is hidden treasures are contained in the internal site search report that even the external search engine report won't tell you. Your job is to monitor that report and put what you discover into action.

Driving sales, not traffic

Internet search engines drive traffic to your site, but the internal search engine can drive conversions. You can pay hundreds or even thousands of dollars when driving traffic to your Web site. Simple site search, by contrast, is free. So, if you're going to bid on keywords at Google, be sure to optimize your site search functions first. Otherwise, you could just be funding the development Google's next online tool.

Site search puts you in the driver's seat. You don't have to depend on being the highest bidder on a keyphrase in Overture. Once users are on your site, you have a captive audience for as long as you can keep them. Site search helps you take visitors by the hand and walk them down the aisles they choose. While you escort them with your site search tool, you can suggest other products and services that compliment what they searched for. For example, if a visitor types *scarlet scarf* in the site search box, you can also bring up scarlet coats and gloves and present them on the same page. This is cross-selling and up-selling at its best.

But wait, there's more! Using Web analytics to monitor your internal site searches can also uncover opportunities to sell products or offer services that customers want but that you don't yet offer. You can also drill down into your reports to discover what products you offered that visitors searched for but couldn't find. (How tragic! You just lost a customer!) You can use a visitors own words to fine-tune your product and service descriptions and even identify emerging customer service issues.

The bottom line from the top down

Here's the bottom line: According to WebSideStory stats, visitors who use internal site searchers spend 270 percent more moolah on a Web site than visitors who don't use internal site search. Need we say more? Great navigation isn't enough, folks, especially if you have lots and lots of stuff to navigate through. Yes, pay attention to your *clickstream analysis* — the recorded path, page by page, of the pages that a visitor requests while navigating through a Web site. But also pay attention to your internal site search.

Allow us to put it to you in another way: For all the hoopla over SEO and SEM, another method could dramatically increase conversion rates for e-commerce players: *site search*. Site search can be as much as three times as likely — yes, we said three times — to convert site visitors to buyers, according to a WebSideStory study. In fact, site search conversion rates can easily run 6 percent compared with the rather typical 2 percent standard for most industries.

Before you begin . . .

Before you begin monitoring your internal site search efforts, be sure to do some quick comparisons and record what you find. Assess the quality of your site search results. Did visitors leave the searcher empty-handed? Are your visitors using your search box to dial up contact information? Did the site search queries your visitors use convert? What is the *conversion rate* (the percentage of visitors who take the desired action) for internal site searchers — and how does that compare with visitors who didn't use the internal search box?

Here's how to calculate your conversion rate:

1. **Determine the number of visitors to your site.**

   Look at the number of unique visitors in your Web analytics program.

Selecting site search technology

Plenty of site search vendors are on the market, but you don't necessarily need to use one. If you have but a few items on your site, you can rely some of the free solutions on the market, like FreeFind (www.freefind.com) or FusionBot (www.fusionbot.com). If you're serious about making the most of site search, however, you should consider investing in a paid solution. Some solid paid tools include Pico Search (www.picosearch.com), SearchBlox (www.searchblox.com), and SLI Systems (www.sli-systems.com). Of course, those are just a few leads. You'll need to check out these solutions for yourself, keeping these points in mind:

✔ **Scalability:** Site-search solutions need to grow with your business.

✔ **Pricing model:** The pricing should be flexible, determined by the size of the Web site being searched.

✔ **Optimization features:** These should offer greater managerial control over your own site search.

✔ **Indexing and templates:** These should keep the engine fresh. The templates are important because they offer a support design system to help control the layout of your search results page. Choose a vendor whose templates can match your site's look and feel.

2. **Determine the number of conversions.**

   Not all Web analytics programs do this for you. If you use Google Analytics, though, you can count the number of *Thank you* pages, or whatever page displays after the visitor takes the desired call to action.

3. **Divide the number of visitors by the number of conversions.**

   This is good, old-fashioned arithmetic. Your answer will offer you the conversion rate for your Web site.

WebSideStory's data suggests that you should be converting site search users at nearly three times the rate of average site visitors who don't use site search. If that's not the case, you might need to look for another site search technology vendor, changing the way you associate keywords with your content or make some other adjustment.

Searching for Accuracy and Relevancy

Internal site search is critical in the Google Age, where searchers expect to get highly relevant results. Going to an e-commerce site and searching in the internal engine only to come up empty is a frustration for visitors, especially when they know that you sell what they want. Getting inaccurate or irrelevant results can be even worse.

You've probably heard it said that your visitors are only a few clicks away from your competitor. That was a popular cliché that developed in the Web's early years. It was true then, and it's still true now. Again, you can't rely solely on navigation. You need relevant internal site search results to help harried visitors cut through the clutter and find what they are looking for quickly. Don't try to be slick and offer them a page of boots when they typed in *sweaters* just because you don't sell shirts. It's one thing to cross-sell or up-sell; it's quite another to get pushy with irrelevant products.

Put on your customer-colored glasses again. Every time a visitor types a keyword or keyphrase into a site's internal search engine, he expects to find results that match his search term. Wouldn't you? If a trend arises in the search terms that visitors use — no matter how strange that trend may be — the internal search parameters should be tweaked to ensure that visitor gets the results that she is expecting.

Creating Targeted Landing Pages

We're about to let you in on one of the newest trends in site search: using the results as a landing page. Your advertising or e-mail campaigns will drive traffic to your site, but you can decide what pages they go to. Of course, being the savvy Web analytics analyzer that you are, you are going to review your internal site search report and send visitors to a page with relevant site search results.

An e-commerce vendor could launch a campaign around a particular brand, for example. If the vendor offers a link that delivers relevant site search results to visitors, he can more easily find the desired brand or product. Clinique, for example, sells more than cologne. A landing page of site search results could display information about all related or available products, which could also lead to cross-selling opportunities. For more information about landing page optimization, read Chapter 15.

Similarly, if you have an e-commerce site, you can enhance your SEM campaigns by indexing site search pages. Typically, spiders don't index site search results because they are automatic user agents. Also known as *Web crawlers, bots,* or *robots, spiders* are automated scripts or programs that browse the Web. Search engines use robots to gather up-to-date data as they index the Web. Search engine spiders can't manually enter keywords in search forms. You can get around this, though, by adding related searches on your product pages. That lets you provide a path to the site search page for various items.

Using this technique makes it easy for spiders to index the site search page and then follow the related search links to get thousands of new pages indexed and optimized for the search terms people are actually using on your site. Brilliant, isn't it? Thank you very much. We thought so, too. Remember the rule of relevancy, though, and keep analyzing your Web analytics reports to determine the appropriate listings.

Your Search Yielded Zero Results . . .

A WebSideStory study of 34 million internal site searches discovered that nearly 12 percent of them led to 0 results. As you review your internal search reports, pay close attention to these goose eggs. Site searches that yield zero results can clue you in to new product or service opportunities. Maybe your competition is already offering the product, and the visitor was doing a little comparison shopping to check out your price. If you run a customer service site and the customer's queries yield zero results, he'll either get angry, pick up the phone and call, or send you an e-mail — or all the above. In any of these cases, your job is to react — and react quickly — to zero results.

Here's an example to drive home our point. We take a quick look at one of the top Web properties that Sostre & Associates (an interactive firm) operates. (If the name Sostre sounds familiar, it's no coincidence. Check out the co-authors of this book!) The Web site, FreeBookClubs.com, is a book club directory that aims to simplify avid readers' search for clubs that offer the authors, genres, and titles they crave.

Mix and match internal and external search

Web analytics allows you to do some interesting experiments in your search for profitable keywords and keyphrases, and it's one of the easiest experiments to execute and measure. First, review the most popular search terms that your visitors used to find your site. Then review the most popular search terms that your visitors entered into your internal search box. Are they the same? Or are there some vast differences? Chances are that at least some minor differences are worth noting. If you see a preponderance of internal site search keywords that convert visitors into buyers, members, subscribers, or otherwise satisfied customers, you need to exploit those keywords to the fullest and use them in your PPC campaigns.

Although FreeBookClubs.com offers an internal site search tool, the Sostre & Associates development gurus realized they could better understand user behavior by tracking the specific terms that visitors used in the search box. What they discovered was that six of the Top 10 most popular search phrases, including the most popular search phrase on the site, were for authors that weren't mentioned anywhere on the site. So even though FreeBookClubs.com did offer book clubs that featured books by those requested authors, the visitor was presented with zero search results. Translation: Most of those visitors left because they thought the site didn't offer what they were looking for.

By adding information about those authors as well as which book clubs they were associated with, FreeBookClubs.com was able to provide visitors with the information they were looking for, keep more visitors on the site, and convert more book club browsers into book club subscribers.

Chapter 13

Increasing Web Site Visibility

*I*t's one thing to use Web analytics to better understand those customers — or readers — you already have. It's quite another to use Web analytics to increase your visibility to new customers and partners. That's what we show you how to do in this chapter. If you haven't considered the power of this software to assist you in your target marketing efforts, now's the time.

Target marketing is a simple concept and one with which you may be familiar: It's merely communicating with a specific group of people who share similar characteristics. By knowing what your visitors are doing on your site, you can carve out markets and target new customers who want what you have to offer. You can do this through *visitor segmentation* — analyzing users grouped by similar characteristics or traits — which we discuss at length in Chapter 9. But that's not the only way to use Web analytics to drive new customers. You are about to discover several other ways to generate new revenue streams.

By the same token, Web analytics can help you discover new partners, or allies. It's a competitive World Wide Web out there. Believe us: You need all the help you can get. The more Web sites that refer visitors to your Web site, the better. It helps your *page rank* — a numeric value created and calculated by Google that's designed to indicate the importance of a page — and it delivers the potential of more conversions. We discuss strategies for reviewing site referrers in Chapter 8, but you'll see these strategic allies in a new Web analytics light in the paragraphs to come.

To put it plainly, this chapter is where you discover how to increase the number of potential customers who come through your site as well as partners who can help get the word out. Whether you are a socialite or a recluse, an expert marketer or still wet behind the ears, you'll discover how to use Web analytics to unlock new opportunities to drive revenue. As an added bonus, we show you how to keep tabs on your Google PageRank so you can watch how your new partnerships and traffic building efforts make your site more attractive to the biggest search engine out there.

Finding New Customers

Face it: Repeat customers are welcomed friends, and they are easier to keep than new customers are to acquire. But that doesn't mean that you shouldn't seek new friends, does it? After all, your existing customers, subscribers, members, and others will only purchase, read, or visit so much. You need a steady flow of fresh blood, so to speak, if you want to see that line on your revenue chart climb higher and higher. You need to find some new customers.

You'll find strategies, tips, and tricks throughout this book on connecting with new customers, but this chapter zeroes in on some Web analytics activities that are specially designed to help you attract more visitors.

Attracting new visitors is only one part of the equation. You can spend half your Internet life driving traffic to your site. If that traffic isn't relevant to what your site has to offer, you'd be better off watching old reruns on *Nick at Nite.* In other words, if you aren't identifying customer trends in your Web analytics report and targeting a like-minded Internet population, you're just using up bandwidth.

Scanning your search engines

Knowing which search engines send you the most converting visitors — who then qualify as customers — helps you make smart decisions about online advertising aimed at attracting more of the same. If you discover that Google sends you virtual truckloads of duds but Yahoo! sends visitors who subscribe to your RSS feeds or fork over cash to buy your widgets, it would seem that the latter also gives you a better shot at finding new customers who will do the same.

Using your Web analytics applications to segment visitors and discover which search engines send you the highest percentage of paying customers allows you to focus your efforts on those engines. After all, your *search engine marketing* (SEM) budget isn't unlimited. (SEM is a method for increasing the visibility of a Web site in search engines through improving rank in organic listings, purchasing paid listings, or a combination of these as well as other search engine-related activities.) Web analytics offers you opportunities for efficiency. Skip to Chapter 14 for more relevant info on how to measure these metrics.

Improving your search rankings

One way to find new customers is to extend your reach online by improving your search rankings. According to a Pew Internet & American Life study, few people look beyond the first page of results. Don't let that get you down. Obviously, not everybody can rank on the first page of search results for a given search term or phrase. And you shouldn't toil and spin trying to get your site on the first page of results for anything and everything you peddle or produce. You need to decide what you want to be known for or check your Web analytics and play off what customers already know you for. Then optimize your Web site's content around those keywords.

To that end, you might engage in any number of search engine optimization (SEO) activities. SEO is a method of improving the rankings for relevant keywords in search results by making changes to the content or navigational structure of a Web site. Web analytics can help measure every one.

Optimizing your Web site so that it ranks well in search engines is one of the first steps in improving your search engine rankings. But how do you know which keywords to target in your quest for higher rankings? Web analytics can help.

- ✔ **Benchmark your search engine standing.** You can't improve your standing on the search engine front if you don't know how you're doing to begin with. The first step for any good SEO campaign is to figure out where you stand in the here and now.

- ✔ **Determine your top converting keywords.** Some analytics applications track conversions and the associated keywords that those buyers, subscribers, leads, and so on use to find your site. WebSideStory's HitBox Professional (www.websidestory.com) and Google Analytics (www.google.com/analytics) are two popular options that offer this feature. After you know which keywords work for you, you can focus on optimizing your site for those keywords. To learn more about the various tools available, check out Chapter 4.

- ✔ **Find new keywords to target.** The *long tail,* a concept coined by *Wired* editor Chris Anderson, refers to the keywords that fall outside your top referring keywords. These are terms that don't send you much traffic individually, but taken together might outnumber your high-traffic keywords because there are so many of them. The idea is that you look beyond your Top 20 keywords and start developing content and pages for those niche, lower-traffic keywords. Generally, they represent more very-targeted areas that are less competitive, making it easier for you to rank well for and *monetize* (generate revenue from) these keywords. For more in-depth insight in the long tail concept, read Chapter 12.

What you'll find as you venture into the world of SEO is that there are more strategies than there are hours in the day to implement them. That's why you need to focus your efforts on what will pay the highest rate of return. Web analytics will help you do just that so that you aren't merely spinning your wheels when you could be driving to the bank.

Measuring your SEO efforts

If you spend any time at all exploring SEO strategies, you'll surely want to know how they pay off in the grand scheme of things. Hopefully, you will notice lots of new visitors, but it's likely that there will be at least a short lag between your site's search engine ranking improvement and the fruit of your labors. Or it could be that your SEO efforts completely fail to boost your search engine rankings at all. Either way, you'll want to know what effect your efforts are making, so we are going to take a side step for a moment to talk about two non-analytics–based metrics: Google PageRank and Alexa Ranking.

Indeed, your Web analytics tools will tell you how your site is performing, but the software won't tell you how well your site is performing compared with your competition. It's true that Nielsen//Netratings, Hitwise, and comScore offer industry rankings, but unless you are rolling with the Fortune 500 clan or have caught the wave of a major emerging trend and become the next YouTube or MySpace, those benchmarks don't offer useful comparisons. All that said, you can still determine how your Web site really ranks against the rest of the World Wide Web.

Google PageRank

Google PageRank, named after Google founder Larry Page, is Google's system for ranking pages. Although the specific algorithm for calculating PageRank is somewhat guarded, we do know that it's based on several factors, including number of incoming links, length of time online, and others. And although it doesn't tell you much specifically, the PageRank can give you a general idea of how important Google thinks your Web site is. The number is based on a 1 to 10 scale. A PageRank of 1 or 2 would indicate that Google does not see your site as very important, and a 9 or 10 means you're playing with the big dogs. If your site does not have a PageRank, it has not been indexed by Google (in which case you can go to `www.google.com/addurl/` to submit your URL to be crawled at a future update).

When you want to find your PageRank, you have two options:

- Use the Google toolbar or another browser toolbar or extension that offers this functionality.
- Use PRChecker (`www.prchecker.info`) or another online PageRank checking service.

To use the Google toolbar:

1. **Go to** `http://toolbar.google.com`.

2. **Click Install Google Toolbar.**

3. **Follow the onscreen instructions to download and install the toolbar (see Figure 13-1) in your browser.**

   The Google Toolbar consists of:

   - An enhanced search box that makes suggestions, spelling corrections, and offers a history as you type

   - Safe browsing features that offer warnings about Web pages that may be unsafe

   - SpellCheck, a tool that checks your spelling automatically as you type in Web forms

   - AutoFill, a feature that automatically fills out forms for faster online shopping

4. **After the installation is complete, just browse to your Web site to see a PageRank indicator on the toolbar. (See Figure 13-2.)**

Figure 13-1:
The Google Toolbar adds functionality to your IE or Firefox browser.

Figure 13-2:
The Google
Toolbar
displays the
PageRank
of any page
you visit.

Checking with PRChecker

Several Web sites also offer online tools to check your PageRank if you want to avoid installing the Google toolbar. Those options are as simple as typing in your URL then and pressing a button. Using PRChecker as your example, here is the quick step by step:

1. **Point your browser to**

   ```
   http://www.prchecker.info/check_page_rank.php
   ```

   You'll see a heading that reads Check Page Rank of Any Web Site Pages Instantly and a box underneath prefilled with `http://`.

2. **Type your URL in the box (just enter**
   http://www.*yourwebsiteaddress*.com**) and then click Check PR.**

3. **Review the results.**

   A bar and your numeric PageRank accompany the results, as shown in Figure 13-3.

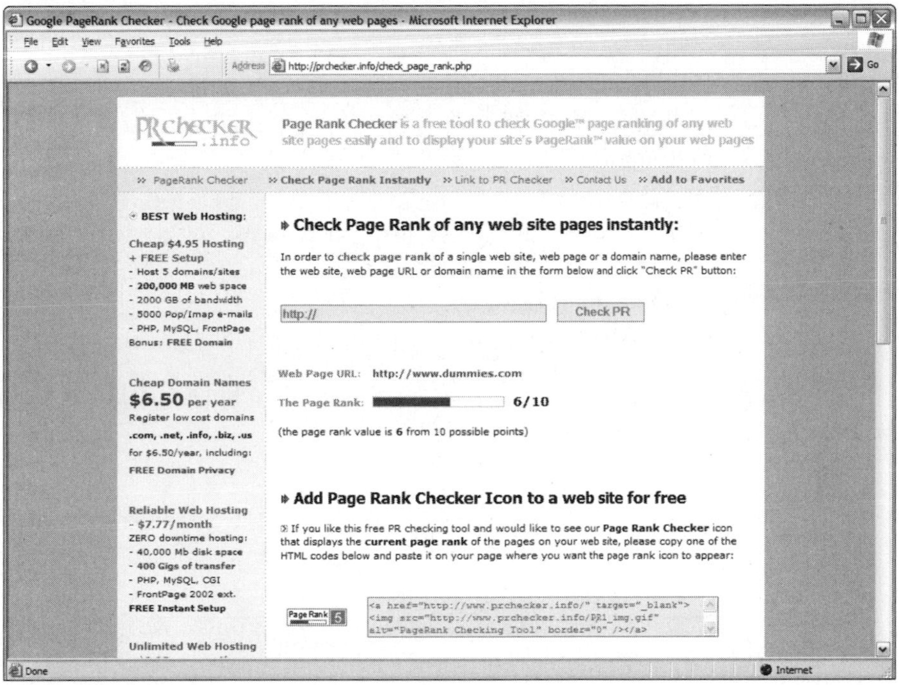

Figure 13-3:
Website
PageRank
as seen in
prchecker.
info.

Alexa Rankings rate you well

Alexa Rankings attempts to give every Web site a numeric ranking. Based on traffic numbers generated by Alexa toolbar users, the ranking assigns every site a position. The most heavily trafficked site is in position 1. At the time of this writing, the site in the number 1 position is Yahoo.com, followed by MSN.com at number 2, and Google.com at number 3. All the other sites fall in some ranking below that.

With Google PageRank, the higher the number, the better; with Alexa, the lower the number, the better.

Because the numbers are based on toolbar users, they are admittedly skewed (see www.alexa.com/site/help/traffic_learn_more for more info). Overall, they are another indicator of where your site falls in the grand scheme of things. And if your search engine campaigns are working well, your ranking will usually increase accordingly.

Here's how to use Alexa Rankings:

1. **Point your browser to**

   ```
   http://www.alexa.com/site/ds/top_500
   ```

   See Figure 13-4.

2. **Type your URL in the box (in the main search box, enter your Web site, with or without the http, such as _yourwebsiteaddress.com_) and then click Get Traffic Details.**

3. **Review the results.**

   Results include Traffic Rank for

   - *Your domain:* This is your place in the list. Remember, the lower the number, the better.

   - *Sites in the top 100,000.*

   You'll also see graphs for Daily Reach, Daily Traffic Rank, and Daily Pageviews. (See Figure 13-5.)

Figure 13-4:
Alexa.com
traffic
rankings
page.

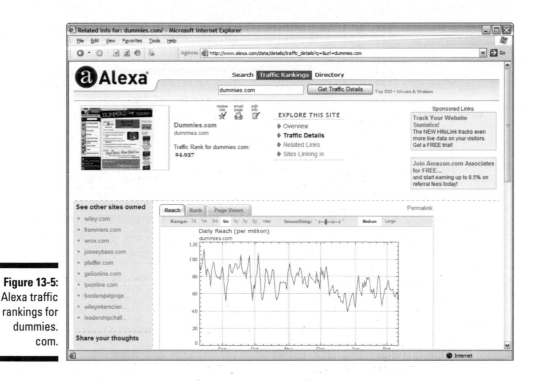

Figure 13-5:
Alexa traffic
rankings for
dummies.
com.

SEO services can take some time before you see any results. Expect to wait four to six weeks before your analytics metrics start to show improvement. You might need to wait even longer for PageRank and Alexa Rankings to reflect those new traffic numbers.

Extending your geographic reach

When you read the preceding heading, you probably said, "Huh? How much further can you extend? The World Wide Web already reaches the world." Yes, but does it cater to potential customers in various countries around the world? If your Web site content displays in English only, you limit yourself dramatically. Depending on which encyclopedia you favor, there are about 190 countries in the world and 6,800 languages.

Approximately 65 to 75 percent of all Internet content is in English despite the fact that English-speaking Internet users number only 35 percent of the world's Internet users, according to Revising. English is still the most widely spoken language of all Internet users, but 14.1 percent of current Internet users speak Chinese, 9.6 percent speak Japanese, 9 percent speak Spanish, 7 percent speak German, 4.1 percent speak Korean, and 3.8 percent speak French.

Now, hold your horses. We aren't suggesting that you blindly translate your site to every known language on the face of the Earth, or even the most common ones for that matter. We are suggesting that you review your Web analytics data to see whether multitudes of visitors come from certain countries looking for certain products. If they are, you can make them feel more welcomed by adding content in their native tongue, adding discounted express shipping, or even creating a subsection of the site just for the products they seem to care about most.

Reviewing your country statistics is one of the easiest and most exciting Web analytics activities because you suddenly realize that half the world is watching, or at least visitors from a few dozen countries. If you are truly going to leverage this data to find new customers, you need to go beyond exploring the interesting flags from the foreign ambassadors who travel through your virtual doors to looking at the hard figures behind them. Here's how:

1. **Point your browser to the control panel.**

   Generally, you can access your cPanel installation by typing in your URL followed by a slash and panel. Here's an example:

   ```
   http://www.yoururl.com/cpanel
   ```

   That URL will probably direct you to another URL that corresponds with your Web hosting provider, so don't be alarmed if the URL changes. If you know your hosting company offers cPanel but the preceding instructions above don't take you anywhere, you might need to contact your hosting company to get the URL for your cPanel installation.

2. **Enter your username and password and click OK to gain access to the control panel.**

   You are greeted with a pop-up box that instructs you to enter your Name and Password. (See Figure 13-6.) You may choose to select a check box that offers to remember your password so you don't have to enter it the next time around. (If you've already forgotten your Name and Password, of if you never knew what it was to begin with, contact your Web hosting provider for details.)

3. **Locate the AWStats section.**

   You can find this in the center column — the second category called Web/FTP Stats.

4. **Open AWStats.**

5. **Find the Who data.**

   At the column to the right, close to the top, is the Who category. Under that is the Countries link.

Figure 13-6:
cPanel
login box.

6. Click the blue Countries link.

You are well on your way to a journey through the nations. (See Figure 13-7.)

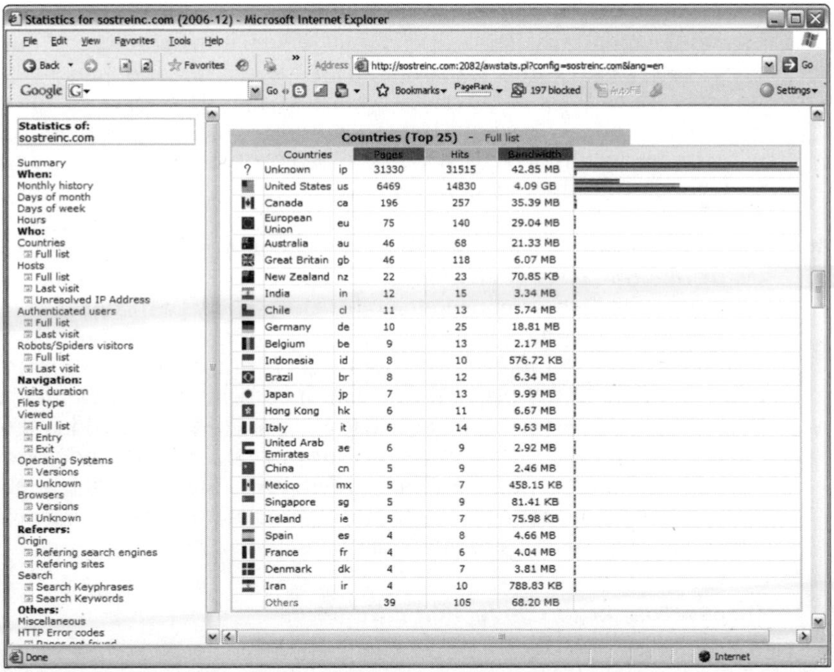

Figure 13-7:
Countries
list from
AWStats.

With your analytics program open, review your country statistics and ask yourself the following questions:

✓ **How many English-speaking countries are on the list?**

✓ **How many Spanish-speaking countries?**

✔ **Do you have a large audience of Asian visitors?**

✔ **What percentage of your visitors come from other countries?**

✔ **What countries convert at the highest rates?**

You need to do some visitor labeling in ClickTracks or a similar application to track this. Read Chapter 9 on segmenting your visitors to discover more about this technique.

You might discover you can extend your geographic reach by catering to these visitor groups that have high conversion rates or by working harder to convert repeat visitors who aren't converting, or even by launching campaigns in search engines and online magazines that target those country groups. Are you starting to get the Web analytics picture? Knowledge applied is power.

Targeting high conversion categories

Every organization has its most popular items. Content portals often display lists of the most e-mailed stories for all to see, for example, and customer support sites typically offer a list of the most asked questions in a convenient list up front. Much the same, service firms have marquee services and e-commerce and affiliate marketers have hot ticket items. Web analytics lets you find out what items, whether FAQs, articles, blog entries, products, or services, so you can play off that success.

Imagine that you sell 30 different products online. Analyzing your Web analytics results reveals that customers who purchase electronics and garden supplies have the highest conversion rates and also make the most purchases after the first sale. Based on your Web analytics reports, it's clear that you've built a name for yourself in electronics and gardening supplies. You should make it a priority to not only target those customers with special campaigns to get them to return, but to find more customers just like them. Visitors trust you and/or the brands you've stocked. Your prices are good, and your site is user friendly for those types of shoppers. Whatever the case, Web analytics has just offered up an opportunity to target new customers in those categories with your advertising and marketing initiatives.

Discovering high conversion categories

You don't need to rely on Web analytics to discover high conversion categories of products. Rather, just look at what you are selling. You don't need to rely on Web analytics to discover popular services, either. Just make a note of what your Web leads hire you to do the most. If you are a content portal, blog, online customer service venue, or some other type of information-based site, you can discover what your most popular content is by looking at your Pages report. In AWStats, this report tells you how many times individual pages on your site were viewed as well as how many people entered your site and exited your site on that particular page.

Milking Multichannel Sales

As Web analytics software matures, these technologies are beginning to find ways to integrate online data with offline data to unlock multichannel opportunities. If you have a brick-and-mortar presence and use the Web as an additional sales channel, listen up: We've got good news for you. Web analytics firms such as Coremetrics are trying to answer the question, "How can I leverage knowledge of my customers' online behavior in my offline marketing activities?" If you are wondering why on Earth this matters, consider a Forrester Research that reveals multichannel customers spend three to ten times as much as single-channel customers, and they have an income that's $10,000 per year higher.

Advanced tools such as Coremetrics Live Profiles allow you to import and export data from offline sources into a data warehouse that will correlate online and offline data for a comprehensive multichannel analysis. If that sounds complicated, don't worry. The bottom line is that multichannel analytics programs offer the best of both worlds: They help you sell more to existing customers and target new customers who share the defined characteristics. If you have the budget to pay the diggers, there are vendors who can do the digging. If you don't have the budget, you can still glean quite a lot by studying certain key performance indicators (KPIs) as they relate to brick-and-mortar trends.

You could collect any number of KPIs and compare them with in-store behavior. Which KPIs you choose depends on your goals. For this exercise, you need to either follow individual users through the site or segment them. (You can read more about segmenting your visitors in Chapter 9.) Check your site referrer report. For example

- ✔ Track navigational paths to see what pages visitors are browsing the most.
- ✔ Discover which items are browsed or purchased.
- ✔ Calculate the lifetime value of the customer.
- ✔ Review data on registration forms to glean demographic information.

The point is to merge what you know about your offline customers with what you know about your online customers and tap into the synergies that this knowledge unveils.

Reach Out and Touch Your Referrers

You have friends, family member, or colleagues who are master networkers. They carry around a stack of business cards with them everywhere they go and reorder frequently. Networking on the Internet is a much different ball game and requires different strategies. It's true that the Internet has created a globally interconnected environment that offers never-before-seen access to potential new customers. However, you can also use that network to discover potential new partners. These strategic allies are other Web site owners — and there are plenty of them.

Indeed, as of December 2006, at least 105,244,649 sites were on the World Wide Web, according to Netcraft. That figure represented an increase of 3.8 million hostnames from the previous month. All in all, the Web added 30.9 million sites in 2006, shattering the previous one-year record gain of 17.5 million sites in 2005. Let us put it to you this way: The Web grew by 41.5 percent in 2006. Could it be possible that there might be some sites who are speaking to the same or similar audiences as you, but who aren't competing for market share? It's more than possible.

Like needles in the proverbial haystack

Your challenge is to find allies. Of course, you can do keyword searches and the like to uncover sites that serve the same niche. That's part of building a good link campaign, and we encourage that. However, with more than 100 million sites out there and probably thousands that you could partner with, you aren't likely to find them all on your own, no matter how proficient you are with your favorite search engine.

Web analytics meets the challenge with referrer logs that allow you to identify the Web sites that sent visitors through your virtual doors. You can discover Web sites that purposely linked to yours because they were either interested in your products and services, enjoyed your content, or just thought your Web site was pretty to look at. In any of those scenarios, you have the opportunity to establish formal link partnerships with those sites.

As we say in Chapter 7, it's possible that not all the sites in your referring sites list actually sent you traffic. The occurrences of *referrer spam* (sites that fake sending traffic to you so that you will visit their site when you check your referrer logs) are becoming more widespread. So if you see sites in your list that don't make sense (these sites are often of the "adult" or gambling genre), just cross them off your list of potential partners.

Here's how to review your referrer logs:

1. **Access your Web analytics tool.**

   You can review instructions for getting into your control panel in the earlier section, "Extending your geographic reach."

2. **Look for the Referrers section.**

   This is the area within the tool that collects detailed information about traffic partners. With AWStats, the Referrers section can be found about three-quarters of the page down on the left side, below the navigation section.

3. **Review sources of Web traffic.**

   Referrer information is usually grouped into various categories, such as traffic from bookmarks, newsgroups, search engines, and external Web sites. For this exercise, ignore everything other than external Web sites.

4. **Make a list of external referrers.**

   Here's the payoff of the exercise. If you already have link partners, you'll recognize them quickly by cross-referencing these links with your partner list. After you eliminate links incoming from e-mail campaigns (these usually have an ISP name, such as `aol.com`, `hotmail.com`, or `bellsouth. net`, in the URL), search engine referrals, affiliate marketers, and Web ring partners, you'll have a list of new potential partners who linked to your site for one reason or another.

Pondering strategic alliances

Now it's up to you to visit the referring site and determine whether you'd like to cement the relationship with a mutually beneficial link exchange or some other arrangement like content sharing, ad banner exchanges, and so on. Consider the following questions as you ponder whether to forge a strategic alliance with a particular site referrer.

- ✔ **Is the referring site talking about your product or service directly or indirectly?** If so, the referring site might already be sold on it. Perhaps you could offer products in exchange for traffic.

- ✔ **What has the referring site already said about you?** Whether the site has positive or negative things to say, contacting it might be useful. If the site dislikes your product or service, this could be a great chance to start a conversation and find out why.

- ✔ **Is the referring site of higher or lower quality than yours?** Although *quality* can be a relative term, you can use metrics such as Alexa and Google PageRank to see whether the site is much better or worse off than your own. Getting strategic links from sites that are more highly regarded than your own helps to raise your rankings.

✔ **What does the referring site tell you about the types of visitors it could refer to you?** Sometimes you will get a link from a site that talks to an audience who you never dreamed would be interested in what you have to offer. This can be a great way to discover new markets.

✔ **What are you willing to give?** It's a give-and-take world. Before you start approaching Webmasters with ideas about what you want, be prepared with a list of things you are wiling to give. Are you willing to offer links back to their sites? Are free products a possibility?

Qualifying the leads

When you walk through a shopping mall, you'll notice that many of the stores in the mall might have similar appearance in terms of pricing, quality, signage, and so on. Still, everyone has seen that one out-of-place store. Sometimes it looks unusually dirty, or maybe it even looks too expensive. It goes without saying that the store that doesn't fit in usually doesn't last very long because it's not what shoppers in that area are comfortable with.

Think of referring sites as your neighboring stores in a mall. Users from those sites are comfortable with those sites, and maybe they just happened across your site along the way. If your site isn't up to par with the other shops in the mall, it could hurt your sales to visitors passing by. By the same token, if the site that's referring customers to you is like that dirty, run-down store in the mall, the quality of customer might not validate an official partnership.

This isn't to say that you need to redesign your Web site based on every referring site you see in your report. The idea is to keep a bird's-eye view of who your visitors are in relation to where they are coming from. You'll be surprised how this can open up new markets for you. Then when you recognize a potential new market, you can implement a special category or offering for that particular clientele, which should then reward your insight with more sales.

A qualified example

Here's a "qualified" example of how to qualify leads. The Sostre & Associates property Audiobookdeals.com (a site that offers information about and places to buy audiobooks), identified its primary target market as career persons who have lengthy work commutes. Although that market was working well, the Webmaster began to notice lots of incoming links from sites that target teens. It seems that teenagers like listening to books on CD or MP3 just as much as their commuting parents. This was a marketing strategy that Audio bookdeals.com had not previously considered, which opened up a new and profitable market for the site.

Understanding Strategic Alliances

Before you can ink a deal with a link partner, you should understand the general concept. Our use of the word *partnerships* in this context is loose. You aren't partnering with another Web site like you would partner with a person, establish a corporation, and share a bank account. Think of it more as a strategic alliance in which you each offer something valuable to the other. In the online world, you should be aware of several different types of partnerships, from simple link exchanges (where most of the process is handled automatically and little interaction is required) to complex content licensing and co-registration agreements. Here are a few of the common types of partnerships, along with how to measure their effect in your Web analytics.

Affiliates

Affiliate programs abound on the Internet. If you sell widgets, it might be a valid option to sell more by signing up affiliates who will put a banner or link on their site (see Figure 13-8) that opens the door for visitors to clickthrough to your site.

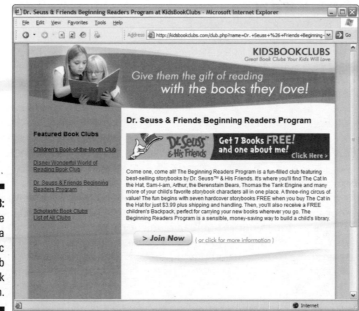

Figure 13-8: Affiliate banner for a Scholastic book club on kidsbook clubs.com.

Being able to connect sales to their referring affiliate is essential for an affiliate program to work. Affiliates will stop sending you traffic if they aren't being paid for their sales. When you decide to start an affiliate program, you also need to decide whether you will be running the program in house or through an affiliate network like Commission Junction or Linkshare. Affiliate networks come with their own statistics to help you keep track of your programs performance. For more information, read Chapter 14.

Link exchanges

You could visit a link exchange directory and weed through its listing to see whether you can find complementary Web sites to exchange links with. Remember, you are looking for high-quality links. There are even link auctions and link brokerages you can sign up with. Link exchanges are big business because quality links help boost your ranking with search engines. You can recognize your link exchange partners by making a list of your partners' URLs and referring back to it to see who is sending you the most traffic. If it turns out that certain partners aren't doing you justice, you might want to drop them like a hot potato and add another link partner instead.

Content sharing

Some sites will let you use their content on your site in exchange for linking back to them (see Figure 13-9). This can be beneficial when you need more content for SEO purposes. You can also write articles in free online article banks, and they will usually link to you. This can help boost your traffic and position you as an expert in your field.

Co-registrations

Co-registrations are online lead-generating tools based on opt-in e-mail. This direct marketing strategy allows you to build qualified mailing lists and membership enrollment by placing your advertisement on subscription-based sites. Co-registration vendors such as LiveDoor and CoRegistration.com target ads to precise markets in effort to generate qualified leads. These are paid partnerships, but they can pay off.

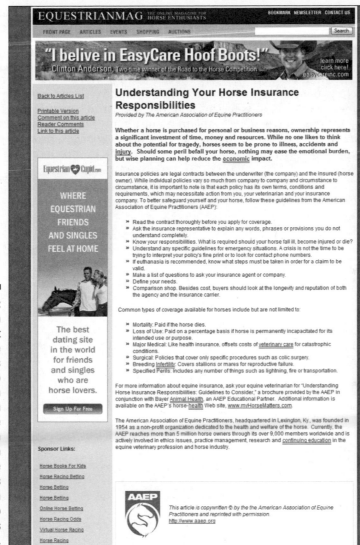

Figure 13-9: Permission to reprint this article was granted to Equestrian mag.com by The American Association of Equine Practitioners as long as a link back to its site was included.

New people, partners, and opportunities

Just think of it. With new people — and new Web sites — coming online literally every day, there are always fresh opportunities to reach out to potential customers and partners who have never heard of you before. Web analytics will help you make your site more visible so that you can target the right customers, get them to your site, and turn them into conversions. That last part — making conversions — might require some Web site optimization. To discover how to optimize your home page, landing pages, product pages, or your entire Web site, check out Chapter 16 for the lowdown on fine-tuning your Web site.

Chapter 14

Revisiting Your Online Advertising Strategy

*I*n a world of dozens of competing search engines, banner ad opportunities, and e-mail marketing service providers, finding ways to spend your money online is about as easy as it is for a kid to spend money in a candy store. Indeed, the number of advertising opportunities available through online advertising networks like DoubleClick, blog advertising networks like PayPerPost, and, of course, *search engine marketing* (SEM; a method that seeks to increase the ranking and visibility of a Web site in search engine results pages) have sky-rocketed in the recent years.

Online ad revenue just keeps climbing higher and higher. Internet advertising revenues for the first half of 2006 totaled a mind boggling $7.9 billion, according to the Interactive Advertising Bureau. That was a record, folks! It was also a 37-percent increase over the first half of 2005.

Of course, every online advertising platform offers "unbeatable" advertising rates and promises a strong return on investment (ROI). But here's the rub (and a very sad rub, at that): Not all those ad dollars reaped a return. There's no telling exactly how much of that money went down the dot-com drain — unless you use Web analytics to calculate it. Web analytics empowers you to find out the truth about your ad campaigns, often with more clarity than offline advertisers could hope to receive.

In the brick-and-mortar world of print, radio, and television advertising, you can't really tell how many people saw and responded to your ad. Sure, you can distribute coupons in Valpak and get some measure of the effectiveness of that particular campaign, but how do you really know how many people responded to that billboard you rented on the highway or how many listeners really responded to your ad on the radio? (Um, you don't.) Nielsen tries to measure TV audiences, but face it: It's still not an exact science. Despite some admitted X-factors, Web analytics comes closer to the truth.

In this chapter, you discover how to track online advertising campaigns of all shapes and sizes. You also get a heads-up on some special tools and services that aim to help you get to the bottom of your ad campaign performance before you get to the bottom of your budget. Whether you're an affiliate marketer, as search engine marketer and e-mail marketer, or you engage in some other form of online advertising, you'll find some valuable nuggets you can use immediately to optimize your ad campaigns.

Many Ad Types, Many Analytics Tools

Before we get into the nitty-gritty of measuring online ad and marketing campaigns, we need to lay a foundation about online opportunities. For all the hype over SEM and *pay per click* (PPC; also called *paid search,* which retrieves listings based on who paid the most money for keywords to appear at the top of the search heap), many other forms of online ads are available, such as banners, pop-ups, e-mail campaigns, and affiliate marketing. Web analytics can help you figure out not only which campaigns are performing but also which types of initiatives your target audience tends to respond to.

Just like the various forms of online advertising and marketing, you can also use various ways to track the success of your initiatives using Web analytics. In fact, different Web analytics tools use different methods to track online ads. Other Web analytics tools work in conjunction with offline databases to tap into multichannel customer experiences. If you're planning for forge into this territory with both guns blazing, make a review of ad tracking methods part of your decision-making process before you choose a Web analytics tool.

To read more about the basics of choosing a Web analytics program, see Chapter 5. Or, if you want special Web analytics software that's designed to track PPC campaigns and the like, be sure to check out some additional top options in Chapter 6. Whatever you do, don't get stuck in the paralysis of analysis while you ponder over tools.

The bottom line is this: If you engage in online advertising and marketing, you need to engage Web analytics tools to track it. A simple tool is better than no tool at all.

Tracking Efforts with Tracking URLs

We start the journey into online advertising and marketing measurement with some practical tips on tracking SEM, banner, pop-up, and pop-under ads. *Pop-under ads* are like pop-ups except the viewer doesn't see them until she closes the browser window. That can make it difficult for the viewer to discern what site snuck up on her with an advertising message.

Running a quick-and-dirty Google search makes it abundantly clear that there is no lack of free or low-cost online tools to help you execute the many different aspects of online marketing and online advertising. You can find free tools to create banners, choose combinations of keywords, manage your bids . . . you get the idea. (Of course, you still have to pay for the advertising and marketing campaigns that you eventually execute.) Unless you are an SEM expert, you need all the help you can get, so use these resources wisely. As you use these tools, you'll find that Web analytics tools become useful once again because you can measure the efficacy of the keyword combinations or banners that these free tools created. You may find out you're better off hiring a pro or educating yourself with some other book in the *For Dummies* series.

Using tracking URLs is fairly foundational to tracking your online campaigns. Google defines *tracking URLs* as "URLs appended with parameters that provide information about the source of the click, the search query used, and other advertising metrics. Tracking URLs help advertisers determine the effectiveness of their ads and/or keywords on non-AdWords channels." Simply, tracking URLs do just what they sound like: They track your ads so that you can tell which ones work and which ones merely cost you money.

Tracking URLs are largely independent of your analytics application; however, your analytics application uses them to tell you how each individual ad or marketing initiative you've launched is performing. Tracking URLs are fairly simple to implement. Imagine that you sell everything under the sun having to do with golf. You decide to place a banner ad on Golfersmag.com because it targets your audience precisely. Sounds like a great idea, but you want to *know* that it's a great idea. That's where tracking URLs come into play.

Here's how it works: Instead of using your standard link to your home page (www.*yoursite*.com), use a tracking URL.

1. **Assign a number to your campaign.**

   If the ad in Golfersmag.com is your one and only ad, you might call it ad1. If you have a slew of ads across the Web, it might well be ad29.

2. **Create a tracking URL, using the number.**

   Append a tracking variable that identifies the campaign number to your URL. One example might look like this:

   ```
   http://yoursite.com/?src=ad1
   ```

   In the example, we used "src" as the name of the variable. The "src" variable is short for "source." The actual variable can be whatever you want. The tracking URL would be just as effective any of the following ways:

   ```
   http://yoursite.com/?ad=1
   http://yoursite.com/?campaign=ad1
   http://yoursite.com/?ref=ad1
   ```

   The URL will still go to your home page (or the landing page of your choice if you use something like

   ```
   http://yoursite.com/landingpage.html?src=ad1)
   ```

   but it will log the variable that was used. This is the URL that you give to your account manager (or enter into a Web-based ordering system).

3. **Check the results of the campaign.**

Now you can

✔ **Segment visitors who enter your site with that parameter.** Use ClickTracks or another analytics application that allows for this kind of visitor segmentation to compare the traffic from this campaign against your nonpaid traffic and traffic from other campaigns. (*Visitor segmentation* means grouping users based on similar traits or activities.)

✔ **Compare the following:**

   • *Bounce rates:* This metric shows the percentage of entrances on any individual page that resulted in the visitor's immediate exit from the site.

   • *Average time on site.*

   • *Conversion rates:* This is the percentage of visitors who took the desired call to action.

Tracking keywords with Google Analytics

Although you can use tracking URLs for banners and pop-ups, Google offers a neat tool — *URL builder* — specifically for its AdWords users. All you have to do is fill in a simple form and then click the Generate URL button. Of course, you need to know how to tag links in order to leverage this tool. If your Google Analytics account has been linked to an active AdWords account, you don't need to tag your AdWords links. An auto-tagging feature will do it for you automatically. In order, here's how to do it in conjunction with Google's URL builder.

Pesky pop-ups and blockers

Plenty of debate abounds, swirling around the intrusiveness of pop-up ads. That's why browser makers such as Microsoft and Mozilla offer pop-up blockers. Pop-up ads introduce some interesting problems for Web analytics. For starters, using pop-up ads can skew the traffic stats because they can automatically open windows to sites regardless of whether the user really wants to see them. And pop-up ads make it impossible to determine whether a visitor intended to visit a site or was ushered there through a pop-up ad that was closed with annoyance. If the tracking URL in your pop-up ad reveals that users left within 20 seconds of being escorted to your site unaware, you haven't succeeded — and, in fact, could be alienating visitors.

Don't get us wrong: We aren't against pop-up ads, per se. The bottom line is they might send traffic to your site, but it's not from folks who chose to go there, so the hit probably won't convert as well as from traffic that choose to clickthrough to your site through a traditional banner ad.

Tag only what you need

Some links don't need tagging. Others, though, such as *organic keyword links* (links that are naturally associated with certain pages on your site) can't be tagged. You don't need to tag links that come from referral sites, such as portals or affiliates, because Google Analytics is smart enough to automatically detect the name of the search engine and the keywords from those sources, usually under Organic listings. Google Analytics also displays referrals from other Web sites, regardless of whether you tagged them. This will save you a lot of hassle in the tagging process.

Create tracking URLs in URL builder

You do need to create tracking URLs for your non-AdWords–paid keyword links, your banners and other ads, and the links inside your promotional e-mail messages. If you use this tool, you won't have to worry about where the question mark, the parameter used to separate variables in a URL, goes or other syntax issues. (See the previous section for step-by-step instructions if you prefer not to use a tracking URL tool.)

Use only the campaign variables you need

Google Analytics' link tagging capabilities let you uniquely identify any and all of your campaigns by virtue of its five fields:

- ✓ **Campaign Source:** Banner ad, e-mail campaign, PPC keywords

- ✓ **Campaign Medium:** Banner, e-mail, cost per click

- ✓ **Campaign Term:** A descriptive phrase or keyword to identify the ad

  ✔ **Campaign Content:** Used to differentiate ads for the same company

  ✔ **Campaign Name:** Product, promo code, or slogan

Google recommends using Source, Medium, Term, and Name for most campaigns.

Click the Generate URL button

Click the Generate URL button. If you make a mistake or want to change any of the variables, click the Clear button.

Tracking URLs cons

Tracking URLs are beautiful — when they work. Unfortunately, their simplicity is also their weakness. Plainly put, if the tracking variable is replaced or removed by an ad serving platform or script, the tracking will not work. In the vocabulary of Webmasters, the link can "break."

Imagine that you're a writer and want to generate more leads for your copywriting services. You might choose to run a banner ad on a popular site where your target audience frequents, such as MediaBistro.com. If the publisher has a system that tracks clicks on its end, the code that it uses to track the click and then redirect them to your site might affect the tracking URL on your end. That makes using tracking URLs less than 100 percent accurate.

So before you run to the publisher and complain that your ad isn't generating any hits, keep the imperfections of tracking URLs in mind. However, for the most part, tracking URLs do work well. Again, using an imperfect tool that tracks most of, but not all, your advertising referrals is better than not using a tool at all. If you're really concerned, you could include a drop-down menu on the conversion page that asks how the visitor learned about you.

Adding Campaign Analytics to the Mix

Campaign analytics is a subset, or niche, of Web analytics. *Campaign analytics* track ad and marketing campaigns specifically and can come as part of a robust Web analytics program or be sold individually from niche players. In Chapter 6, we offer CampaignTracker and BlackTrack as two examples of campaign analytics just to whet your appetite for these focused tools. However, if you're serious about online advertising, you'll want to review a few additional tools to make sure you choose the one that's right for you.

Although the baseline functions are typically the same, you'll find that each tool has its own unique features. CampaignTracker, for example, offers competitive reporting and engine-to-engine comparisons. BlackTrack offers live analysis. Check out these tools to find out what else is available. During your journey, you might discover that some tools are a better fit for the type or depth of your campaigns, or just your personal data digestion preferences. Here is a short-list of vetted tools you might choose to put your magnifying glass to.

Openads points you to profits

www.openads.org

Openads bills itself as the most popular online advertising software. It's essentially an open source ad server with an integrated banner-management interface and tracking system that gathers statistics. If you offer banner advertising, this software has some attractive features. For example, you can rotate paid banners with your own in-house advertisements. You can also integrate banners from third-party advertising companies into the measurement mix. Openads also tracks all types of banners, from buttons to pop-ups to text ads and even Flash banners. The software is free although donations are accepted.

TrackPoint ad tracking

www.alentus.com/hosted-applications/trackpoint.asp

TrackPoint boasts performance tracking dollar-by-dollar, click-by-click on all your online advertising campaigns. This is a hosted service developed by Alentus. Whether you have a single campaign or dozens of different campaigns of various types (such as PPC, banners, newsletter links, and so on), this program lets you see the big picture on the total spend or drill down to individual campaigns.

The software also reports exactly which keywords and keyphrases visitors typed into all major search engines to arrive at your site. You can use these reports to add keyword density to your site. *Keyword density* is the ratio of the number of occurrences an individual keyword to the total number of words on a page. This is one aspect of *search engine optimization* (SEO; a method of improving the rankings for relevant keywords in search results by making changes to the content or navigational structure of a Web site).

This program integrates with a shopping cart for easier conversion tracking. TrackPoint costs $9.95 per month or $99.95 per year.

Clickalyzer's marketing co-ops

`www.clickalyzer.com`

Clickalyzer has some interesting features from the SEM perspective with eight real-time reports. Beyond all the basic analytics and visitor segmentation capabilities, Clickalyzer actually tells you how much of your marketing copy a visitor read. You can see the last page your visitor saw before he accepted or rejected your offer. You can even run a marketing co-op with several other marketers who all promote the same product. Just combine your advertising budget and use Clickalyzer's split testing to accurately divide the visitor's between your URLs.

The program costs $29.95 per month, $299.95 per year, or $599.95 for a lifetime account.

Bid management and keyword optimizer tools aren't Web analytics, but you can use them in tandem with your Web analytics tools — and you probably should if you spend lots of money on PPC advertising. Keyword optimizers can help you discover the best keywords for your campaign. Bid management tools can help you organize your online ad spending. Instead of logging in to three or four search engine marketing interfaces, you can log in to one service and execute your campaigns. If you don't have much experience in the PPC game or aren't getting good results despite your best efforts, consider checking out some of these online tools.

Combating Click Fraud

Even though we briefly mention *click fraud* — purposely clicking ad listings without any intention of making a purchase from the advertiser — other places through this book, we couldn't write a chapter on revisiting your online advertising strategy without a thorough review of click fraud and the tools available to prevent it. Click fraud has been called one of the biggest threats to the continued growth of SEM, and we agree. It's also opening up new opportunities for vendors to generate revenue, or add value to existing products, by helping you fight it.

Listen, the cost of click fraud isn't chump change. Market researcher Outsell estimates that advertisers wasted over $800 million on click fraud in 2005 alone. Surveyed advertisers say they believe about 15 percent of all clicks are bogus, and 75 percent have been victims at least once. (That means some were victims more than once!) Click fraud has prompted nearly 30 percent of advertisers to stop spending on click-based initiatives. Outsell figured that Google and Yahoo! have lost $500 million because some advertisers have drawn back from this form of advertising.

The official online ad guide

In November 2004, the Interactive Advertising Bureau (IAB) Measurement Task Force issued a global standard for counting online ad impressions. It was the first time that any advertising medium developed a measurement standard that measures the ad itself, as delivered to a consumer. In other words, using this measurement standard tells you in no uncertain terms whether folks viewed your ad or not. Other forms of advertising (such as radio, TV, or magazines) can only rely on the number of potential viewers. The guideline standardizes how and when an ad impression is counted and has offered the global media buying community consistent and accurate data. Keep in mind that these guidelines do not measure paid search, rich media, or broadband commercials. Measurements for those forms of interactive advertising, though, are in the works. Behind all of this, of course, is Web analytics.

Here's the deal. Click-based advertising works. You just have to be wise as the proverbial owl in this day and age where cyberbandits are turning the World Wild Web into the Wild Wild West, organizing virtual hold-ups designed to leave your advertising budget stranded on the side of the dusty trail. Don't get into your covered wagon without your weapons. Instead, ride with a posse (in the form of click fraud tools) that can stop those crooks before they have a chance to rob you blind. Click fraud perpetrators could be competitors trying to bleed your PPC campaign dry or angry customers trying to take revenge *incognito*.

Check into your SEM providers' policies. Google, for example, launched its Cost Per Action service (available by invitation only at the time of this writing). Advertisers pay only when a user takes a demonstrable action after clicking. Still, that might not be enough. That's why vendors are emerging with an arsenal of click fraud tools to combat this slick debauchery. Check out these weapons and wield them boldly.

Need detectives on your case?

www.clickdetective.com

ClickDetective monitors clickthroughs from PPC campaigns to help you detect and deter potential click fraud and manage your PPC advertising campaigns. Think of it as a one-stop shop for the serious PPC advertisers. With real-time monitoring and e-mail alerts to warn you of suspicious click activity as well as a starting price of $49 per month, this application could save you thousands in the long run. (And you gotta love the name.)

CFAnalytics: Free and plenty of perks

www.cfanalytics.com

CFAnalytics is a free click-fraud reporting and monitoring service from Click Forensics. You can't beat the price, and the features of this page tag-based click-fraud reporting system are pretty keen, too. You can track up to 100,000 clicks per month and get a free weekly e-mail report with an overview of your PPC campaigns. You can also access reports online to help you manage your PPC campaigns and access the Member's Only section of the Click Fraud Network, where you'll find a Click Fraud Index and campaign reports detailing click fraud threat level by term and search provider. This is advanced stuff — and, again, it's free.

AdWatcher adds it all up for you

www.adwatcher.com

AdWatcher does it all. It monitors your ad campaigns for fraudulent activity, helps you track your ROI, and manages your online advertising from one central location. This tool claims that it can save you up to 50 percent in click fraud charges. This solution will not only detect suspicious activity, but it also works with search engines to recover money that click fraudsters ripped from your clutches. This program offers over 20 metrics to analyze your campaigns, organizes your campaigns by group, and reveals which keywords convert best in your PPC campaign. This service costs $25 to monitor up to 3,000 clicks per month.

WhosClickingWho?

www.whosclickingwho.com

WhosClickingWho claims to be the first pay-per-click detection service. We won't deny or substantiate that claim, but we can tell you that the software cuts to the point in a hurry. After five repeated clicks from a PPC listing to your Web site, a ClickMinder tool pops up to deter potential abusers. (You can set the parameters to warn clickers at the number of clicks you decide upon.) Pop-up blockers won't block ClickMinder, which tells the clicker the following:

> You appear to be abusing our search engine listing. YOUR ACTIONS ARE BEING LOGGED. Please stop clicking on our search engine listing.

You can also select a custom message that isn't so "in your face."

The tracking offers proof you need to take to search engines to get your money back. The fee is $30 per month for up to 5,000 clicks.

Remote Tracking 101

Clickalyzer is mentioned several times in this chapter and for good reason. It has plenty of options tweaked just for search marketers like you. One unique feature that might appeal to marketers who promote cost per action (CPA) offers and don't actually make the sale on their sites is Remote Tracking. Clickalyzer coined the term that refers to the ability to track activity on a Web site that you promote but don't own. In other words, you no longer have to be content just sending traffic to a site and tracking how many clickthroughs you generated for that site. Now, you can actually see what the traffic you sent the advertiser did after they got there — all the way to the point of sale. Remote Tracking lets you verify that the advertiser credits you for the sales you sent.

Evaluating E-mail Marketing Campaigns

Despite the growing number of spam messages jamming up e-mail boxes, direct marketers still find value in legitimate opt-in e-mail marketing campaigns. Web analytics can add tremendous value to e-mail marketers by making way for more targeted e-mail communications that are based on measured visitor behavior. Although *server-side* analytics (analytics software installed on the Web site's server) offers only limited information about e-mail marketing campaign success (you can view your site referrer report to discover links from URLs with ISP names, like AOL or Hotmail, in the code), a maturing client-side analytics market is opening up possibilities to integrate Web analytics and e-mail marketing.

This is an important development because much like PPC, you can spend bundles of money on e-mail marketing in a hurry. What's more, you can also come off as an irritant to the recipients. If you don't believe us, just ask the Direct Marketing Association (DMA; www.the-dma.org). That makes e-mail marketing analytics programs vital to the online direct marketer. Of course, the market for e-mail analytics is still shaking out. Right now, large analytics vendors such as WebTrends, Coremetrics, and Digital River are integrating metrics with e-mail. Here's a look at some of the capabilities available today.

WebTrends targets markets

www.webtrends.com

WebTrends works with ExactTarget, a third-party e-mail solutions provider. Customers can view Web metrics on top of e-mail campaign performance and drill down to the clickstream level to create visitor segments that ultimately allow more targeted marketing. You can compare the performance of your campaigns and capture the *key performance indicators* (KPIs; metrics that illustrate how well the site is performing against goals) and conversion events that are most important to measuring your success. You can also use the data to create more targeted lists.

```
www.coremetrics.com
```

Coremetrics has been perhaps the most aggressive in this area. The firm works with Responsys, Digital Impact, Yesmail, and CheetahMail to measure e-mail marketing success. Coremetrics automatically feeds behavioral data into these e-mail marketing platforms so that you can deliver targeted campaigns based on a customer's recent behavior, such as what categories the visitor clicked or what was in her shopping cart before she left the site.

```
www.digitalrover.com
```

Digital River now owns Fireclick and BlueHornet and offers an integrated product designed to enhance e-mail marketing opportunities. The company also wraps bid management tools into its package, along with message wizards that guide you through the e-mail message creation process as well as a spam rating tool that lets you check your content and layout for factors that have been proven to trigger filters and event-triggered messaging for greater relevance. This is a comprehensive package for the Internet marketer.

Reaching for relevancy

Sometimes — well, actually most of the time — you need to exercise some good, old-fashioned common sense to interpret your Web analytics. Case in point: More is not always better when it comes to e-mail marketing. If you expect to get clickthroughs that lead to sales but get no action or even opt-outs, you might be bombarding subscribers with too many messages. A DMA survey reveals that the *opt-out rate* (the percentage of recipients who request to be removed from a mailing list) for recipients who were contacted via e-mail every month was below 1 percent. Recipients who were contacted on a weekly basis were more likely to become disinterested. The result: a 2.5 percent opt-out rate.

The good news is that the more relevant your content, the lower the opt-out rate — and, by default, the higher the chances that the recipient will click-through and take the desired action on your site. DMA research proves it: As e-mail messages have become more targeted and relevant, clickthrough rates have improved. Two-thirds of e-mail service providers experienced opt-out rates of less than 0.5 percent in 2006 compared with 44 percent in 2005.

E-mail marketing KPIs to monitor

When you launch your e-mail marketing campaign, you'll receive what amounts to an analytics report from your e-mail service provider. This report tells you the fate of the e-mails you sent, such as

- **Bounces:** The number of e-mails that didn't get delivered
- **Opt-outs**
- **Open rate:** The percentage of recipients who opened your e-mail
- **Clicks**

Your job is to review that report with KPIs in mind. (You can read much more about KPIs in Chapter 11.) You'll want to keep track of these KPIs while you seek to measure the effect of your e-mail marketing campaigns.

Open rate: Facts and myths

Modern technology is so wonderful that it can tell you not only how many e-mails were opened but also which recipients opened the message. Of course, you can't tell whether the recipient actually read the message or engaged with your e-mail. Sometimes, a recipient does indeed open — and even read — your e-mail, but it doesn't get recorded. We won't bore you with the techno mumbo-jumbo. Suffice it to say that if the recipient has text-only e-mail, your system may not be able to track that the email was opened. What's more, some programs will count a new Open each time the recipient opens the message, even if that's several times a day.

Thus, you can see that using an Open rate isn't an exact science (and that's putting it kindly). For all these reasons, don't think of the Open rate as the be-all-end-all measurement. However, Open rates are good for comparing the apparent success of different e-mail campaigns. Higher Open rates could mean more relevant messaging, more effective subject lines, or a more targeted list from an e-mail service provider.

If you switch providers and see massive drop-offs, consider switching back to your original vendor. If you switch subject line strategies and it leads to more Opens, you've hit on something that works. Maybe you changed to an action verb or a popular keyword for that market. If your Open rate to AOL accounts is 50 percent but your Open rate to Hotmail is 0 percent, there's probably an issue with Hotmail users receiving your message. If they don't receive the message, open it, and read it, you've wasted your time.

Clickthroughs in context

After you have a handle on the Open rate, you can put the clickthrough rate in context. Visitors can't clickthrough if they don't open the e-mail. A high number of clickthroughs could mean that your e-mail message hit home. Your price was good, your copywriting was keen, or the reader saw some other benefit to clicking through. Still, that's not the bottom-line story.

Calculating cost per lead

The cost-per-lead generated via e-mail is a key metric to watch. Because an e-mail recipient might initially clickthrough to your site but then visit several times before taking the desired action (downloading a file, registering, purchasing, and so on), you need to know how much you are paying to drive traffic to your site. To determine this metric, divide the number of leads into the cost of the e-mail campaign. To keep it simple, if you pay $100 to send out the e-mails and generate 500 leads, it costs you $.50 per lead. If you spend $500 to get 100 leads, it costs you $5 per lead.

Calculating cost per conversion

At the end of the day, what you ultimately want to know is the cost-per-conversion generated via e-mail. To determine this metric, divide the number of conversions into the cost of the e-mail campaign. Once again, to keep it simple, if you pay $100 to send out the e-mails and you generate $500 in sales, it costs you an average of $5 to make each sale. You came out on top. Alternatively, if it costs you $500 to send out the e-mails and you generate $100 in sales, you are upside-down. You lost.

More e-mail marketing KPIs

Here's a list of a few more e-mail marketing KPIs that you might want to track. Like with any KPIs, your goal is to choose a select few that make the most effect on your campaigns. You'll notice that many e-mail marketing KPIs depend on Web analytics work together to tell you the whole story.

- ✔ Campaign over campaign open rates
- ✔ Campaign over campaign clickthroughs
- ✔ Send to a friend
- ✔ Average order value
- ✔ Number of site visits
- ✔ Average page views
- ✔ Length of site visit
- ✔ List growth

Measuring mobile marketing

Many believe that mobile advertising is the wave of the future. Indeed, it's already gaining momentum. Market researcher M:Metrics (www.mmetrics.com) launched a definitive metrics for mobile advertising in late 2006 and found that a sizeable percentage of mobile subscribers are responding to short codes placed in advertisements or in other media. The firm compares the state of mobile advertising with what we saw in e-mail response during the mid-1990s as the Web emerged as an advertising medium, with as many as 29 percent of mobile subscribers responding to text message ads. The data signals that multimedia convergence is a reality today — and a growing one.

This data, combined with the fact that Smart Phones are becoming pervasive, makes it easy to imagine targeted ads strategically served to your mobile device while you walk through the Macy's. The retailer could alert you to a special in the furniture department as you approach the second floor. The movement, dubbed *m-commerce (for mobile-commerce),* is coming to a cell phone near you. Google has already created a mobile AdWords platform, complete with the ability to set daily spending budgets, establish schedule marketing messages and make payments only when consumers click, so it seems only a matter of time before the concept takes off.

The next question is: How do we measure it? WebSideStory HBX Analytics platform allows publishers and marketers to measure both streaming media and mobile device user behavior. With this tool, you can measure mobile devices used by visitors, with details about the device brand, model, and service provider. This is an area of analytics that's sure to mature as the market demands more robust solutions.

Tracking Offline Responses to Online Ads

Web analytics is not just for the Web anymore. As the technology matures, these tools are being used to track what is happening in multiple channels. (You can read more about milking multichannel sales in Chapter 13.) Beyond philosophical talks of how online ads generate brand awareness even if the consumer doesn't act upon them, you can certainly track how your online ads led to online sales. This is important, with comScore estimating that 60 percent to 90 percent of all conversions happen offline. Tracking the return on your ad spend, then, is critical to understanding your profit margins.

Tracking an offline response to online ads taps into a concept *delayed conversions,* which start online but conclude offline some time later. Say that your online conversion rate is 4 percent. If you take delayed conversions into account, it could really be 5 percent. That means what you are doing online is more effective than you thought it was. Tracking offline responses to online ads — or mere site visitors for that matter — gives you the big picture. The delayed conversion concept is especially prevalent with lead generation sites where, even though there might be an online registration form, customers tend to call a week later to sign up for that new bank account or inquire about that new car.

Using coupon codes

Using coupon codes can clue you in to a conversion process that began online but escaped the boundaries of the World Wide Web and continued in the physical world. The travel industry offers a strong example of using coupon codes in connection with reservations. If Hotel ABC runs an online banner ad campaign on a popular online travel portal, it might instruct the viewer to use booking code XC#89. The viewer picks up the phone and calls the agency to book the reservation. That booking code ties the viewer to that specific ad. This takes some offline database expertise because the sales agent needs access to online promotional information to tie the viewer in with the booking code. By the same token, any retailer could offer an online coupon code that offers 5 percent off the purchase price and can be used online or offline.

Using unique URLs

You can use unique URLs in your offline advertising and see whether it triggers an online response. Say you run a print ad in a women's fashion magazine for a new line of handbags that you sell exclusively online. Tracking the success of that specific ad is as easy as

- ✔ **Including a unique URL in the ad:** *Hint:* Make it easy to remember, like www.*mycompany*.com/europeanbags.
- ✔ **Using the URL only for that particular campaign.**

If that landing page features the handbags and offers mentioned in the ad, it will ensure a quick connection in the consumer's mind, and you are well on your way to converting the visitor. If visitors did not convert, perhaps your landing page was not making the connection, and they really didn't want to spend the money on a European handbag. At least you know the ad got them there, though.

Using unique toll-free phone numbers

Another strategy for tracking ads that publish online but convert offline is to include a unique toll-free number in the ad. When operators answer that line, they know that the caller viewed your ad on the Internet and can relate it to the specific offer she saw. Again, this takes some database integration if you have heavy call volumes. (And, of course, you can afford it if your phones are ringing off the hook with new sales, right?) Still, this tracking can help you know exactly how well your online ad worked. Although it's possible that the consumer remembered your company name and not the phone number and called your general toll-free number, this method offers you the possibility of tracking offline conversions.

Ferreting Out Ad Stats that Don't Work

Measuring your online advertising strategies is an ongoing process. That's why the title of this chapter is "*Revisiting* Your Online Advertising Strategy." What brought high-targeted traffic that converted at record numbers last year might or might not work again this year. And that's why it's important to benchmark your data so you can compare last year's data with this year's data to uncover hidden trends. Read more about how to do that in Chapter 15. For now, we help you concentrate on some current comparisons that will help you ferret out ad strategies that don't work.

Comparing engine to engine

If you're trying to ferret out paid search campaigns that threaten to rob your children's inheritance, use your Web analytics report to compare search engine to search engine. Some simple metrics can tell a lot about the quality of the traffic you are receiving, and one of the easiest ways to compare those metrics is to use the ClickTracks Labels feature. Labels are ClickTracks' way of segmenting visitors, which is quite powerful in that it allows you to group users by traits. You can segment visitors based on behavior such as what search engine or site they came from, what page they entered on, what time of day they came, and more.

Labeling for entry pages

The following steps show you how to use your tracking URLs for each campaign you ran to group visitors by those tracking variables. Then you will see in no uncertain terms which SEM campaigns performed well and which ones didn't. To set up visitor labels for certain entry page parameters in ClickTracks Analyzer, here's all you have to do:

1. **Open the ClickTracks application.**

2. **On the home page or dashboard of your ClickTracks application, click the Advanced Labels button (center of the page).**

   This opens the Advanced Labeling Visitor Wizard; see Figure 14-1.

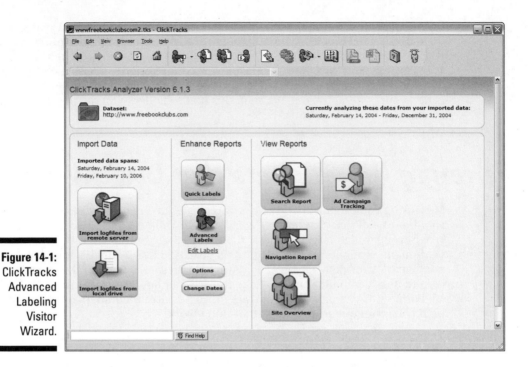

Figure 14-1:
ClickTracks
Advanced
Labeling
Visitor
Wizard.

3. Select the Entered at a Certain Page radio button and then click Next.

See Figure 14-2.

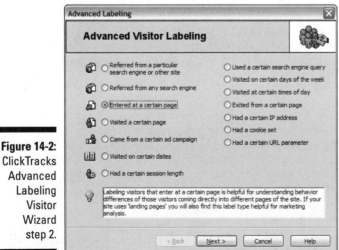

Figure 14-2:
ClickTracks
Advanced
Labeling
Visitor
Wizard
step 2.

4. From the drop-down list, choose Contains the String.

5. In the second drop-down box, enter

```
?src=XXX
```

where *XXX* is substituted for whatever your variable your tracking URL uses. (See Figure 14-3.)

Figure 14-3:
ClickTracks Advanced Labeling Visitor Wizard step 3.

6. Click Next.

7. Leave the Inverse (Count if Criterion NOT Met) check box clear. Then click Next.

8. Make sure that all the check boxes under Display Options are enabled. Then click Next.

9. Choose a display color and name for this label and then click Finish.

You can follow the preceding steps to define a label for every campaign and tracking URL that you use. That will segment out those particular users. The next step in your engine-to-engine comparison activity is to use the data generated by Labels to conduct a side-by-side comparison of traffic quality.

Comparing your traffic quality

To determine how the traffic quality from one search engine compares with the traffic quality from another search engine, follow these steps:

1. Open the ClickTracks application.

2. On the home page or dashboard of your ClickTracks application, click the Site Overview button (lower right of the page).

This opens the Site Overview page.

3. Scroll down slightly.

You see a section for Average Time on Site and Page Views Per Visitor. (See Figure 14-4.)

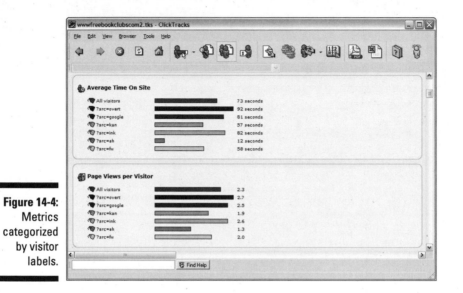

Figure 14-4:
Metrics
categorized
by visitor
labels.

These two metrics are a great way to quickly evaluate the traffic you are receiving from your different campaigns. For the most part, the longer that users stay on your site and the more pages they visit, the higher the quality of the traffic.

Comparing keyword to keyword

You could just as easily drill the above example down to the keyword level even if you're using only one search engine. Suppose you put your entire advertising budget into Google. (That might or might not be a wise decision. Fortunately, your Web analytics program will tell you.) You can then choose to compare the performance of one keyword against another keyword by segmenting your site's visitors based on those keywords.

Practically speaking, if your site sells comic books and you ran AdWords campaigns with Batman, Superman, Spiderman, and X-Men, your task is to segment your users based on the keywords through which they entered the site. You'd have one segment, then, that was looking for the bat cave, another that loved to leap tall buildings in a single bound, and so on. After segmentation, you can analyze the behavior of those visitors up to the point of conversion. If you find that X-Men blew Spiderman away (figuratively speaking, of course), you might want to up your spend on X-Men at Spidey's expense.

Determining the cost of traffic

Here's another example from the Sostre & Associates Web property, FreeBookClubs.com. The affiliate marketing publisher was running several separate online keyword campaigns with different SEM vendors promoting the site. Using Web Analytics, the team was able to segment the visitors based on what campaign they were coming from. Specifically, that meant segmenting Yahoo!, Google, Miva, Kanoodle, and a few other second-tier search engines.

The results revealed that as a whole, the traffic that came to the site from one of the engines had an 80 percent bounce rate. Google and Yahoo! were just about even, posting a 30-percent bounce rate. Those figures made it clear that money was being wasted on some of the second-tier engines. Even though the cost of the traffic was far less on the lesser-known engines, the quality of the traffic was too poor to keep the return on the investment out of the red.

Web analytics gives you raw metrics. You still need to use some common sense and sometimes some street smarts, too, to determine what those numbers really mean. While you are making these comparisons, keep external market influences in mind. What works one summer might not work in the winter. For example, if a new Spiderman movie comes out in the summer months, it's only natural that those keywords would perform better. That fad might die out in a few months when people get sick of all things Spidey and move on to the next cool comic. The same goes for generators during hurricane season or perfume around Valentine's Day. (Even Homer Simpson could figure that one out. D'oh!)

Unraveling Conversion Process Breakdowns

You might spend $1,000, $5,000, or more on a campaign, but when you're done, you don't have a single conversion to show for it. The immediate assumption is that the ad campaign belly flopped in the pool of SEM. (Ouch!) But could it be possible that other forces at work caused your visitors to bail out on you? It's not only possible, but it's likely. Before you rush to judgment, you need to examine your conversion process for breakdowns as it relates to the keywords you chose for your campaign. That means that the problem could be on your site rather than on the search engine that sent the visitor to your site. It's been said that blame is the guard to change. So don't point fingers at Google, Yahoo!, and others until you examine your site.

Possibly, your paid search or banner traffic didn't convert because of some disconnect in the visitors' minds between your advertising campaign and what they found on your site when they clicked through. So it might be your own stinkin' fault instead of the search engine that sent the visitor to your site.

Understanding the conversion funnel

Google describes *conversion funnels* as a series of pages through which a visitor must pass before reaching the *conversion goal* (desired visitor action). In the Google Analytics world, the name comes from a graph of visitors who reach each page. The first page in the funnel counts the most visitors. Each successive page shows fewer visitors as they exit the site before reaching the finish line.

Read more about conversion funnels in Chapter 17.

Tracking the pages represented in the conversion funnel is important. One reason is to see how efficiently your pages direct your heard-earned visitors to the final destination you have in mind. You can discover quite a bit about specific pages by reviewing the conversion funnel. If you see visitors moving right along until they get to a certain page but then witness dramatic drop offs, perhaps the design of your page isn't user-friendly. Or, perhaps your prices are too high, your information isn't satisfying, or some other negative visitor perception is amiss.

Cueing in to conversion funnel issues

Imagine that your visitor lands (enters your Web site) on the home page. From there, he clicks through to a product or service page that interests them. Your snazzy photos and/or compelling copywriting did the trick. The visitor wants what you've got. So he moves on to the next step: conversion. (That's the conversion funnel in its simplest form. In reality, it doesn't typically happen that fast. Visitors might click around and around, leave, come back, place items in the cart, abandon the cart, come back again later, and repeat the process several times before actually converting.)

Now, put your math mind on. We're going to associate some numbers with the simplified funnel we just took you through. If 100 percent of your visitors hit the home page but only 25 percent continued on to the product or service page, you lost 75 percent of your traffic before they even had a chance to see your diverse array of products and services. There could be many reasons for this. Maybe your home page is poorly designed, or your shopping cart is difficult to navigate, or the page could simply be failing to make that keyword connection. By setting up specific KPIs for each of those areas, you can determine where you can start plugging the holes in your funnel. See Chapter 11 for the lowdown on KPIs.

Examining Google's Conversion Funnel

As we discuss, you can discover at what point in the conversion process your visitor bailed out on you by looking at certain reports in your analytics data. Google Analytics, as well as other analytics providers, offer visual views of your conversion funnel and other metrics that indicate where users bailed out. If your site is having trouble closing the sale, you'll want to become best friends with this report as you make site changes and watch how they affect your funnel. We'll show you how to get started with goals and funnels with Google Analytics. For an extensive lesson on how to use this program, pick up a copy of *Google Analytics* (Wiley Publishing, Inc.).

Suppose you're trying to drive visitors to a particular landing page. That could be a product page, an e-mail registration page, or a page that describes your stellar services. You can track the number of successful conversions using goals and funnels in Google Analytics. Each profile can have up to four goals, with a defined funnel for each goal. With your Google Analytics program open, here's how to set up goals and funnels in Google Analytics:

To enter goal information, follow these simple steps:

1. **From the Analytics Settings page, find the profile for which you will be creating goals and then click Edit.**

2. **Select one of the four goal slots available for that profile and then click Edit.**

3. **Enter the Goal URL.**

   If your visitor reaches the goal page, congratulations. You made a successful conversion. Examples of goal pages include registration confirmation pages, a checkout complete page, or a thank-you page.

4. **Enter the Goal name how you want it to appear in your Google Analytics account.**

5. **Turn the goal On or Off.**

   This tells Google Analytics whether you want to track that specific goal.

The next step is to define a funnel. Here's how:

1. **Enter the URL of the first page of your conversion funnel.**

   The first page of your conversion funnel should be a page that is common to any visitor moving toward your conversion goal. If you track user flow through your checkout pages, for example, don't include a product page as a step in your funnel. You are measuring only shopping cart issues in that type of funnel.

2. **Enter a Name for this step.**

3. **If the step you just named is a Required step in the conversion process, select the check box to the right of the step.**

   If this check box is selected, any visitor that reaches your goal page without traveling through this particular required funnel page will not be counted as a conversion.

4. **Continue entering goal steps until your funnel has been completely defined.**

   Google lets you enter up to ten steps.

Finish by configuring additional settings:

1. **If the URLs entered in the funnel definition are case sensitive, select the check box.**

2. **Enter a Goal value.**

   Google Analytics uses the goal value in its ROI calculations. You can set a goal value for the page, or a dynamic value pulled from your e-commerce receipt page.

   - *If you are setting a goal value for a page:* Enter the amount in the field.

   - *If you are entering a dynamic value pulled from your e-commerce receipt page:* Leave this field blank.

     You'll need to get some additional insight from Google from its support site.

3. **Click the Save Changes button to create this goal and funnel or click Cancel to exit without saving.**

Employing Conversion Tracking Tools

If you don't want to go through the brain damage of setting up conversion funnels but you still want to track the conversions of your PPC campaigns, you can employ conversion tracking tools. Google offers AdWords Conversion Tracking, which is different from Google Analytics but yields similar end results. Google is not the only one that has these tools. ROI Tracking, Conversion Ruler, and Hitbox Professional offer them, too.

If you're already using Google AdWords, though, the search giant's Conversion Tracking tool is a good bet. Conversion Tracking works by placing a cookie on a user's computer when she clicks one of your AdWords ads. The way Google explains it, if the user reaches one of your conversion pages, the cookie is connected to your Web page. Then, when a match is made, Google records a successful conversion for you.

Be wary of this potential caveat to conversion tracking tools: They don't always work well with cookies. Pretend that a visitor comes to your site through a Google search. She likes what she sees, but she has to rush to a business meeting before she has an opportunity to accept your call to action. That same visitor types in your URL the next day and purchases a subscription to your online magazine. Some applications won't recognize that visitor as a Google-referred conversion, so Google gets a raw deal because it really sent you a converting visitor but doesn't get the credit for it. Google says that its cookie doesn't expire for 30 days, but if the visitor logs back on to your site from a different computer or doesn't use cookies, the root of the conversion is a mystery.

Optimizing Your Ad Campaigns

We talk more about how to use analytics data to optimize for these types of issues in Chapter 16. The point here as it relates to advertising is this: The keywords that you use in your advertising campaign are targeting a specific audience. Those keywords and concepts need to be clearly reflected on whatever landing pages they are associated with. It's not just about choosing the right keywords, then, it's about making sure your site connects with what the reader was searching for when he gets there. Copywriting and other content should be optimized with keyword and keyphrases that you used in your advertising campaign.

You might wonder how to use your newfound knowledge of the keyword connection to optimize your ad campaigns. Pretend that you operate a site for your business consulting firm, and you target small businesses that are trying to take their company to the next level. Instead of sending the visitors to your home page and hoping that you've adequately communicated your value proposition, why not send them to a landing page that lists all the strategic services that you've provided to other small businesses? Because you never have a second chance to make a first impression — some clichés are true, okay? — why not make the most of the money you paid for that clickthrough by getting right to the bottom line with your visitor with a specially crafted landing page designed to compel them to convert? We can't think of any good reason.

Here's another example. You sell watches. You run a banner ad campaign that promises free shipping on orders greater than $100. The watcher customer decides to take you up on your offer and clicks through to your site. The only problem is when he gets to the product page, the content does not reflect the free shipping offer you promised in the banner ad. He might feel like you've pulled the old bait and switch (like the used car dealer's ad for a low-mileage, fully loaded Cadillac, that turns into a run-down bare bones lemon when you show up on at the car lot). If the visitor feels slighted, she might not only decide to exit your site, but she might not trust your next banner ad promising a free charm bracelet with the sale of a Rolex watch.

As you can see, you have many different ways to track your online advertising and marketing campaigns. We don't want to sound like nags, but our advice bears repeating:

> Whatever method you use, if you are an aggressive search engine marketer, please, please, please use one or more of these methods to revisit your strategies. You'll be glad you did.

Chapter 15

Chronicling Your Web Analytics History

*I*f seeing the word *history* in the chapter title made you yawn and consider skipping ahead, don't you dare! We promise not to bore you or make you memorize the names of America's presidents, significant wars, or watershed political events. We do suggest, however, that you keep a record of your Web analytics history. You know the adage: History repeats itself. If that's even the slightest bit true, you'd better make a note of what happened in your Web site's past so that can foresee the good, the bad, or even the ugly that potentially lies ahead.

You've probably heard the word *benchmark* used in connection with any number of industries, from investing to education to NASCAR racing. Simply put, a *benchmark* is merely a point of reference from which measurements can be made. Because Web analytics is all about measurements, benchmarking — in this context — is critical to applying the data properly. Just as racecar drivers time their speed around the track in what's often called a *benchmark race* that gauges their performance on a specific track with a specific vehicle and a specific crew, you can use Web analytics to benchmark your *key performance indicators* (KPI) on your site or sites. KPIs illustrate how well your site is performing against goals; read all about them in Chapter 11.

Regardless of whether you enjoyed history in high school, you'll have to admit that it does offer valuable insights. From the annals of history, we all learn about the successes and failures of great leaders and great nations. Much the same, if you chronicle your Web analytics history, you have a strong frame of reference to compare your Web site's performance today with its performance last month, last year, or even five years ago. You can clearly see the effects that seasonal shifts, economic conditions, market changes, product trends,

Web site redesigns, marketing initiatives, and other activities had on your site. You can see what did and what didn't work and then forecast how external factors that are beyond your control could affect your site so that you can plan accordingly.

Don't pooh-pooh this chapter. Instead, embrace it. You are about to see first-hand the importance of

- ✔ Benchmarking your data
- ✔ Which numbers you absolutely must save
- ✔ How to save them
- ✔ How to use this historical data to see what would otherwise remain invisible

If you study your history, you'll be prepared to pass the tests that come your way as customers, partners, products, services, content, and strategies change.

Name, Rank, and Serial Number

Some people love numbers, and some people don't. Some people are pack rats, and others throw away anything they haven't used for six months. For you data-loving packrats, chronicling your Web analytics history is a welcomed task. Regardless, here's our mandate: Save as much of your analytics data as you can, for as long as you can. Unlike tax paperwork from 20 years ago, left-over paint, and dried-up caulking (and all the other stuff that people nag you to get rid of), your Web analytics history will probably come in handy — and it won't clutter up the garage. In just a bit, we show you how to save it all.

For those of you who begin feeling nauseous at the thought of numbers (much less taking the time to save them), we'll try to make this as painless as your last cavity-free trip to the dentist. All you have to do is save the equivalent of a soldier's name, rank, and serial number. That's it. In the Web analytics world, that includes your

- ✔ **Standard traffic information**
  - *Unique visitors:* The actual number of individual users who came to the Web site
  - *Pageviews:* A record of each time a visitor views a Web page on your site
- ✔ **Top 25 search terms**
- ✔ **Top 25 referring sites**

The three types of Web analytic tools

Server-side analytics tools are installed on the Web site's server. *Client-side tools* are installed on your computer. A service provider on its server hosts *hosted solutions.* Be sure to read Chapter 4 for the scoop on the pros and cons of each of these delivery models.

✔ **Conversion rate:** The percentage of visitors who took the desired call to action

✔ **Any other KPIs** that you discovered are vital to keeping your Web site humming like a shiny new Lamborghini (or Porsche, if you prefer)

After you decide to save your data (even if it is a reluctant determination), you need to know how to save it. Like many things online, the answer is not cut and dry. Your saving options depend on two factors:

✔ The type of analytics software you use

✔ How long you plan to continue using that service

The three distinct Web analytic tool options you can choose from — server-side, client-side, and hosted solutions — play a role in determining how long your data is stored.

Don't take it for granted that your Web analytics application will automatically save your history by default, or you could lose valuable data. For example, some tools might save your data for only a limited period of time. Just like you check the expiration date on a carton of milk, be sure to find out where your Web analytics software or vendor stands on saving your history, or you could be in for a sour experience.

Saving data on the server side

Server-side analytics applications tend to put a cap on storing your historical data automatically, maybe storing it for only three or six months. Other server-side analytics programs might limit the amount of data that you can save based on how much storage or hard drive space you purchased with your hosting package. The latter issue is easier to clear up:

✔ **Pony up:** Spend more money to get more storage.

✔ **Watch your pennies:** Gauge how much you much data you can save before you go over quota and run into costly overage charges or experience server downtime.

If it's just a matter of the provider putting an expiration date on your data, talk to your Web host to determine how you can download your raw access logs and save them to a permanent location.

Saving data with client-side solutions

If you use a *client-side solution* (a log-parsing application that is installed on your personal computer), your only limitation in terms of space is the size of your hard drive. With the prices of storage drives as low as they've ever been, upgrading your capacity or buying a new storage device when your data gets really large is a no-brainer.

However, think about this when you're saving data on your computer: What happens if your computer dies or is lost or stolen? If you choose to save important data to your local computer, you should have a backup plan in place so that when (because it's not really a question of *if*) something bad happens, you can still access your data.

Saving data with hosted applications

If you use a hosted analytics application, the service provider will most likely save your historical information for as long as your account is in good standing. You can enjoy easy access to your historical data anytime you need it: that is, until you change providers. Like changing Web hosts, switching hosted Web analytics providers can cause major headaches. Beyond the fact that statistics can vary from application to application, you typically lose all your historical data. There's no need to stock up on aspirin as long as you get in the habit of recording your KPIs in a spreadsheet. We talk more about that in the next section.

Saved by the spreadsheet

Even if your historical Web analytics data is available on a server, your desktop, or a host indefinitely, it never hurts to compile an additional backup. You can do this using a simple spreadsheet program like Microsoft Excel, as shown in Figure 15-1. Be sure to check out Wiley's *Microsoft Excel 2007 For Dummies,* by Greg Harvey, if you need help with this program.

Not only does saving this data to a spreadsheet serve as a backup for your vital metrics and KPIs, but it also offers another way for you to review and compare your historical data. You don't need to record each and every metric, but you should make it a habit to review your analytics info and record the important metrics to an Excel file at least every few months. This can be a life-saver — or at least a marketing-saver — should your normal data storage plan fail for any reason.

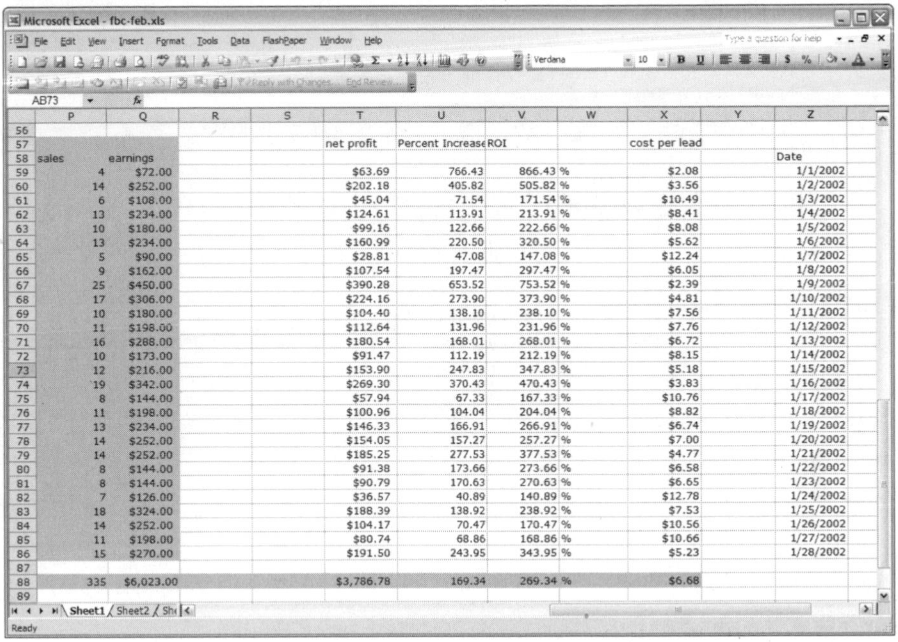

Figure 15-1:
A Microsoft
Excel
spreadsheet
with key
metrics
saved.

	sales	earnings			net profit	Percent Increase	ROI		cost per lead		Date
59	4	$72.00			$63.69	766.43	866.43 %		$2.08		1/1/2002
60	14	$252.00			$202.18	405.82	505.82 %		$3.56		1/2/2002
61	6	$108.00			$45.04	71.54	171.54 %		$10.49		1/3/2002
62	13	$234.00			$124.61	113.91	213.91 %		$8.41		1/4/2002
63	10	$180.00			$99.16	122.66	222.66 %		$8.08		1/5/2002
64	13	$234.00			$160.99	220.50	320.50 %		$5.62		1/6/2002
65	5	$90.00			$28.81	47.08	147.08 %		$12.24		1/7/2002
66	9	$162.00			$107.54	197.47	297.47 %		$6.05		1/8/2002
67	25	$450.00			$390.28	653.52	753.52 %		$2.39		1/9/2002
68	17	$306.00			$224.16	273.90	373.90 %		$4.81		1/10/2002
69	10	$180.00			$104.40	138.10	238.10 %		$7.56		1/11/2002
70	11	$198.00			$112.64	131.96	231.96 %		$7.76		1/12/2002
71	16	$288.00			$180.54	168.01	268.01 %		$6.72		1/13/2002
72	10	$173.00			$91.47	112.19	212.19 %		$8.15		1/14/2002
73	12	$216.00			$153.90	247.83	347.83 %		$5.18		1/15/2002
74	19	$342.00			$269.30	370.43	470.43 %		$3.83		1/16/2002
75	8	$144.00			$57.94	67.33	167.33 %		$10.76		1/17/2002
76	11	$198.00			$100.96	104.04	204.04 %		$8.82		1/18/2002
77	13	$234.00			$146.33	166.91	266.91 %		$6.74		1/19/2002
78	14	$252.00			$154.05	157.27	257.27 %		$7.00		1/20/2002
79	14	$252.00			$185.25	277.53	377.53 %		$4.77		1/21/2002
80	8	$144.00			$91.38	173.66	273.66 %		$6.58		1/22/2002
81	8	$144.00			$90.79	170.63	270.63 %		$6.65		1/23/2002
82	7	$126.00			$36.57	40.89	140.89 %		$12.78		1/24/2002
83	18	$324.00			$188.39	138.92	238.92 %		$7.53		1/25/2002
84	14	$252.00			$104.17	70.47	170.47 %		$10.56		1/26/2002
85	11	$198.00			$80.74	68.86	168.86 %		$10.66		1/27/2002
86	15	$270.00			$191.50	243.95	343.95 %		$5.23		1/28/2002
88	335	$6,023.00			$3,786.78	169.34	269.34 %		$6.68		

Benchmarking Your Conversion Rate

Because operating a Web site is all about conversions, if you make no other effort to chronicle your Web analytics history, benchmark your average conversion rate at the very least. Whether you sell pet supplies, offer an online self-service support kiosk, or generate leads or serve up information, your conversion rate is the bottom line, and Web analytics doesn't beat around the bush. It tells you the way it is.

To calculate your conversion rate

1. **Determine the number of visitors to your site.**

   Look at the number of unique visitors in your Web analytics program.

2. **Determine the number of conversions.**

   Not all Web analytics programs calculate conversions this for you. If you use Google Analytics, you can count the number of "Thank you" pages, or whatever page displays after the visitor takes the desired call to action (see Figure 15-2).

3. **Divide the number of visitors by the number of conversions.**

   This is good, old-fashioned arithmetic. Your answer will offer you the conversion rate for your Web site.

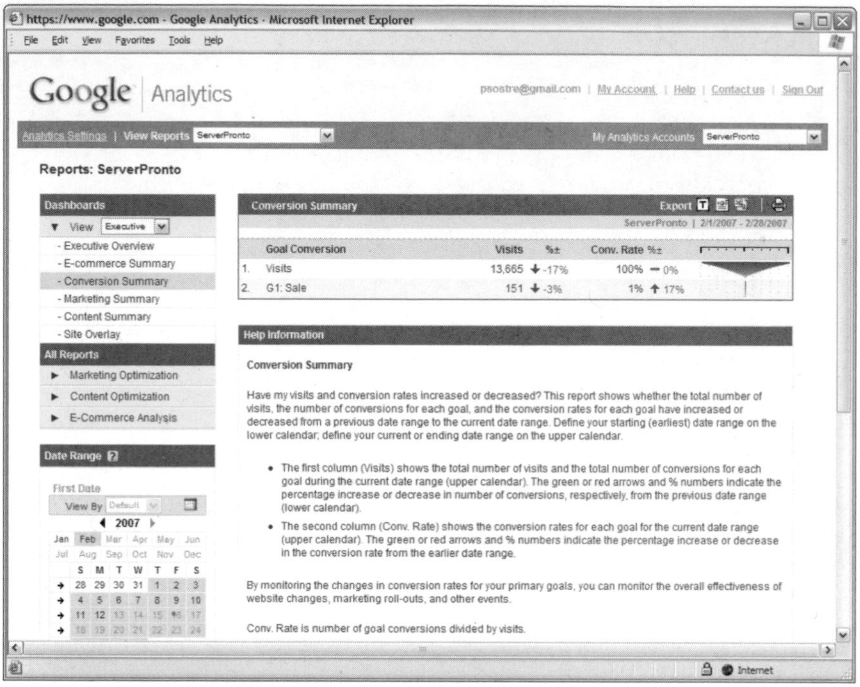

Figure 15-2:
Conversion Summary report from Google Analytics.

4. Make a record.

Now make a record of your conversion rate and note the date. That is your benchmark.

5. Monitor your conversion rate.

Your goal now is to monitor your conversion rate on a monthly basis (or more often if you choose) and see how well your site is performing against that benchmark. If you run an e-commerce site, you could also choose to benchmark against special promotions or holiday shopping seasons. If you are an accountant, you could benchmark against tax season or year over year. Tailor your benchmark against your business goals.

A declining conversion rate won't help you diagnose an ailing Web site, but it at least offers a warning sign that you are headed toward the edge of a cliff. Much the same, a rising conversion rate won't tell you what you've done right, but it at least gives you peace of mind that your overall efforts are paying off. Benchmarking your conversion rate, then, helps you keep a pulse on your site's overall ability, over time, to maintain peak performance.

Oh, what difference does it make?

Do you know what your conversion rate is today? Do you know what it was a year ago? Two years ago? Most people don't. In fact, a survey conducted by the e-tailing group, a shopper-centric e-commerce consultancy, found that 58 percent of retailers say the conversion rate is an important metric in understanding how well a Web site performs. (In our minds, that's a low number: It should be 100 percent.) If that's not bad enough, 19 percent didn't even know their conversion rate.

Failing to benchmark your conversion rate can spell disaster with a capital *D*. In this fast-paced world, you might not be too concerned over even notice a conversion rate that slips half a percentage point month after month. However, if you keep tabs on your historical data, you'll avoid that slippery slope. If you ignore your historical data, you could wind up with a 2.5-percent decline in your conversion rate over a four-year period. That's the equivalent to a wake up call delivered by the worst ever performer on "American Idol." It's a rate change that not many businesses can afford to miss.

Benchmarking against the masses

Sometimes folks in the Web analytics world consider benchmarking a comparison between your site and competitive sites. That's one way to look at it, and it's a valid way despite the variations in how analytics tools measure metrics and how often they fluctuate. However, most Web sites don't generate enough traffic to rank next to the mass retailers and content providers that major indexes like what comScore and Neilsen//NetRatings measure.

If you are really interested in how your Web site performs in the broad category that you serve, check out the Fireclick Index instead of beating your head against a brick wall (perhaps Wal-Mart or Amazon.com).

Fireclick (`www.index.fireclick.com`) is a Web analytics provider that taps its database to offer a publicly available Web analytics benchmark index (see Figure 15-3) across a variety of segments, such as fashion and apparel, electronics, catalog, specialty, outdoor and sports, and software.

WebSideStory (`www.websidestory.com`) offers a benchmarking service called StatMarket that offers critical comparison metrics — from checkout start rates to new and repeat visitor conversion rates — against five e-commerce categories, including apparel, toys, computers, sports, and leisure, as well as all categories together. StatMarket is only available by subscription and pricing starts at $750 for two-weeks' access and $1,500 for an annual subscription.

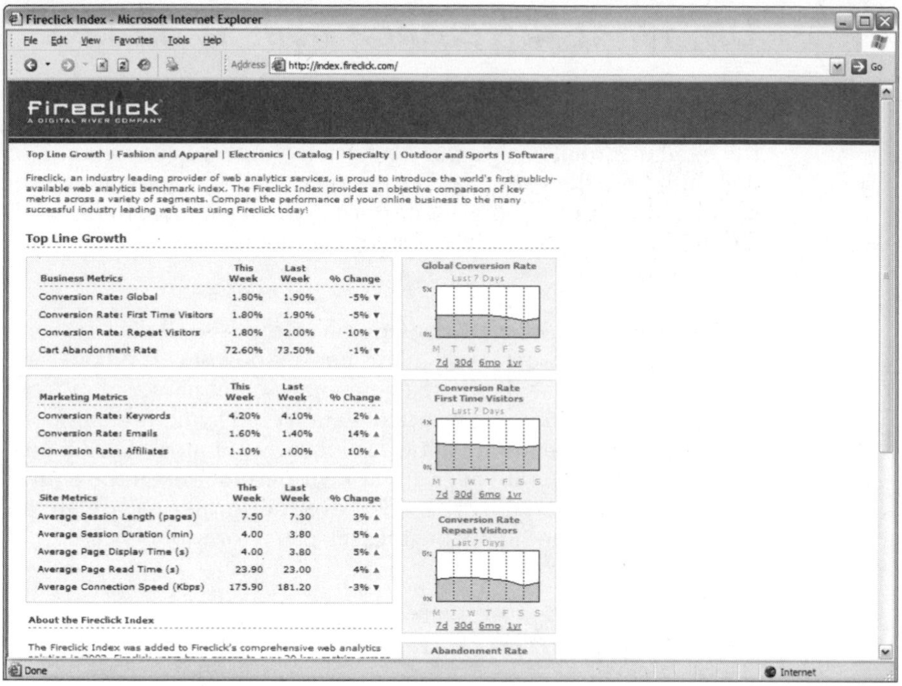

Figure 15-3:
Top line growth metrics from the Fireclick Index.

Some big analytics firms, such as Omniture (www.ominiture.com), don't believe in industry benchmarks at all because of the fluctuations we mention. The bottom line should always be making your site perform to its highest standards. Focusing too much on what your competitors are doing could ultimately distract you from your own agenda.

Benchmarking Your KPIs

As we list earlier in this chapter, your baseline comprises unique visitors, pageviews, Top 25 search terms, Top 25 referring sites, and conversion rate. Depending on what type of site you operate, you want to benchmark critical KPIs. E-commerce sites, for example, want to benchmark the *shopping cart abandonment rate* (the number of visitors who put items in the shopping cart but did not complete the sale). Content producers might want to benchmark metrics such as time spent on site. Customer service operations would want to benchmark *support ticket abandonment rates* (the number of visitors who started the customer support process but did not complete it). A lead generator might want to benchmark search-marketing KPIs. Are you catching on yet? For an exhaustive list of KPIs and how to take action on them, read Chapter 11.

Benchmarking Times and Seasons

If you're wondering how often you should look back at your Web analytics history and compare your benchmarks against your site's current performance, that's a valid question. Your answer depends (don't you hate when people say that?) on how much traffic you have, for one thing. If you get 500 hits per month, you aren't going to see dramatic changes in your KPIs, so reviewing your history on a monthly basis is probably sufficient. If you get one million hits per day, your KPIs could be skewed widely on a day-to-day basis, and you should have someone in your organization who monitors the metrics daily, if not more often. If you are aggressively spending on *pay per click (PPC)* campaigns (also called *paid search*; this method retrieves listings based on who paid the most money for keywords to appear at the top of the heap) across various engines, you need to monitor your analytics just as aggressively.

Here's the bottom line: Even if you can start only on a quarterly schedule, starting to track and record your important metrics as soon as possible is vital. Looking at the data every once in a while isn't good enough if you're serious about using analytics to improve your e-business. Get on a schedule that works for you and stick to it.

Month-to-month monitoring

Regardless of how aggressive your Web strategy is, you want to keep a pulse on certain benchmarks every month. Unique users, pageviews, and top search engines and keywords can see dramatic fluctuations month-over-month, even if you aren't doing anything to your Web site. This is because Google, Yahoo!, MSN, and the other search engines constantly tweak algorithms which can cause your listings to fall and rise unexpectedly. If you fail to take notice of those changes, your business could suffer. On the other hand, if your traffic numbers are increasing but your sales are not increasing proportionately, reviewing your data could point you in the direction of increased profits. Who would willingly pass on that opportunity?

Scoping history season-to-season

To everything, there is a season. If your business is seasonal, you want to be sure to review your Web analytics history accordingly. We mention accountants earlier. Although accountants could use a Web site to generate leads all year long, every year holds the tax season during which that accountant might generate most of his leads for the entire year. Likewise, if you run an e-commerce shop that sells sporting goods, you are likely to see sales spikes in basketball gear during basketball season and camping gear during the warmer months.

Much like how traditional brick-and-mortar operations review their seasonal data to make predictions for labor, advertising, merchandising, and other business functions, you can use the historical data in your Web analytics software to gauge the same factors. The good news is Web analytics lets you take it a step or two further. Not only can you gauge the need to saturate the market with advertising, but you can review search term reports from that period to discover what keywords drove the most traffic to your site and use those while weeding out the duds. You can see which site referrers drove the most conversions your way and make sure that you're still connected. To read more about how to measure traffic generation to your site, read Chapter 8.

Another year goes by . . .

Seasons come and go every year, but comparing seasonal metrics and comparing yearly metrics are two different things. Comparing your Web analytics history year over year gives you the big picture view of the growth of your operation. Ideally, you should be growing each and every year. As you review your year over year history, have your goals in front of you. Did you meet your sales goals? If so, did you spend more on PPC campaigns to get those sales? If so, what was the actual return on investment? You need to determine what those annual analytics comparisons really mean to your business.

The numbers can be deceiving if you don't put them into context. We've heard some Internet marketers claim that they are making $1 million on their sites, and consequently offer to sell their expert consulting services for a pretty penny. But did they neglect to tell you that they spent $950,000 on PPC campaigns to generate that $1 million in revenue?

Revenues and profits are two different metrics. Just like you shouldn't bank on *hits* (also called an *impression;* a hit created when your Web server delivers a file to a visitor's browser), you shouldn't bank on sheer numbers. Always drill down into your Web analytics to get the big picture. Set new goals each year and leverage your tools to truly measure your progress toward those goals.

Too, don't be fooled by an eye-pleasing chart (see Figure 15-4). Some unscrupulous consultants could take numbers out of context in order to impress you. If you are working with a *search engine marketing* (SEM) consultant (one who uses methods that seeks to increases the ranking and visibility of a Web site in search engine results pages) or a *search engine optimization* (SEO) consultant (one who uses methods of improving the rankings for relevant keywords in search results by making changes to the content or navigational structure of a Web site) who offers you graph that makes everything look dandy with unique visitors and pageviews going up, up and up, just remember to ask how much it cost you to get those increased visitors. And are these numbers also bringing increased conversions? Although improving individual metrics is easy, your KPIs are what really tell the story.

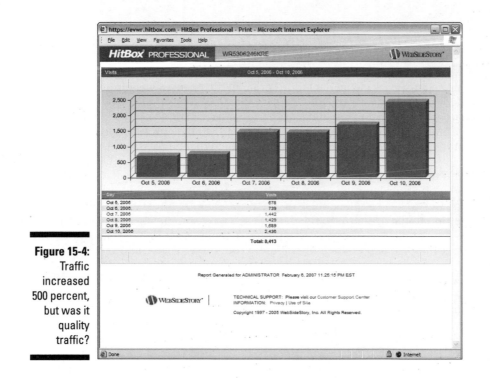

Figure 15-4:
Traffic
increased
500 percent,
but was it
quality
traffic?

Identifying Hidden Trends

If you've read this chapter to this point, you are likely thoroughly convinced of the importance of chronicling your Web analytics history. Assuming that you are indeed sold, we have a bonus for you. Analyzing your historical Web traffic data can help you identify visitor trends and patterns that would be invisible if not seen from the 10,000-foot view offered by your historical data. These could be positive trends or negative trends.

For example, you might not notice that your traffic for a particular keyword is increasing by 2 percent month after month. Still, missing a 24-percent increase in traffic for that keyword after 12 months is hard. Seeing the effect of this new keyword could indicate a growing market for the associated product or service. Or it could mean that some of your online competition is losing its step. Either way, it poses an opportunity that you might have missed otherwise.

On the other hand, say that your shopping cart abandonment rate is increasing by .05 percent per month. One-half of 1 percent would hardly make one flinch. Left unchecked, though, that .05 percent becomes almost 2 percent in the course of three years. Keeping tabs of your historical data lets you identify these trends so you can head off the negative effects before it's too late.

Many Tools, Many Benchmarks

Now we are going to throw you for a loop, but don't worry — we'll help you get your balance back in just a minute. Earlier in the chapter, we talk about three different types of tools (client-side, server-side, and hosted solutions). We also share with you that you could use dozens — even scores — of Web analytics tools. We warn you of the potential pitfalls of switching tools and losing your historical data. Now we answer your question: What if I use more than one tool?

If you use more than one tool to keep tabs on different slices of data, you haven't painted yourself into a corner. For example, you might use server-side analytics to keep a quick pulse on your critical KPIs but also use a hosted solution to dig deeper into the data. That's a reasonable tack because there are pros and cons to each different type of analytics tool. (To discover more about the pros and cons of the different tool types, read Chapter 4.)

Much the same, you might decide that client-side tools are right for you but use more than one vendor because you like the combination of features that using both tools offers. For example, you might use AWStats to monitor your day-to-day fluctuations in traffic but also use a client-side version of ClickTracks Analyzer to determine which user groups are generating the most revenue. Because AWStats is a free, server-based tool, it offers a quick and easy way to pull up your stats from any computer with an Internet connection. And although your client-side ClickTracks Analyzer application might take a little longer to import and process logfiles, it offers visitor segmentation tools that are unavailable in AWStats.

Nothing is wrong with using data from multiple vendors, but let the analyzer beware. You might yield slightly different results — or even significantly different results — from vendor to vendor. Each vendor defines and calculates metrics slightly differently: While one tool says that you had 10,000 unique users last month, another tool might figure that number at 8,000.

Here's how you reconcile using more than one tool: Even if you use multiple tools, be sure that when you benchmark and record your essential metrics and KPIs, you always grab your numbers from the same tool. Switching back and forth can make historical trend watching irrelevant.

Access Log Files: To Save or Not to Save?

Access Log files, also called *raw log files* or just *logfiles,* are generally text-based files that record each and every Web user's interaction with the Web site. In simple terms, a typical logfile records when a user visited, what files they accessed, and a unique identifier such as host address or IP address (see

Figure 15-5). More robust logfiles store additional data that can include where the user came from (or her referring site), what operating system and browser she was using, the resolution of her monitor, and more.

Analytics applications then use the data in logfiles to create reports and metrics that you see displayed in your analytics application's charts or data tables. Logfiles are usually saved on the server that hosts your Web site; depending on your hosting company, they might or might not be available for download.

Figure 15-5:
Access
Log file.

The case for dumping logfiles

Sometimes being a pack rat can leave you without much room to grow. Saving logfiles isn't always a good idea, nor is it always necessary. The downside is that logfiles can get very large. That means they can take up lots of storage space and become hard to manage.

And if you decide to change vendors and you have all these raw logfiles of data, you might not want to transfer them all over. It's not always a simple process. First, you have to locate the files. Then you have to prepare them for importing, which can involve using utilities to uncompress or convert the files to other formats. Finally, you go through the process of importing the files, if your vendor allows it. That can take a lot of time and a lot of computing resources.

Your decision boils down to the importance of your history. If you weren't getting much traffic before the last 6 or 12 months, saving historical data before that point in time can be a waste of time. However, if you have years' worth of logfiles that you feel are critical to keeping tabs on your site's performance, by all means — save, back up, and save again!

The case for saving access logs

Sometimes, being a pack rat can pay off. (Ask anyone who saved their bell bottoms until they came back in style.) The default setting for most hosting companies is to delete logfiles after a certain amount of time. However, you should decide whether you want to save those files. The benefits of saving your logfiles is that they are the raw data files that analytics applications need to generate your metrics. So, if you decide to change analytics applications or upgrade to one of those high-end enterprise solutions in the future, you can run those logfiles through your new application and possibly pull gems out of the data that you didn't know to look for previously.

Deciding whether to save your logfiles depends on how important it is to you to be able to parse this raw data in the future. As the analytics world changes and evolves, it seems that advances in this area will continue to lead to innovation in the way that applications parse and present that data so keeping it around for a while might make the most sense.

A simple way to save your files is to download and save the access logs to your computer. If you don't have the space on your computer, or would feel more comfortable with a more redundant backup, look into an online storage solution — some of which start at just $9.99 a month.

Chapter 16

Fine-Tuning Your Web Site

*W*hen all is said and done, you need Web analytics data to accomplish one overarching goal: Improve your business. If you've read all the earlier chapters in this book, you know that analytics can expose powerful information about your customers and their online behavior, which pages on your site are most popular, what content your visitors look for, where your online sales process breaks down, and more.

Web analytics can help you find new customers and partners, revisit your online advertising campaigns, and identify your most important pages, among other things. However, Web analytics can also help you take a view of your site from 10,000 feet up so that you can see potential problems with the function, design, and content of your Web site that you might otherwise not notice in the day-to-day grind of doing business online.

Indeed, one of the most powerful ways that you can use Web analytics data is to fine-tune your Web site. Much like *search engine optimization* (SEO; a method of improving the rankings for relevant keywords in search results by making changes to the content or navigational structure of a Web site) or ad campaign optimization, the idea behind Web site optimization is (as dear Merriam-Webster puts it) to "make as perfect, effective or functional as possible."

If you haven't already read Chapter 15 on chronicling your Web analytics history, we highly recommend you do that now. Trying to optimize a site without understanding your starting point is like going on a rapid weight-loss reduction program without weighing yourself at the onset. (That's *dumb* underlined three times.) In other words, you can't really measure how far you've come because you don't know where you started.

In this chapter, we make concepts such as redesigning your Web site based on solid analytics data, optimizing your home page and landing pages, minimizing shopping cart abandonment, and measuring the effect of site changes come to life with practical examples that will help you relate to your dear Web designer in a whole new way.

Understanding Optimization Strategies

If you've traveled in Web circles for any length of time, you've probably heard the word *optimization*. Optimization simply means to make as perfect, effective, or functional as possible. That definition in and of itself clues you that various optimization strategies exist for Web sites. Before we share strategies for using Web analytics data to make your site the best possible online business ambassador it can be, then, take just a minute to understand some common optimization strategies and how they relate to the challenge at hand.

Search engine optimization

We mention SEO throughout this book, defining it as a way to beef up your rankings for relevant keywords in search engines by making changes to the content or navigation. If you want to know more about SEO, pick up *Search Engine Optimization For Dummies,* 2nd Edition (Wiley Publishing, Inc.; Peter Kent) for everything you need to know about this popular optimization strategy. For our Web analytics purposes, if you engage in SEO projects, you want to keep track of a few metrics to measure your success against your goals. If your SEO strategy is working, you should be getting more traffic to your site.

- **Percent of User Growth this Period:** The total number of users this reporting period, divided by the total number of users in last reporting period. (Periods are usually measured in months or years.)

- **Percent of Traffic Growth this Period:** The total number of visits this period, divided by the total number of visits in last period. (Periods are usually measured in months or years.)

- **Percent of Traffic from Search Engines:** The number of visits referred from search engines divided by the total number of visits.

- **Percent New Visitors:** The number of new users divided by the total number of users. Getting return visits is great, but making sure that your site is being exposed to new visitors on a regular basis is also important.

After you have these stats in hand, you have two options:

- Conclude that your SEO efforts have paid off and move on to the next conquest in life.

- Decide that you have more work to do and get to it.

Reviewing the Robot Report

A *Robot Report* may sound like something the Jetson's maid (Rosie) would offer at the end of a long day of dusting high-tech gadgetry. In the world of Web analytics, though, this report tells you which bots visited your site, the date of the last visit, how many times they visited, and how much bandwidth they consumed. Also known as *Web crawlers, bots,* or *spiders,* a *robot* is an automated script or program that browses the Web. Search engines use robots to gather up-to-date data as they index the Web. This report is helpful for several reasons. For example, if you determine that the Googlebot darkens your virtual doors once per week, you can push through any new changes to your site between visits to bolster your page rank (determined by how many links point to a Web site together with the quality of the sites providing the links). Also, if you notice that the Yahoo! bot visits your site every month, but you don't get any traffic from Yahoo!, you might want to research search engine optimization techniques specifically for that search engine.

Web analytics doesn't measure some aspects of SEO, at least not directly. If you are gung ho about SEO, you also need to watch your Google PageRank. Your *page rank* is where your Web site falls on Google's scale of 1–10, with 10 being the highest. You also want to check your *link popularity,* which measures of the total number of Web sites that link to your site. Link popularity can dramatically increase traffic to your site and can also generate additional search engine traffic.

Calling on conversion design

Whether you are building a Web site from scratch, redesigning your site, or just improving certain pages, conversion design is an optimization strategy you'll want to employ. *Conversion design* is a design philosophy that combines business goals with aesthetics. It's bottom-line design with a single goal in mind: to turn online traffic into online sales (or subscriptions, registrations, leads, or whatever your desired call to action is). Conversion design describes the business of design and encompasses critical Web design elements that spark increased conversions, such as color theory and usability.

For our Web analytics purposes, if you execute conversion design concepts, you want to use A/B and multivariate testing to compare how one landing page performs against another. These tools help you take the guesswork out of site changes. You could literally test hundreds of different variations in the placement of Buy Now buttons, product images, copyrighting, and the like to figure out which site variations do the best job persuading visitors to take action.

✔ **A/B testing:** Also called *split testing, A/B testing* allows you to compare different versions of your site and measure the effect that they make on conversions.

✔ **Multivariate testing:** *Multivariate testing* goes a step further to let you test multiple versions of the same Web site.

With these niche software tools, cousins of traditional Web analytics, you could literally test hundreds of different variations in the placement of Buy Now buttons, product images, and the like to figure out which site variations do the best job persuading visitors to take action. Check out Chapter 6 to read more about these tools.

Capturing customers with conversion content

It's been said that content is king, but in a maturing Web world, not just any content will do. Search engines are clogged with blog entries and copywriting that is search engine-optimized beyond coherence. Different from *keyword density* (the ratio of the number of occurrences an individual keyword to the total number of words on a page), the concept of *conversion content* describes the actual content of copywriting, video scripts, PowerPoint presentations, and various forms of rich media that encourage a visitor to take the desired call to action. Conversion content, then, is not merely about drawing traffic to your Web site. Nor it is not merely about telling the visitor what to do when he gets there with a clear call to action. Rather, conversion content includes the meat of multimedia elements that accurately depict clear user benefits, communicating answers to unasked questions that could lead to consumer objections — and, in doing so, compelling visitors to respond to your offer.

For our Web analytics purposes, again rely on A/B and multivariate testing to optimize around conversion content. For example, an attorney might find that a version of his site that offers an introductory video that talks about the last big case he won generates more leads than the version that merely advertises his credentials, or vice versa. Or, an online catalog might discover that copywriting written in a conversational tone draws more conversions than copywriting written in a formal tone. However, this tack might not be true for a dermatologist's Web site, where potential patients might feel better about a doctor's big vocabulary. Indeed, how your visitors respond to your content can tell you much about who your visitors are as well as how to further optimize your site to meet their needs.

Optimizing Your Home Page

Before you attempt to optimize your home page, you need to understand its purpose and importance. Your home page can often be the first impression that the world gets of your company. It's the doorway to the rest of what you have to offer; its design and content can cause a visitor to enter or slam the door of opportunity in your face. The home page has to balance visual appeal with usefulness. Of course, you can accomplish that goal in any number of ways, but you certainly want to include standard elements about who you are, your unique selling proposition, and a clear navigational framework to help visitors explore the site efficiently. Then, use Web analytics to help you measure the most effective combination of elements so that you can increase revenue from your home page.

Before you start any optimization project, be sure to record your key metrics' *key performance indicators* (KPIs). KPIs illustrate how well the site performs against goals. You can read much more about KPIs in Chapter 11. Users enter your site from many different pages. When you track users who enter your site from the homepage, here are some important metrics and KPIs that you'll want to measure:

- ✔ **Average Time on Site:** The average amount of time a visitor stays on your site (see Figure 16-1). Users who come through your home page should be immediately understand what you offer and should feel a sense of trust for your site that will encourage them to hang around and see what all you'd like to show them. If this number is under 30 seconds, you didn't get their attention. You need to make some changes to your home page.

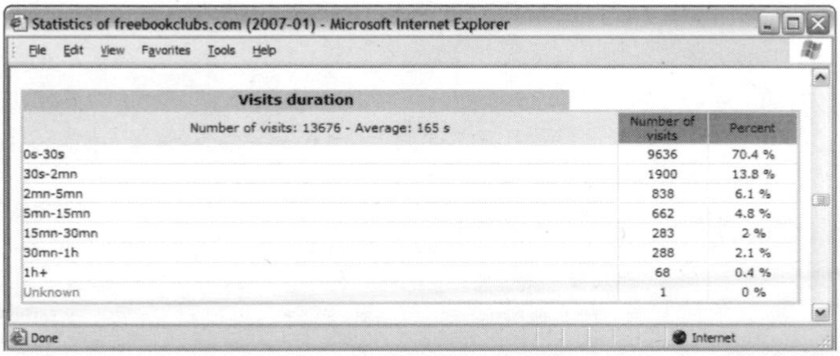

Figure 16-1: Average Time On Site report.

Visits duration		Number of visits	Percent
Number of visits: 13676 - Average: 165 s			
0s-30s		9636	70.4 %
30s-2mn		1900	13.8 %
2mn-5mn		838	6.1 %
5mn-15mn		662	4.8 %
15mn-30mn		283	2 %
30mn-1h		288	2.1 %
1h+		68	0.4 %
Unknown		1	0 %

- ✔ **Average Number of Pageviews:** The average number of pages a user visits on your site (see Figure 16-2). This metric is similar to average time on site except instead of measuring seconds and minutes, it measures how many pages your users visit before ultimately making a purchase or leaving. If this number is low (less than two or three pages), you might need to address problems with your navigation.

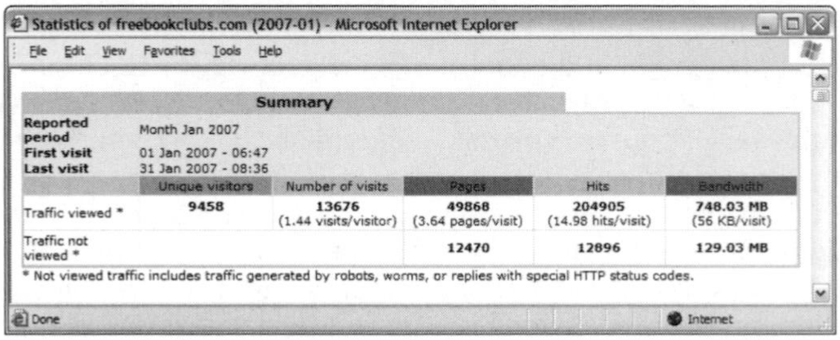

Figure 16-2:
Average number of pageviews report.

✔ **Bounce Rate:** A metric that shows the percentage of entrances on any individual page that resulted in the visitor's immediate exit from the site (see Figure 16-3). Visitors can decide in a flash whether you have what they need just by how your site looks. They could be wrong, but if you have a high bounce rate, perhaps the first impression scared them away. If that's the case, you need to make some changes to your home page.

Figure 16-3:
Bounce rate report.

What Sends Visitors Running?

Before you can optimize your home page, you need to understand some of the issues that can send visitors running to your competitor's front door. It could be any number of issues. As you set out to optimize your site, make changes in these areas if you feel that they apply to your site:

- **Unclear selling proposition:** If your home page does not quickly tell the visitor what your site sells, why she should buy from you, and how she can accomplish that goal, she could decide to move on to the next virtual outpost. For example, if your site's main focus is to sell shoes but your home page is cluttered with everything else that could fit into a closet, a visitor could easily get confused. Try repositioning the most important elements at the top of the page for the world to see; then measure the results with your analytics program.

- **No images:** If your e-commerce site's home page doesn't display images of your company's best-selling products, you are wasting an opportunity to cash in on the visit. What's more, if visitors came looking for that best-selling product and didn't see it within a few seconds, they might not clickthrough to the product pages where you proudly display your profitable goods. Try adding attractive photos of your prime time products and measure the results.

- **No contact info:** Even on the home page, it should be evident how to contact your service firm, register for your newsletter, or add items to the shopping cart. If your visitors can't find out how to contact you, they can easily leave as fast as they came. Try adding prominently displaying phone numbers and/or registration and contact forms on your home page; then measure the results.

- **Too much navigation:** If you present too many navigation options, it's difficult for the eye to pick any one thing out, much less what's really important. Visitors might miss what they came for and leave without digging. Try narrowing down your categories based on groups of complementary products. You might have to rename the buttons. That's okay! Try it and then measure the results.

- **Unclear navigation:** When your navigation options are unclear, the visitor might be forced to guess which category the products and services his heart desires are hidden behind. Visitors can get frustrated and leave if they guess wrong. Try to get more specific about your navigational scheme; then measure the results of your efforts.

- **Uncommunicated trust:** If the visitor can't trust you, he won't walk through your door. Your home page should exude authority, trust, and credibility. If your site is outdated, is unprofessional looking, or offers copywriting that, well, sounds like your younger brother wrote it, you probably aren't exuding these qualities. It might be time to remake your home page and rewrite your content. Try it and measure the results.

An informational example

Sostre & Associates worked with an information portal for new fathers. The site featured articles, pregnancy tools, a shopping directory, and various other valuable resources. The home page was jam-packed with more navigational options than you could shake a stick at. (Where does that statement come from anyway?) Although the number of unique visitors was healthy, the conversion rate was ill. The Web site owner, of course, was trying to increase his conversions by offering everything possible on the home page. Instead, the result was a cluttered, confusing, jumbled mess.

Using the conversion design concept (read about this earlier in this chapter), Sostre & Associates redesigned the home page, grouping the content into clearly defined categories so that visitors could easily move through the page. The designers used more white space between informational elements, cut the number of navigational buttons and moved them to another position on the site, used fewer colors, and added a registration function on the home page. When the owner measured his analytics reports again, he discovered a major boost in his KPIs, including 20-percent higher affiliate commissions and 40-percent greater advertising revenues.

Even if your home page isn't a jumbled mess, you can still toy with smaller elements of the design and see substantial improvements. It could just be that you need to rework your copy because it's not compelling the visitor to enter. Or your navigation might not appear user-friendly. It can surely be the little foxes that spoil the vine. Be sure to measure your metrics and KPIs to judge the impact of your changes.

The preceding list comprises just a few of the obvious issues that can cause visitors to turn tail and run. There are many others, including poor use of photos, wide text columns that are difficult to read, cryptic icons. . . . The list goes on. Your job is to assess the potential problems, make some changes, test, make some more changes, and test again. This, our friends, is the process of optimization.

Optimizing Your Landing Pages

A *landing page* is the specific Web page on which a visitor first arrives in response to advertising or paid search initiatives (see Figure 16-4). If you are driving traffic to specific pages, such as product pages, promotional pages, registration pages, or some other page you want them to land on, you want to optimize that page for optimum results: conversions. If you have plenty of visitors hitting your landing page but they aren't converting, something is obviously wrong somewhere. Don't spend another penny on SEM or another hour on SEO until you optimize your landing page.

Figure 16-4:
An example
of a landing
page.

Measuring landing page KPIs

Although you have only one home page, you might have many landing pages. You could run customer-only ads on a hidden URL that's not accessible to mainstream visitors and another similar promotion that is publicly available to anybody and everybody. You want to measure the KPIs of each individual landing page that you're planning to optimize rather than measuring overall site metrics as a benchmark of success. Before you begin, make a record of these landing page metrics and KPIs so you can measure your results:

- ✔ **Average Time on Site:** If your average time on site is high but conversions are low, it could be that you don't have a clear call to action. Visitors need to be told what to do in a way that compels them to do it. You might need to add a Buy Now button, do a better job of highlighting your super-low prices, or more prominently display your price. Perhaps you have too much content altogether.

- ✔ **Bounce Rate:** If your bounce rate is low and your conversion rates are also low, maybe your visitors are either confused or are engaging in a long game of eenie, meenie, minie, moe. You need to compel them to convert with design and content. Following the conversion content concept, you might need to add in some product images, write stronger headlines, descriptions, body copy, or bullets.

✔ **Conversion Rate:** If your conversion rate is low, perhaps you don't have the right products. Too, consider some of the aforementioned reasons. You could be losing thousands of dollars over a few simple changes. Keep testing until you figure out what works.

If visitors don't love the landing page

Before you can optimize your landing page, you need to understand some of the issues that can prevent your visitors from falling in love with your presentation. Any number of issues could be the reason. As you set out to optimize your site, you should make changes in these areas if you feel they apply to your site:

✔ **Poor design:** Poor design is one of the leading reasons why visitors don't love your landing page. Design includes text and link color (some colors are difficult to read onscreen), image choices and positioning, the layout of the page, navigation, and even the font and the size of the font. If you suspect that any or all of these elements hinder your conversions, begin making changes and then measure the results.

✔ **Unclear price:** If the price of what you sell isn't positioned clearly and accurately, visitors might not like — much less love — your landing page. Make sure that the price is easy to find and is consistent with any promotions you've launched online.

✔ **Content considerations:** A myriad of content considerations can hurt your landing pages chances of conversion. If your landing page copy rambles on and on like your second cousin whose phone calls you avoid, you could have a problem. If you fail to mention the benefits of what you're selling (benefits are different from product and service features, mind you) or fail to mention them quickly enough, your landing page conversions could suffer. If any of your content isn't up to professional par or isn't consistent with your promotions; or if your captions, headlines, and blurbs aren't attention-getting, you might need to make some changes. Then, measure the effect.

✔ **Cluttered page:** If your landing page is as cluttered as your kid's bedroom, how do you expect visitors to find what they're looking for? Organize your content into chunks that are easy for the eye to scan and then measure the results.

✔ **No call to action:** If you don't tell the visitor what to do, she might not do it. You need to make a clear call to action. Try adding Buy Now buttons and adding copy that states to respond to this limited-time offer or some other promotional strategy. Then measure the results.

A healthy example

Here's a good e-commerce example for you. Sostre & Associates worked with a Web site owner who provides salary information, medical testing and advice, and a medical industry job search to med students. The site didn't have a tagline or any images to convey what it was about, so it just looked like a list of links. The site didn't encourage visitors to come again, either, or register for updates. After adding a simple photo of medical students at the top of the site, a logo update with a clear tagline, a few text links to help visitors find what they are looking for more quickly, some calls to action to bookmark the site and register for updates, the site took on a whole new look — and a lot more conversions.

The Web design team demonstrated that just a few changes could lead to dramatic results. The same probably holds true for some of your landing pages. The key is to dive in, make the changes, and then test, change, test change, and so on.

Optimizing Product Pages

Your product (or service) pages are where your bread is buttered. These pages are where you spotlight what you have to offer the world. If the bright light turns up ugly flaws or noncompelling content, you could lose the sale.

Not all product pages are landing pages. Landing pages are pages you design for search engine visitors or visitors responding to some other promotion to land on so they can take advantage of what you are marketing. You will have a product page for each product (or service) you offer but perhaps only a few landing pages.

Measuring product page KPIs

Unless you operate an information site or an online customer support center, most of your site is made up of product (or service) pages. Keep these metrics and KPIs in mind at the onset, and then measure against them:

- ✔ **Percent Low/Medium/High Time Spent Visits:** The percentage of visitors who stayed on your Web site for under 30 seconds (low), between 30 seconds and 2 minutes (medium), or longer than 2 minutes (high). Knowing how long a visitor was at your site can be an important piece of the puzzle that when solved, shows you how effective your site really is. If your product pages are doing their job, your visitors should be willing to stay and shop or read.

- ✔ **Shopping Cart Start Rate:** The number of users who started a shopping cart (by adding one of your products to their shopping cart) divided by the total number of visitors who viewed your product page. This is important because one of the main goals for your product pages is to encourage users to add the product to their shopping cart. If only 1 percent of users who hit your product page add something to their cart, you might not be clearly communicating what makes your product better than what your competition offers. You can read much more about minimizing shopping cart abandonment later in this chapter.

✔ **Conversion Rate:** The number of conversions divided by the total number of visitors. Converting visitors into buyers, members, or subscribers is the name of the game. This is the core metric around which everything else ultimately revolves. Your product pages should have a clear call to action. If not, add one and measure the results. Add some calls to action in various places on the page and measure the before and after.

Perking up poorly producing product pages

Before you can optimize your product pages, you need to understand some of the issues can prevent your visitors from browsing long enough to respond to your call to action (if you've made one). It could be any number of issues, as we discuss earlier in this chapter in the landing page section.

As you set out to optimize your product pages, start with the page that gets the most traffic so that you can discover more quickly how the changes impact performance. After you hit on some winning optimizations, you can use them on your other product pages and really get your conversion rate rising.

Here's another good idea: If you're making changes in waves, begin your changes *above the fold* — the area of the Web site that visitors see in the first section of the browser screen (without having to scroll down). If you have limited time, those changes are bound to make the greatest immediate impact because some people won't scroll down if they don't like what they see initially.

Just a few words about optimizing customer support sites. If your goal is to help users get answers to questions about your products or services, you need a well-organized site with searchable information. Site search and clear copywriting are integral to your efforts. To read more about site search, see Chapter 12. You'll also find a list of critical KPIs for customer support sites in Chapter 11.

Likewise, if you seek to optimize your content portal or blog, consider your article or blog post pages as your product pages. Although shopping cart metrics don't apply, your articles are the products for content sites. Make sure that those are optimized to sell users on coming back to your site often.

Starting with a Clean Web Slate

In rare occasions, you might need to crumble up your Web pages and throw them in the virtual wastebasket. If your site looks like it came right of out the early (or even the late) 1990s and you haven't spruced up your site in five years, the content and the design are likely in sore condition. If your navigation is a list as long as your arm, you are confusing visitors in many cases. (There are always exceptions to the rule, of course. Some sites, like news portals, can get away with lots of options. Folks expect that, though, and the navigation is clearly expressed.)

If you decide to totally redesign your Web site, it's time to go back to the basics and review your goals. The issues we discuss earlier about landing pages, product pages, and the home page apply here as well. You have two options:

- **Redesign your site page by page while it's live.**
- **Design a completely new site offline or in a *development environment*** (a location that is online but hidden from the view of most users) and then make it live it when it's complete.

Either way, your focus should be on improving your KPIs.

Don't get in a hurry with Web site optimization projects. You should make sure you have clear goals in mind and think through each and every change and its potential consequences before you decide to invest the time in making them. You can take a good guess by reviewing your Web analytics data.

Determining Why Your Customers Abandon You

Shopping cart abandonment is one of the plagues of e-commerce. *Shopping cart abandonment* happens when a visitor puts items in the virtual shopping cart and initiates the checkout process, only to leave the site before the sale is complete. In the brick-and-mortar world, this is akin to going to the grocery store, filling up the cart, and leaving it stranded in the produce section (filled with rapidly melting ice cream, among other things) as you walk out the electric doors. This is one of the most frustrating statistics to review because you were oh-so-close to hearing the welcomed cha-ching sound of your virtual cash register — and instead, you heard the door slam shut in your face.

No one likes to be abandoned, but instead of getting offended, you need to put on your customer-colored glasses and get to the root of the problem. There could be any number of reasons why your customers walked away from the deal. It's your job to find out and to correct the problem. Of course, most of the time you can't chase the customer out of those electric doors and ask him why he abandoned the sale. However, your handy-dandy Web analytics serves as a stealth detective who gathers clues at the scene of the crime and delivers them to you in the form of navigational paths and numbers.

Customers bail out on the transaction for any number of reasons. Here are some of the most common ways. As you read these reasons, consider whether they might apply to your Web site.

✔ **The visitor was comparison shopping.** Visitors often browse before they buy, comparing your price, shipping price, return terms, and the like before actually making the sale. With this scenario, the visitor might go through this process with several vendors before choosing one and abandoning the others.

✔ **The visitor might plan to return.** Not all customers who abandon a shopping cart abandon it for good. A ScanAlert study demonstrated that the average time delay between a consumer's first visit to a Web site and the first purchase was just over 19 hours. Some took days or even weeks to return and close the sale.

✔ **The visitor was concerned about security.** The visitor might have gotten cold feet when it came time to enter his credit card number because the shopping cart area did not instill consumer confidence. Some reasons why a shopper might get cold feet are a lack of security seals from trusted firms, such as VeriSign, TRUSTe, or the Better Business Bureau, not seeing https in the URL, which means a secure connection has not been established, and not offering a contact phone number on your site.

✔ **It takes too long to seal the deal.** Online shoppers demand convenience. That's why they let their fingers do the walking rather than driving to the store and buying what they want immediately. If it takes too long to close the deal — say, they have to jump through pages of hoops masquerading as lengthy registration forms — they might decide it's not worth it.

✔ **Your site loads too slowly.** If the visitor, virtual arms overloaded with products, clicks the Order Now button and watches (and watches and watches) as the order processes, he might get impatient and decide to click the Stop button on the browser, effectively canceling the sale.

✔ **Shipping charges are too high.** You might have great prices on your products, but if you charge an arm and a leg to ship it, potential customers might abandon the sale. You can avoid this by offering a shipping calculator before the visitor puts the item in the cart. It won't help you close the sale, but it will help you determine in your analytics report whether they possibly decided not to buy the item based on the shipping charges.

✔ **Shipping time is too long.** By the same token, if you don't offer express mail services and the visitor needs the product overnight, he might abandon the sale.

✔ **The product is backordered.** The time to tell a customer that the product is backordered is not when she goes to close the sale. That's just annoying. Your Web site should let visitors know when they go to enter the item in the cart that it will not be available until next month, and then give them the opportunity to have it shipped when it is available.

✔ **The visitor changes her mind.** It's a woman's prerogative to change her mind — and a man's, too. Quite possibly, the buyer got cold feet and decided to abandon the transaction. That might be a better outcome than buyer's remorse that leads to returns. There's no way that Web analytics can tell you this. It's pretty advanced, but it doesn't read minds.

✔ **You lack a return policy.** If you don't have a return policy, the visitor might choose to not take a risk. If you do have a return policy, the visitor might not agree with the terms. If your Web analytics show that the visitor abandoned the sale after reading your return policy, that's a strong clue.

✔ **Too much personal info is required.** Sometimes visitors don't want to register with your site if they are required to ante up too much information about themselves, such as annual income, birthdate, and gender. If your site doesn't offer a quick checkout opportunity that lets them make a purchase without anteing up too much personal information, they might go to a vendor who does.

✔ **Your checkout process is confusing.** Your shopping cart process should be easy to wade through. If it's not clear where to enter information or how to redeem gift certificates or how to ship to a different address than the billing address, your would-be customers could bid you farewell instead of sending you their credit card information.

✔ **You don't offer order tracking.** Some consumers want to know where their package is every step of the way, especially if they need it in a hurry or are nervous about online shopping to begin with. If you don't have order tracking, they might back out of the sale.

Reducing Shopping Cart Abandonment

At this point, we have some good news and some bad news. You will never be able to completely eliminate shopping cart abandonment. It is a sad fact of life that you must learn to live with. The good news is that you can tap into the power of your Web analytics software to find ways to reduce abandonment — and, at the same time, increase your conversion rate. In fact, you can learn more about what your customers expect from your site by paying attention to these metrics.

What you'll find as you fine-tune this aspect of your Web site is that a little common sense goes a long way. At this critical turning point in the conversion funnel, it's imperative that you get your customer-colored glasses out of your drawer and onto your face. We recommend that you visit some leading e-commerce retailers to see what they are doing. Read this section first, though, so you can understand the why behind the what.

Finding out why shopping carts are abandoned

Before you set out to put the kibosh on shopping cart abandonment, you need to clearly define what that really means to you. Sure, at a broad level, you understand that shopping cart abandonment simply means the customer had "stuff" in the online shopping cart but decided for one of many reasons not to complete the sale. You need to narrow that definition a bit, though, or you could be spinning your optimization wheels.

Especially with expensive items, a visitor might return to your site multiple times to do research before making up his mind. With inexpensive items, it not be worth including the abandonment in your overall rates because it doesn't affect your business enough to justify making changes to your process. Perhaps some visitors treat the shopping cart like a bookmark to save items they want to go back and look at again but might not be ready to buy. (Sites like Amazon.com implemented wish lists for customers who are browsing but perhaps not ready to make a purchase. Amazon then takes that information to personalize e-mail campaigns or product offers that appear when you first enter the home page. Pretty clever, eh?)

You can set some parameters in place to account for those types of situations so that you don't get inflated numbers that are meaningless. By determining how long a cart can sit empty before you label it abandoned or the total dollar amount a cart must reach before you consider it worthy of measuring, you can fine-tune this metric and optimize accordingly.

Shopping cart KPIs to watch

Web analytics offers some strategic insights into shopping cart abandonment in the form of KPIs. After you have a handle on these metrics, you can determine which of the strategies we offer for reducing shopping cart abandonment later in this chapter are the best options for your site.

✔ **Cart Completion Rate:** The number of users who completed the shopping cart process, usually by clicking a Checkout button, divided by the total number of users who started a shopping cart. If this number is high, you've either made it very easy for your visitors to close the sale, or they wanted what you were selling badly enough to jump through pages of hoops to get through the buying process. If this number is low, your buying process might be too complex. Try to limit the number of steps to three.

✔ **Checkout Completion Rate:** The number of users who completed the checkout process, usually by finalizing and paying for an order, divided by the total number of users who started the checkout process. This might sound a little bit like the conversion rate, but they're different:

- The *Checkout Completion Rate* compares how many people completed the checkout process with how many people actually started the checkout process.

- A *conversion rate* in the traditional sense of the word compares how many people completed the shopping cart process with the number of people who visited the site.

The Checkout Completion Rate metric is important because if only 10 percent of people who start a cart actually complete it, your shopping cart process might be too long, your shipping charges could be too high, or you have one of the other reasons we outline earlier. Either way, it tells you that something about your shopping cart process causes people to leave.

✔ **Ratio of Checkout Starts to Cart Starts:** The number of users who start the checkout process compared with the number of users who added items to their shopping cart. People add things to carts all the time, and then they never start the actual checkout process for whatever reason. There are things you can do to push people toward the checkout after they add items to their shopping cart. Make sure that your Checkout button is clearly evident. If you offer free shipping, really hammer that message after a user adds something to his cart. Talk up your return policy (if it's good). This is an important and sometimes easily improved metric for e-commerce sites that want to ratchet up the conversion rate.

Sealing the shopping cart deal

Finally, the section you've been waiting for — the ways to reduce your shopping cart abandonment rate. Besides fixing all the problems we outline earlier, you can also take these measure steps (notice we said *measure steps*) to increase your chances of sealing the deal. Try some or all of these tactics and then measure your shopping cart KPIs again. We bet you'll see improvements.

Offering multiple payment options

Visitors might abandon their shopping cart (and your opportunity for greater profits with it) if you don't offer multiple payment options. In fact, Quality Research Associates polled 147 of the leading online retailers last year to determine the benefits of offering multiple payment options and concluded that sellers who accept four types of payments (such as credit cards, online checks, PayPal, and similar services) have more visitors convert to customers than merchants who offer a single payment method. In fact, merchants can covert as many as 20 percent more customers by offering them more payment types to choose from, according to the study. This is true, the study concluded, because Internet shoppers now include more people who might not have credit cards. Or for security purposes, people might choose to use an alternative payment service such as Google Checkout or Bill Me Later instead.

✔ **Streamline the checkout process.** How many steps are in your checkout process? Two, three, five, nine? Some believe the fewer steps, the better. Others believe it doesn't really matter as long as it's not confusing. We believe that less is more in this case. If you can condense the number of steps without making it confusing, you should. And there shouldn't be any reason not to. You don't need a visitor's life history in order to fulfill the product order.

✔ **Use a progress indicator.** No matter whether your checkout process is one step or ten steps, let visitors know what to expect along the way. Tell them they are on *Step 3: Address Information* or *Step 8: Payment Information*. Make a way for them to click the Back button so they can change information without losing everything they've entered on later pages in the process.

✔ **Offer a link back to the product.** Make it easy for visitors to check back and make sure they are getting what they thought they were getting. If you offer a link back to the product page, you can ease their minds by making it easy for them to review the product description one last time before authorizing the credit card swipe. If the visitor has to leave the shopping cart area and wander back through the navigation system or search function, she might never make her way back.

✔ **Use thumbnails.** You use images on your product pages, so why not use them in the shopping cart? Using thumbnail images of what the customer ordered can ring that mental bell so he doesn't have to even click the link back to the product page. By the same token, be sure to include the quantity and size in the product description that appears next to the thumbnail.

✔ **Change quantity.** Make it easy for your visitors to change the quantity of the items they are buying. Don't make them start the checkout process all over — or worse, empty the cart and start the entire visit over. They might forget to put some items back in the cart — or not even bother at all.

✔ **Use clear error messages.** Make error messages easy to understand rather than cryptic or difficult to follow. It's a frustrating exercise to try to convince a computer to accept the expiration date on your credit card when it wants that info in some newfangled format previously unknown to man. Make sure the bugs aren't your fault or that what you are asking for isn't in some strange format.

✔ **Provide purchase options.** Even if the visitor is halfway through the process, she might decide to pick up the phone and call instead. Make it easy by providing a phone number on every page along the way.

✔ **Use live chat software.** Live chat software can help minimize shopping cart abandonment. If the visitor gets confused, your live chat rep is there to answer questions. Don't let your reps barge in on the process, though. Always let the visitor initiate contact. You don't want them to feel like Big Brother is watching — even if he is.

✔ **Don't advertise.** Don't place advertising banners or other forms of marketing in the shopping cart area. You don't want to distract shoppers. You've got them right where you want them, why risk that they'll click a banner that will take them somewhere else?

✔ **Promote return policies.** Make it clear within your shopping cart that you offer a no-risk guarantee. You want visitors to feel comfortable buying from you. Let them know they can return or exchange the item if it doesn't satisfy them when they see it in real life.

✔ **Reassure about privacy.** Any time you ask for personal information, include language alongside the request that ensures the visitor that you will not sell his private information but will protect it. Four simple words *We value your privacy* — can go a long way toward reassuring would-be customers.

✔ **Send a pop-up message.** Technology allows you to send a pop-up message that reminds the visitor that they have items in their cart. Perhaps they forgot and will thank you for the gentle nudge. You get the sale. The worst thing they could do is close the message. But at least you gave it a shot.

✔ **Don't empty the cart.** Technology also allows you to not immediately empty the cart when the visitor leaves. It could be that their computer crashed. They will be grateful that they didn't lose all the items in their shopping cart — and so will you.

✔ **E-mail customers.** If you save the cart contents, you could e-mail customers and remind them that you've done so, or that their cart is about to expire. Again, you have lots to gain and nothing to lose.

✔ **Run a dummy test.** Have someone who isn't well versed with e-commerce try to make a purchase on your site to see how did he fares? If he makes it through with all his hair, good for you. If he abandons the cart, go back to the top of this list and choose some additional changes to implement.

These are all good tips, but your site isn't like any other, and your site doesn't have the same challenges as any other. It's important, then, to review your Web analytics to discover exactly at what point your visitors abandon a sale. After you identify your weak spots, you can focus your attention on strengthening those areas.

Measuring the Effect of Site Changes

Don't make the mistake of working up a sweat making changes to your site without measuring the impact of your toil. Throughout this chapter, we give you some pointers about what to look for along the way. Now, we take a big-picture view of your site that takes all the potential changes in perspective and offer a few tips for the road. Keep in mind that you typically need at least four weeks of Web analytics data to really discern the impact of the site changes you're making. Also keep in mind the many X factors that can give you false positives and traffic boosts, such as seasonal events, societal trends, and other things that you can't control — and, therefore, cannot replicate.

When you work on enhancing an individual page, we recommend that you make several versions of the same page. Each version should have different combinations of design enhancements or content changes. You can test one page each week until you run through the lot of them, and then aggregate your Web analytics results to determine which pages performed the best. You might discover that three out of the eight pages you created were top performers. That's good; now narrow it down even further by taking combinations of those design and content elements and creating three more test pages until you have a clear winner. Alternatively, you could choose to make one minor change at a time and measure the results, but that can leave you with slowed results, at best.

Clickalyzer (`www.clickalyzer.com`) makes some bold promises — and delivers. This software tells you why people leave your Web site without buying, which traffic sources are truly profitable to you (even before they ever convert), exactly how far down a page someone reads, and what happens on your affiliate's Web sites right down to the point of sale. This is interesting software that's worth the buck you pay for a seven-day trial. After that, you'll pay $29.95 a month or $299.95 a year (you save $60 by paying up front).

Clickalyzer puts you in the driver's seat. You can tell the program what you want to see and what you don't want to see. *Split testing* is another keen feature. You can rotate the URL of a single Web address between several different Web site addresses. That allows you to test the effectiveness of different sales copy, pricing strategies and various other options.

If you want to kick-start your testing, you could choose to launch a paid search campaign. It will send plenty of traffic your way and allow you to come to some conclusions in a matter of days rather than weeks. That said, don't be too hasty with your final decision. Review your metrics, put them in context, and then decide. What you'll discover is that Web site optimization is an ongoing process. It never ends. Your search for statistical treasure that will continually improve your conversions is a lifetime proposition. Happy analyzing.

Part V
The Part of Tens

The 5th Wave   By Rich Tennant

"We have no problem funding your Web site, Frank. Of all the chicken farmers operating Web sites, yours has the most impressive cluck-through rates."

In this part . . .

*N*ow that you've got the basics of Web analytics under your belt, this final part of the book will help you implement best practices, avoid common pitfalls, and utterly convince you that this software will revolutionize your e-business.

We talk about a number of myths, pitfalls, and mistakes that are common in the Web analytics realm. You may have made some assumptions about how Web analytics will work for you — and they may be all wrong. You're not alone. There are plenty of stumbling blocks on the road to Web site optimization. We'll help you avoid them.

Of course, it's one thing to avoid pitfalls. It's another thing to find a road that's been freshly paved. In this part, we also illustrate some Web analytics best practices. These approaches to interpreting the data are tried-and-true and will work for you. Finally, we make a convincing case for the overwhelming impact Web analytics could have on your Web site today — and tomorrow. With Google and Microsoft getting into the game, the industry is bound to see even further advancements.

Chapter 17

Ten Web Analytics Myths, Mistakes, and Pitfalls

In This Chapter

▶ Six of the most erroneous Web analytics myths

▶ Two of the most horrific Web analytics mistakes

▶ Two of the most pitiful Web analytics pitfalls

*P*lenty of Web analytics myths circulate online, and there are probably as many mistakes to make as statistics to measure. If you aren't careful, you could end up in the fairy-tale world of Neverland with Tinkerbell interpreting your data, and Peter Pan making changes to your Web site. Make no mistake — the real world of Web analytics isn't a place where the data is black and white but rather can be sliced and diced in many different ways.

As you begin to put what you've read in this book into practice, remember to go in with your eyes wide open. Don't listen to just anybody and everybody's latest "strategies" for how to wade through your data more effectively. Any black belt karate master will tell you this: The strength is in the fundamentals. The same is true for Web analytics. Straying from the fundamentals will lead you into pitfalls that can be hard to escape.

You'll be tempted to look at averages, Top 10 lists, and monthly visitor trends. Go ahead and look, but don't let these reports muddy your decision-making process. Just like world-changing events in a history book, Web analytics data has to be put into context in order for the reader — that's you — to truly understand what has happened in his world.

Like we said, there are plenty of Web analytics myths circulating online and dozens of mistakes you could make. Although this list is certainly not exhaustive, it does offer insight into some of the most common mistakes. These universal errors are based on wrong perspectives that, if corrected, will help you avoid the many other blunders.

Averages Are the Analytics Answer

Oh, what a wonderful world it would be if Web analytics offered a single digit to describe your Web site's performance. Imagine the glorious ease of a figure that took into account every possible analytic — from unique visitors to length of stay to page views, and more — and offered an arithmetic mean to portray your site's performance on a scale of 1 to 10. A 1 might indicate that your paid search campaigns are failing miserably and that your traffic is shrinking month by month. A 10 would offer a picture of perfection, where visitors respond to organic search strategies, make large purchases, and return again and again. Unfortunately, one number does not fit all.

It's a fallacy, or at least an online urban legend, that averages are the answer. True, Web analytics software offers plenty of averages, such as average time on site, average visitors per day, average pages per visit, and so on. However, these median figures might not be as telling as they appear. You have powerful technology at your fingertips, so why settle for averages when you can drill down to specific data points that help you outline action plans?

Before you throw your averages out the window, allow us to explain. Averages are helpful when you use them in tandem. It's discouraging to learn that visitors who find your Web site through *organic search* — a search that retrieves results by indexing pages based on content and keyword relevancy — spent an average time on site of only 35 seconds. However, say you can glean that your *paid search* or *pay per click* (PPC) traffic — namely, visitors who are drawn to the site through search engine listings that you pay for — post an average time on site of 180 seconds. When you compare one group of visitors with another, you can easily see that your PPC campaigns draw the more valuable traffic.

Just like there is no such thing as one number that fits all, there is no such thing as an average visitor. Like the people those metrics represent, many different types of users will use your site differently. Visitors who come to your site through organic search might have knocked on your virtual door by mistake and left in chagrin when they realized the error. Paid search visitors know exactly where they are going, and then it's up to you to deliver the goods after they get there. Weekend visitors might have different habits than weekday visitors, morning visitors than late night visitors, and so on.

Monthly Visitor Trends Tell All

When you turn the pages of women's magazines, you see the latest trends in fashion design. When you explore a business magazine, you learn about the latest management trends. Much the same, when you delve into Web analytics, you discover visitor trends. Identifying trends is a key to data deciphering, but it's the trends you watch that make the difference. Watch the wrong trends, and you'll end up making the wrong decisions.

Here's the myth: You can determine visitor trends by simply reviewing your monthly visitor report. Perhaps you can indeed determine overall traffic trends — whether page views, unique visitors, and length of stay is up or down for any given 30-day period — by scanning the charts and graphs in your monthly visitor report. But wait: Don't get too excited about an upward trend in traffic and begin increasing your PPC dollars arbitrarily.

Trends based on the monthly visitor report alone can be somewhat of an optical illusion, tricking your eyes into seeing something that is not really there or incorrectly perceiving what is there. In other words, the surface data can be deceptive. For starters, the monthly visitor report draws you into a time warp, of sorts, because the time intervals depicted don't reflect real-world events. The report surely offers a snapshot of how your site performed but doesn't take into account the e-mail campaign you released in week one or the site optimization project you completed six weeks ago. Likewise, your Web analytics software clearly depicts traffic ebbs and flows, but the numbers alone cannot tell you the reasons behind those spikes.

Instead of watching monthly trends and monthly trends alone, define the trends that matter most to your site. You do that by segmenting the time periods your software is evaluating. Don't let your software dictate the timing: Put the clock in your own hands by setting your own dates based on events (such as weekend promotions) and activities (such as blogging updates). For example, if you send out an e-mail blast on January 15, compare your conversion rates two weeks before and two weeks after the campaign. (The *conversion rate* is the percentage of visitors who completed a transaction; filled out a membership; or, in the case of lead generation, requested additional information.) Those real comparisons speak undiluted volumes.

Pinpoint Precision Is Paramount

The "accuracy" myth is hard to wrap your head around, especially in the realm of data. After all, who wants to make business decisions based on inexact statistics? Would Microsoft Chairman Bill Gates tolerate approximations in his boardroom meetings? If he's measuring how many visitors used MSN portal in June, "close" might have to be good enough.

Determine ROI improvements

You can determine the effect of your Web initiatives by measuring the *key performance indicators* (KPIs), which is information viewable from the Web analytics dashboard that illustrates how well the site is performing against goals at strategic time intervals. You can not only determine the impact but also get clues as to the lingering effects of the campaign.

Here's a rough overview:

1. Measure your KPIs before your promotion to establish a baseline.

2. Measure your KPIs the day of your promotion to measure the immediate effect.

3. Measure your KPIs two weeks after your promotion.

4. Measure your KPIs three weeks after your promotion.

You can read much more about KPIs in Chapter 11.

The accuracy myth states, in no uncertain terms, that pinpoint precision is paramount to determining how your Web site is performing. The fact is, though, that no Web analytics software is 100-percent accurate. Many factors can skew the data, such as proxy servers, tabbed browsing, dynamic IP addresses, ever-changing security enhancements, and other emerging technologies. Web analytics software does offer close estimates: Certain metrics, such as unique visitors, are more valuable than other metrics (such as hits). Before you throw your software program out the window — and this book along with it — take a deep breath and consider what matters: whether the overall metrics are improving or declining.

At the end of the day, it doesn't matter too much whether 25,000 or 25,500 visitors navigated your well-designed Web pages. You shouldn't be too concerned one way or another over 500 visitors (unless your site is only getting 500 visitors a month because it then may be time to break out the aspirin to ease your aching head). On the other hand, you should be extremely concerned if your visitor count drops from 25,000 to 10,000. That would qualify as a *bona fide* emergency that requires your full attention to diagnose a disease and determine a cure.

Top-level data is not nearly as powerful as contextual data. Drill down from the top-level conclusion that says, "Search engines send me the most traffic" to the more specific "Google sent 60 percent of my unique visitors last month." But don't stop there. You won't hit oil until you compare this month's Google traffic with last month's Google traffic to discover that your Adwords campaign is a gusher. Contextual data might also compare search engine to search engine in light of *search engine optimization (SEO)* initiatives that were launched on various engines. (SEO comprises methods to improve the rankings for relevant keywords in search results by making changes to the content or navigational structure of a Web site.)

Unique Visitor Data Tells the Truth

It's true that unique visitor counts can offer a more accurate metric of site traffic than pageviews or hits, but the notion that all unique visitor tracking is accurate is a new wives' tale in the Web analytics era. Web analytics applications track unique users in two basic ways, by

- ✔ An *IP address*, which is a unique numeric identifier assigned by a user's Internet service provider (ISP)
- ✔ *Cookies*, which are small text files that hold defined visitor information

Because of proxy servers and dynamic IP addresses, counting IP addresses isn't entirely accurate. And when it comes to cookies, you have to face the possibility that users will delete their cookies or have their security settings set to block cookies.

Analytics applications that rely entirely on IP addresses to track unique visitors fall short in two ways: when a user's ISP assigns a dynamic IP address and when a visitor is surfing your site from behind a proxy or network IP. A *dynamic IP address* is one that changes each time a user connects to the Internet; or, in some cases, when they browse the Internet. *Proxy* and *network IP addresses* let several users connect to the Internet through the same IP address at the same time.

Analytics applications count each individual IP address. So if an individual user is browsing your site from several IP addresses, your unique visitor counts are automatically inflated. Comparatively, if several visitors access your site through a proxy or network IP address, your analytics program might count them all as one unique visitor.

All Web Analytics Software Is Alike

Saying that all Web analytics software is alike is akin to saying that all word processing applications are alike. Sure, they share some common denominators, such as text entry and formatting. Similarly, all Web analytics software tracks fundamental metrics, such as hits, pageviews, unique visitors, and site referrers. And, just like how sophisticated word processing programs offer much more than the ability to type text onto a digital page (such as internal, dictionaries, grammar checking, and even layout tools), sophisticated Web analytics software offers much more than the fundamentals. In fact, the most advanced programs on the market run complex analytics systems that parse data in real-time and present 3-D page-traffic reports.

When the cookie crumbles

For all the Web analytics myths and mistakes, misconceptions about cookies are making it more difficult to measure unique visitors. *Cookies* are small files that can hold information on the times and dates when a user visits your Web site. Examples are log in or registration information, online shopping cart data, user preferences, and the like. Cookies allow Amazon.com to recognize you and offer a list of personalized product recommendations. You don't even need to register or submit any information for Amazon to start tracking your Web site behavior and targeting its marketing efforts to your sweet spots.

However, cookies don't take into account the possibility that one person could be using several different browsers, such as Firefox and Internet Explorer, to access the same site from the same computer. That single visitor, then, would register as two unique visitors when technically only one person viewed the site. Likewise, cookies don't take into account that one person can call up the same sporting goods Web site from several different computers in several different locations all in the course of a single day. Further, cookies don't take into account that several people could use the same computer and the same browser to visit the same site on the same day. Can you see the cookie crumbling?

Another important consideration in the cookie tracking method is cookie deletion issues. If one individual deletes the cookies from a Firefox browser but doesn't delete them from an Internet Explorer browser, the number of unique visitors is skewed, depending on which browser the visitor is using. One individual can accept cookies on one computer yet reject them on another. There are more than a dozen different scenarios that could cause the proverbial cookie to crumble.

Although cookies are invaluable to Web site owners and can be convenient for users, the fear of adware and spyware leads many consumers to rid themselves of these files. In fact, a survey conducted by JupiterResearch (www.jupiterresearch.com) found that as many as 39 percent of U.S. Web surfers delete cookies from their computers at least once per month, with 17 percent erasing cookies once per week and 10 percent cleaning them out daily. That means that if your Web analytics software uses cookies alone to track unique users, the sheer number of your unique visitors could fluctuate dramatically over a 30-day period.

Cookies are a great asset to Web analytics software, but they can also be a liability in some cases if you don't measure your metrics *in context*. If you compare groups of visitors with each other, such as visitors who found your Web site through Google with visitors who found your Web site through Yahoo!, the cookie issues become less of an issue. Sure, you still have to deal with the multiple browser issue, but you are mitigating the cookie deletion dilemma.

Because Web analytics terminology and methodology is still evolving, interpreting metrics offered by one application might require a different approach than interpreting metrics offered by another. Analytics such as pageviews, visits, and unique visitors are slightly different from system to system. Making matters more confusing, different products from the same vendor might count in different ways.

A key reason for the discrepancies is how the products are delivered: client-side, server-side, or hosted. You can read about the differences in detail in Chapter 4. Another reason for the inconsistencies is how the software is configured. We recommend that you configure your Web analytics tools based on data-collection and reporting best practices. Omniture (www.omniture.com) launched a Best Practices Group in 2006 to address some of these issues. Then conduct ongoing accuracy audits to ensure data reliability.

Choosing a Web analytics application because it works well for your friend could leave you with a bullet in your foot. Every Web site is different, with different goals and measures of success. Every Web analytics program is different, with different features and functions. Before choosing a vendor, you need to know what data and metrics are most important to your business. Then you can focus on finding programs that offer exactly what you need.

But Numbers Never Lie . . .

An old adage emphatically states that numbers never lie. That's a half-truth that was probably coined by an accountant type who sees the world in black-and-white digits. It's a half-truth because, well, numbers themselves might not lie. They are what they are. Still, numbers can be skewed to portray an inaccurate picture; and, with mountains of data, statistical perception can be downright deceiving. As we've learned with the corporate accounting scandals of the past few years, numbers have been at the heart of some of the biggest lies of our day.

This is not an accuracy myth; rather, it's a metric myth. Some metrics are downright overrated. The marketing industry might build a buzz around hits, for instance, but advertisers are beginning to catch on to the flaw in this broad figure. So it is true that numbers don't lie. However, your goal is to avoid toiling over metrics that don't really matter to your bottom line. Making decisions about your Web site based on metrics that don't accurately measure online success is a flat-out mistake. An informed decision based on the wrong information is an ill-advised decision.

Take site referrers for example. *Site referrers,* or *referring pages,* are the URLs of the previous Web page from which a link was followed. In the SEO world, these are called *backlinks.* You might have an impressive number of backlinks, perhaps hundreds or even thousands. You might drill down a little further and determine that those backlinks brought 150,000 visitors — unique visitors, at that — to your Web site. Before you get too excited, though, don't forget a couple more metrics that matter:

- **Depth of visit:** Depth of visit shows you how many of your Web pages a visitor viewed.

- **Length of stay:** Length of stay indicates how long the visitor was on your site. If most of those 150,000 visitors stayed an average of 10 seconds and viewed one page, what have you gained? Making a decision to invest more resources on linking partners based on pure traffic generation alone would be erroneous.

Make money with your metrics

There's potential money in your metrics. That's right, if you understand how to analyze your Web analytics, you can uncover revenue-generating opportunities to which you would otherwise be blind. However, there is a rhyme and reason to making money with your metrics. Consider the following steps as you set out to tap your stats for more income:

1. **Determine the type of site you have — e-commerce, lead generation, content portal, and so on — as well as its goals.**

2. **Determine relevant KPIs, such as new account sign-ups, Contact Us form completions, article views, online sales, case study downloads, and so on.**

3. **Combine relevant metrics (such as pageviews, visitors, length of stay, and site referrers) to get a clear picture of what drives conversions as well as where your site needs optimization or your marketing efforts need tweaking.**

4. **Develop a strategy, take action and continue to measure your results to continual improvement.**

A Picture Speaks a Thousand Words

The world of Web analytics is a world of multicolored charts, graphs, and other visuals that are bound to attract the attention of Web site owners who would rather look at pretty pictures than crunch numbers. Whether you prefer pie charts, line graphs, bar graphs, or some other type of picturesque presentation, you'll find it in a Web analytics program near you. But don't get too enamored with session graphs, pageviews graphs, hits graphs, bytes graphs, and the like, or you could fall into a nasty trap: putting too much stock in charts.

Don't get us wrong: Eye-pleasing graphical data is helpful, but there is a tendency to skip the hard data analysis in reliance of the colorful imagery. The problem with graphs is they highlight trends only at a glance. In order to make the most of your Web analytics, you need to dissect the data, run comparisons on various groups, and otherwise gain a deeper understanding of the statistics the technology worked so hard to gather. ClickTracks CEO John Marshall once said in his charming accent, "Data must be clear first, pretty second." We wholeheartedly agree.

For an example of this concept, take a look at Figure 17-1. At first glance, you might see that traffic spike on Wednesday and rush to the marketing department folks to tell them to get the campaign that drove that traffic online again. However, when you dig a little deeper, behind the bar graphs, you'd see that the majority of the visitors from that day stayed less than 20 seconds and did not visit any secondary pages. Obviously, the campaign was great at generating traffic, but this is not the type of traffic that converts to sales. Bottom line: Spending more money on a campaign like this won't pay dividends.

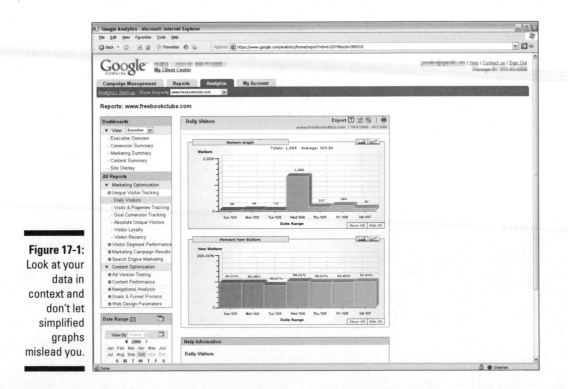

Figure 17-1:
Look at your data in context and don't let simplified graphs mislead you.

After you get more acquainted with Web analytics, you'll begin to understand what the highest-paid analysts already know: Graphics are helpful in persuading decision makers to invest in new initiatives, but flashy imagery without an in-depth comprehension of how those numbers really affect your return on investment are only ostentatious displays of artistic flair. If you insist upon relying on graphics, make sure you understand what the colors — and the shades of those colors — actually mean.

Popular Search Terms Hold the Key to More Traffic

Basing decisions about your organic search or PPC campaigns based on popular keywords and phrases alone could leave you with more than empty pockets: It could put you right out of business. Indeed, in the age where you rack up a large pay-per-click bill in a hurry, this is one of the biggest dangers in interpreting Web analytics data. We'd like to rescue you from this bottomless pit before you ever come to its edge.

We can just hear you now, "Wait a minute! Keywords drive most of my traffic. How can investing in the most popular phrases be a bad thing?" Before your brain goes tilt, allow us to explain. See, there is a fundamental difference between quantity and quality. It doesn't really matter whether the keyphrase *gold tennis balls* drives the most traffic to your Web site if you are selling jewelry. Are you starting to get the picture? When you look at your Web analytics, you'll notice all sorts of strange keywords and keyphrases popping up — some of them with great frequency. But it doesn't do you a darn bit of good if they aren't relevant because visitors looking for gold tennis balls are extremely unlikely to buy an expensive tennis bracelet.

Quality keywords and keyphrases are more likely to lead to conversions, which is the name of the game. So you don't want to merely know what keywords and keyphrases are the most popular. You want to know what keywords and keyphrases are bringing *bona fide* customers to your site.

When you sit down to analyze your keywords popularity to plan your PPC spend, don't limit yourself to what's on the chart. You might need to consider using some new search terms based on new products or services. You also might need to retire popular search terms that don't lead to conversions. There is a whole industry devoted to SEO for a reason. Don't make the mistake of making assumptions based on popularity contest alone. Compare your data with other statistics to get the whole picture.

Funnel Vision Offers a Quick Fix

Like graphs and charts, your funnel report can be fun. The *conversion funnel* outlines a series of linear steps a visitor takes toward a transaction, such as an e-commerce sale or a newsletter subscription. In other words, the conversion funnel shows you many of your visitors expressed interest in your widgets, how many put the widget into the virtual cart, and how many carts were pushed through the checkout lane to seal the deal. Here's the pitfall: Visitors don't always walk in a straight line, and the funnel doesn't offer insight into why they abandoned you midstream.

Like a funnel that you use to pour the contents of a large jug of water into a small bottle of water, the funnel merely channels the flow. The large jug of water represents the myriad of customers who enter your Web site with high hopes of finding what they are looking for. The small bottle represents the few who actually found it and purchased it. Each stage of the funnel gets narrower, winnowing out those who exited before conversion. Funnel vision, though, isn't broad enough to show you how many times the visitor clicked around your site looking for the right color, size, shape, or other product characteristic before the put the item in the shopping cart.

The visitor might exit the shopping cart temporarily to shop for more items, to read the return policy, or to check the shipping charges. That act clogs the linear flow of the funnel, and some funnel reports will put the cap back on the gallon water bottle and start over again. That makes it impossible to truly determine your conversion rate because one visitor is split into two. You can't make smart decisions based only on the funnel because it only tells you half the story, at best. Advanced Web analytics programs offer more robust funnel reports that address some of these issues. Once again, though, just like charts and graphs, relying on funnel reports alone could be a fatal flaw.

Betting the Farm on Top 10 Lists

Billboard magazine, *The New York Times* and even late night show host David Letterman have conditioned us to look to Top 10 lists when making decisions about what to listen to, what to buy, and, well, what to laugh at. Web analytics reports have no lack of Top 10 lists of their own. You can get a list of the Top 10 countries, the Top 10 referrers, the Top 10 robots, and so on.

The keywords and referrer lists are two of the most popular of the popularity records because they tell you what led traffic to your site. Just like keyword popularity alone won't win any conversion prices, these Top 10 lists shouldn't dictate your decision-making, either. Digging for statistical treasure requires deeper excavation because barring any major changes on your Web site, the Top 10 remain fairly constant. It's the trends that are developing below the surface that help you see where small changes could pay big dividends. For example, the 20th most popular keyphrase might lead to more conversions than #3. Following that path of reasoning, the 100th most popular site referrer could actually be the one that pays the bills.

Your goal with Web analytics is to identify the best traffic, and that usually comes from the most targeted efforts. If home-and-garden bloggers are raving about your selection of exotic fertilizer, this accidental viral marketing probably won't bring you large volumes of traffic because the viewing audience is much smaller than the overall online population. Still, the traffic you receive from those blogging recommendations is prequalified. The pump has been primed, and conversions are far more likely even though the blog never makes it in your Top 10 list, or even your Top 50.

The more site referrers you have, the deeper you need to go in your search for statistical treasure. If you have 5,000 site referrers, consider using Web analytics software to help you see how the list is changing from month to month. ClickTracks (www.clicktracks.com) offers a feature called *The What's Changed Report* that quickly tells you just that — what's changed in the past day, week, or month.

Chapter 18

Ten Reasons Why Web Analytics Will Revolutionize E-Business

- -

In This Chapter

▶ Two revolutionary user-oriented action plans

▶ Four revolutionary search and marketing tactics

▶ Four revolutionary sales strategies

- -

*R*evolutionary. It's a term that's almost overused in today's world. You hear about revolutionary new medicines and revolutionary new diets and even revolutionary new laundry detergents. When writing this book, we almost hesitated to use the word *revolutionary* in connection with Web analytics. But then we figured, heck — this is one place where it actually fits. Web analytics is a revolutionary practice that can transform an e-business from an ugly online frog to an Internet prince almost as fast as a fair maiden can pucker up.

Well, okay, maybe not quite that fast. Web analytics does require diligent analysis followed by persistent action with ongoing measurement, testing, measurement, testing, and so on. However, Web analytics doesn't need to take years or even months to pay off. You can see the revolutionary effects of this software on your Web site in weeks — or, in some instances, even days — if you make smart decisions according to the data.

There is little doubt from industry analysts, online marketing gurus, or savvy Internet entrepreneurs that Web analytics will revolutionize e-business as we know it. In fact, it already has for those who have tapped into the power that this knowledge offers. That knowledge is ever increasing with new iterations of these powerful software tools that offer a behind-the-scenes look at customer behavior.

If you still don't believe in the power of Web analytics to transform your e-business, consider this: Google and Microsoft are making their moves in this arena. These companies are known for revolutionary products in their respective fields. Still need some convincing? Take a look at these top ten reasons — oh, there are many more than ten — that Web analytics will revolutionize your e-business.

Truly Develop a User-Oriented Web Site

User-friendly sites were once all the rage. Guess what? They still are. Web analytics can revolutionize your e-business with insights that help you develop a user-optimized site. Your analytics program can reveal what browsers your visitors use, what version of JavaScript they run, what operating systems they use, what their screen resolution and color quality are, what country they are visiting from, and other important metrics.

Different browsers display your Web site differently. Unfortunately, different is not always better. A site that looks great in Microsoft's Internet Explorer browser may not even function in Apple's Safari browser. And a site that adheres to the strict Firefox requirements might look skewed in some of the lesser-known browsers, like Opera.

If you discover that the vast majority of your visitors are viewing your site in a certain browser, consider optimizing your site for that browser and cut your losses on the others. If many of your visitors don't have the latest version of Flash, remove those dazzling elements. Sometimes a site with less dazzle performs better because it offers a friendlier user experience. Although many Webmasters want to build sites with animated eye candy, creating a Web site that converts visitors to customers should always be the priority.

By the same token, you can also use Web analytics to analyze the *clickstream* (the recorded path, page by page, of the pages a visitor requested while navigating through a Web site) and make the navigation through your site more user-friendly. Certain navigational paths inevitably generate more conversions than others. User-friendly sites offer a straight line between point A and point B. In other words, don't make your visitors take detours on their journey to the point of conversion by throwing up untargeted advertisements, unnecessary registration forms, or other obstacles that might cause them to abandon the transaction.

Make the Most of Online Marketing

Whether you are engaged in *guerilla marketing* — unconventional marketing tactics designed to get maximum results from minimal resources — or you spend a tidy sum on traditional online advertising tactics, Web analytics can revolutionize your e-business by helping you make the most of it.

Your goal with online marketing campaigns is to see them generate more money than they cost. Web analytics clarifies your Return on Marketing Investment (ROMI). Before Web analytics, online advertisers figured about half their efforts were paying off — they just weren't sure which half. Web analytics offers the ultimate accountability. If a certain campaign is sucking your bank account dry, you can turn off the vacuum and reinvest in another promotion.

Web analytics is revolutionary because it offers a crystal clear window into what works and what doesn't with greater accuracy than you could ever dream of with offline advertising measurements. What's more, online Web analytics can add value to your offline marketing efforts. All you have to do is use a simple but unique URL in the ad that is used only for a particular campaign.

If you want to measure the effect of magazine ads that sell your new online-only special travel packages, simply create a special URL for that campaign and track the responses by using your handy-dandy Web analytics program to measure traffic, unique visitors, length of stay and, ultimately, conversions. You can take it a step further by comparing that magazine ad with keyword campaigns by linking your *paid search* or *pay per click* (PPC) ad traffic (visitors who are drawn to the site through search engine listings that you pay for) to a different URL with the same promotion. It doesn't take a brain surgeon to cut into the comparison and extract the data that matters.

Save Money on Paid Search Campaigns

PPC is all the rage because it drives targeted traffic to your Web site. The quest to discover which words are driving traffic, which words are driving conversion, and which words are plain ol' duds has shed new light on Web analytics in recent years.

The first order of business is to stop wasting money. One key to efficient PPC campaigns is to first understand which keywords and keyphrases are already driving *organic search* traffic to your site (and which ones are driving conversions). Organic search retrieves results by indexing pages based on content and keyword relevancy. If you pay for search terms that don't historically lead to conversions, you're throwing good money after poor keywords.

The second order of business is to start saving money. PPC depends on sponsored links displayed in a shaded box above the organic search results, or in a column to the right. Doubtless, PPC campaigns drive traffic and often convert to customers. However, searchers know that you paid for this placement and might choose to give more credibility to listings in the organic search box. Unless your PPC campaign is highly targeted and hits the bull's-eye, it will either be ignored, or it will waste your money because the visitors click the link — and you will pay for that — before realizing that your site doesn't have what they are looking for.

This second order is one big reason why so much focus is being put on *search engine optimization* (SEO), which is tweaking your current Web pages and creating new Web pages in hopes of getting ranked higher in the search engines. For a fraction of the cost, you can rely on this technique to produce unpaid search rankings that drive qualified leads to your site. For many Web site owners, this might prove to be a better long-term investment than PPC.

 Google launched Google Sitemaps service in mid-2005 to help Web site owners keep their content current in its search engine index. Google won't admit that its *sitemap* — pages that link to all the other pages on the Web site — has any effect on your page rank, but ensuring that all your pages appear in Google's index with a properly formatted sitemap certainly can't hurt. Visit here for more information about this program:

```
www.google.com/webmasters/sitemaps
```

Online tools like XML-Sitemaps.com that let Web site owners create a Google site map for free have sprung up in response to the Google Sitemaps offering. However, Webmasters have been creating HTML sitemaps for years. If you are wondering why you should bother, consider this: These sitemaps enable search engine spiders to find pages — even the ones linked deep into your site that may otherwise go unnoticed — more quickly.

Cross-Sell and Up-Sell Your Customers

Web analytics is revolutionizing e-business because it identifies ways to optimize your merchandising schemes. Think of a grocery store. There may not be a rhyme, but there is a good reason why retailers choose to combine food types on the same aisle. Dozens of varieties of bread are displayed right next to the peanut butter. On that same aisle, you are likely to find cereal, breakfast bars, grits, and oatmeal. You might even find coffee, tea, creamers, artificial sweeteners, and other things that lend themselves to breakfast fare.

The grocery store gurus know that if you are buying bread, you might also be in the market for peanut butter. If you are buying grits, you might also have a craving for toast and jelly. Of course, what breakfast would be complete without coffee? You could certainly argue that bread might be better positioned next to the deli, and you'd be right. That's why grocery stores stock French bread, pumpernickel, and other varieties there. But they also stock pickles, specialty mustards, and other condiments — sandwich-y *accoutrements*. Are you beginning to get the picture?

Grocery stores *cross-sell* — sell related products or services over and above the original intended purpose — and *up-sell* — sell customers a higher-priced version of the product they intended to purchase. That's why it's so difficult to get out of the grocery store with just those five items on your list.

Web analytics offers insight into how to optimize your merchandizing efforts on product pages. With this data in hand, you can determine which products people purchase together. The trends you uncover might surprise you. After you discover that visitors who bought a sweater also purchased a scarf, you can make changes to your site so that the scarves and sweaters are displayed on the same page. If you have a content site, you can analyze what content departments readers flow between the most. If most of them jump from news directly to sports, it behooves you to make sure your navigation makes it as easy as possible for them to get from one place to another.

Realize Real-Time Opportunities

From instant grits to instant messaging, the whole world wants what they want — and now. Web analytics can revolutionize your e-business by offering opportunities to dissect revenue-generating data in real-time and avoid costly mistakes. Think of it as on-demand actionable data available second by second, as it happens.

Sophisticated programs show you in the here and now where your most profitable customers are coming from. You can immediately glean what content or product pages they are flocking to at any given moment and make changes to your pages on the fly to accommodate daily trends. You will know right away which of your banner ads and keywords promotions are paying dividends so you can decide whether to add more dollars to a particular campaign budget or shut down the promotion for the day.

Imagine if your landing page was throwing an error that was hurting sales of your best-selling product. Real-time Web analytics lets you fix site errors as soon as they occur. Real-time analytics also helps you detect and deter *click fraud,* which fraud occurs when someone purposely clicks your PPC ad listings with no intention to buy from you.

Combating Controversial Click Fraud

There's been plenty of technology news headlines — as well as at least a couple of lawsuits — over the click fraud issue. The clicks can be generated using by *hitbots* or *clickbots,* which are programs that automatically click PPC ads or manually click the link over and over again.

Here are two clear motives for this scam, depending on who is committing it. One, a competitor might click your PPC ads repeatedly to exhaust your advertising budget so that he can benefit from the traffic. Or, it could be an affiliate marketer clicking-through on links from his site to drum up revenue.

Web analytics is revolutionizing e-business by combating controversial click fraud. A variety of indicators can give you a heads-up on suspicious activity in your PPC campaign. If you see an increased number of clicks from countries like Romania (.cn) or India (.in), you might be the target of click fraud. If you see repeat visitors from the same IP address, you might be the target of click fraud. Other suspicious signs are one-page visitors, clicks at unusual hours, visitors who do not accept cookies, and short time-spans on site. Of course, any of these metrics could be legitimate. In combination, though, they could be costly.

Closing the Delayed Conversion Loop

Here's a nagging question in the back of the minds of many entrepreneurs who have both a brick-and-mortar presence and an online channel: How do you tell whether the customer did research online before shopping in the store? The same question holds true for lead generators: Did they learn about your services online before picking up the phone? Web analytics can revolutionize your e-business by tracking what some have called delayed conversions. Just like it sounds, *delayed conversions* are conversions that start online but close offline.

Without understanding the concept of delayed conversions, you might get the idea that that high-cost traffic you've been paying for is a waste and thus stop marketing just at the brink of financial breakthrough. Likewise, with no knowledge of how many of your customers actually began the product or service education process online, you might change navigational paths, rearrange graphical elements, or even undergo an entire site design — all unnecessarily. You've heard the old adage, "If it ain't broke, don't fix it." Well, remaining ignorant to delayed conversions could cause you to break something that is working quite well.

The good news is that you can close the delayed conversion loop. Your Web site can feature a unique toll-free number so that any calls (and sales) coming through that number are sure to have come as the result of Web research. Another popular method involves creating special promotional codes that are available only on the Web site, and then tracking how many of them close. With a little help from a knowledgeable Web programmer, those promotional codes can be tracked back to their online referral source, revealing the quality of the leads coming to your site through various means, whether PPC, organic search, link exchanges, banner ads, or some other promotional activity.

Now you can focus your efforts on the sources that offer the most conversions: immediate or delayed. You can also determine how the quality of the leads generated through your Web site compare with the quality of the leads generated by any one of the other offline marketing methods you are using. You can even compare the length of time it takes for an online generated lead with the time it takes a Yellow Page ad to convert. Getting the whole story might take a few months, but it's worth listening to.

Optimize Self-Support Functions

If making money while you sleep is a dream come true, not having to answer support calls the rest of the time is the ultimate fantasy. Indeed, customer self-service is the Holy Grail of Internet business. Maintaining a large call center is such a costly task.

The Internet has inspired all sorts of innovative technologies designed to do away with traditional customer support functions, such as FAQs, searchable Q&A databases, and customer chat boards. Unfortunately, many dreams turned into nightmares after companies poured big money into customer self-service sites that failed to reduce traditional support call volumes. The bottom line with customer self-service is this: If the user can't find the answers he needs online, he'll pick up the phone and give you a call.

Web analytics can revolutionize e-business by offering key insights into why users weren't able to find the answers they were looking for. Web analytics identifies where the process broke down. Did your internal site search function fail to yield relevant results? Or did the answer itself fail to satisfy the customer's curiosity? Could it be possible that the answer was not to be found at all?

There are countless reasons why self-support functions fail, but proper use of Web analytics helps you understand where the breakdowns occur so that you can build a bridge to true self-support. Although the dream of eliminating call centers entirely might not have been realistic from the beginning, it certainly is possible to significantly reduce the number of support calls your team has to field by using Web analytics to fine tune your online support functions.

Increase Results from E-Mail Campaigns

According to JupiterResearch, Web analytics can make a dramatic effect on targeted e-mail campaigns. According to a Jupiter study, using Web analytics to target e-mail campaigns can produce 9 times the revenues and 18 times the profits of broadcast mailings. (Yes, we said *18 times* the profits.)

David Daniels, a research director for the New York–based research firm, says the study proves that spam and the cluttered inbox have not killed the e-mail medium for marketers. A clear messaging strategy that is built off a lifecycle relationship-driven approach still offers tremendous value.

However, as Jupiter noted, few marketers are sending highly contextually targeted e-mail campaigns. Most are using broadcast and basic personalization tactics that do little to make these marketing messages highly relevant. According to Daniels, the failure of Customer Relationship Management (CRM) systems to centralize all customer insights haunts e-mail marketing; and, in many respects, relegates it to a second-class medium. Because the lack of integrated customer data is the top challenge for large marketers, he adds, these data deficiencies bind many of them to relatively simplistic targeting tactics.

Here's how Web analytics will revolutionize e-mail campaigns: by using clickstream data. With clickstream data, targeted e-mail campaigns on average produced open rates of 33 percent, click-through rates of 14 percent, and conversion rates of 3.9 percent, Jupiter revealed. That compares with average open rates of 20 percent, click-through rates of 0.5 percent, and conversion rates of 1.1 percent for mass mailings.

Better results come at higher costs. There is much more labor involved in applying Web analytics to track e-mail campaigns. According to Jupiter, the average total salary budgets for campaigns using clickstream targeting are 2.5 times higher than those of marketers using mass-mailing campaigns. The average cost per message totals $4.50, excluding Web analytics costs, compared with $3 for untargeted mailings. Overall, Jupiter concluded that the additional costs were worthwhile, pointing to e-tailer Newport-News.com and its six-fold improvement in revenue after using Web analytics to target browsers of three of its worst-performing product categories.

Predict the Future Here and Now

There is no such thing as a crystal ball in the world of Web analytics, but there are predictive analytics, which can revolutionize your e-business. *Predictive analytics* is a type of data mining that focuses on predicting future possibilities and trends. Predictive analytics vendor SSPS (www.spss.com) translates it this way: Predictive analytics ensures that the actions you take today will directly achieve your organization's goals tomorrow.

Predictive analytics works on the premise that there are scores of critical decisions to make at any given moment. Any one of those decisions could impact your ability to convert visitors into profitable customers, members, or readers. Predictive analytics analyzes the mountains of behind-the-scenes Web site data, combines information on past circumstances, present events and projected future actions, and then automates the decision-making process.

Predictive analytics can lead to greater cross-selling, lower marketing costs, reduced click fraud, or increased PPC response rates. Sure, you can gain those advantages by analyzing the data yourself and taking an educated guess, but the beauty of predictive analytics is that it does the heavy lifting for you. This software can predict product preferences and purchasing habits and create relevant marketing messages and target marketing at its best. It's fact-based decision making plain and simple. It's revolutionary because it automates the process so you won't risk drowning in an ocean of statistics.

According to analyst firm IDC (www.idc.com), "Predictive analytic projects yield a median ROI of 145 percent." Of course, the cost of predictive analytics is probably out of reach for most entrepreneurs today, but the good news is that just like other technologies, the prices will eventually come down. When they do, predictive analytics could make one of the biggest impacts on e-business since e-business was birthed. Predictive analytics goes beyond telling you what happened on your Web site last month to what is likely to happen next quarter.

Chapter 19

Ten Web Analytics Best Practices

In This Chapter

▶ Five ways to tie your data into your business objectives.

▶ Five metrics that deserve extra special attention.

*W*eb analytics makes a promise to its users — to capture mountains of data about customer behavior — and the technology never breaks its promise. However, the data is only as good as the person interpreting it.

The good news is that you don't have to figure out the best way to take action on the data you've gathered in a vacuum. Web analytics is a young industry, but it's old enough to have an industry association, a cadre of experts, and some established best practices. You can implement those best practices to get the best possible results from your Web optimization initiatives. In fact, one of the leading Web analytics providers, Omniture (www.omniture.com), launched the industry's first Web analytics best practices group in 2004. The group offers services and methodologies designed to address and drive online marketing return on investment (ROI), ranging from strategic planning and rapid implementations to enterprise marketing optimization.

If you're wondering just how important best practices are, consider what market research firm Gartner's (www.gartner.com) Principal Analyst Bill Gassman said: "As companies acquire or reevaluate a Web analytics solution, many are finding that they don't have the internal skills and resources to quickly and effectively implement online marketing and merchandising strategies. Yet, that expertise is important for maximizing the success of their strategies. The companies that incorporate Web analytic tools in recurring cross-organizational processes, not just occasional projects, will see the highest returns from their Web channel investments. To achieve better results, more quickly and effectively, companies should consider using external expertise to learn about best practices and principles."

Trust us: We're all for getting external expertise when needed. But if you implement the ten best practices we cite in this chapter, you'll be well on your way to becoming an expert yourself.

Define Metrics That Matter

Web analytics can generate mind-boggling amounts of data. Even simple programs offer enough metrics to keep you busy staying in tune with keywords that work and site referrers that succeed in driving traffic for days on end. And the pages and pages of reports that sophisticated programs have to offer could intimidate even the most daring number crunchers.

Whether you use the freebie software or the most expensive enterprise-class technology on the market, your ability to make decisions boils down to measuring the data that matters. After all, you need more than information: You need interpretations that offer actionable insights. Actionable insights are found in the realm of *key performance indicators* (KPIs), which illustrate how well the site is performing against goals. You can read much more about KPIs in Chapter 11.

Here's where many novice Web analytics interpreters miss it: They don't connect the KPIs to clear business goals. Failing to make that critical connection is like starting on a long journey with no map and no address through the countryside to visit grandma's new house. You might see some pretty scenery along the way, but you won't know which way to go or whether you've arrived. In other words, you'll waste a lot of time and money and probably end up frustrated to boot.

Some people go online for fun, and others go online for money. Either way, Web analytics works best when it's tied to your goals. The funster may just want to build a community of friends. The entrepreneur has monetary motives in mind. Ask yourself the following questions to outline your business objectives:

- Is my goal to drive online sales?
- Is my goal to generate traffic so I can win advertisers' hearts?
- Is my goal to generate qualified sales leads for my services?
- Is my goal to streamline customer service so customers can find fast answers or even engage in total self-service?
- How will I know when I've accomplished my goals?

The answers to these questions will help you define the metrics that matter. Then you can monitor only your most vital KPIs.

Monitor Only Your Vital KPIs

There are scads — and scads and scads — of KPIs you *could* monitor. If you are like most time-strapped entrepreneurs, the majority of these metrics will never even become a blip on your radar screen. Realistically, the choice between combing through every last possible metric your Web analytics software offers or keeping up with the PPC campaigns that are generating paying customers is no choice at all.

Your goal is to monitor the most vital KPIs. Think of yourself as an emergency medic. These harried healthcare professionals check a patient's vital signs — the blood pressure, heart rate, breathing, and so on. What we are saying is this: If you have time to monitor many different KPIs, go ahead. But if you're like most Web site owners, you are better off identifying the most vital KPIs to keep your finger on the pulse on the health of your Web site.

✔ If your goal is to drive online sales, you'll want to pay attention to KPIs that illustrate revenue, orders, profit, conversion rates, revenue per visit, profit per visit, and average order.

✔ If you're an online content portal whose goal is to generate traffic so you can win advertisers' hearts, you need to concentrate on KPIs like the average pageview per visit, the percent of returning visitors, conversion rate through subscriptions, registrations, log ins, cancellations, and overall *pageviews* (a record of each time a visitor views a Web page on your site).

✔ For lead generators who seek qualified prospects, you need to focus on KPIs that highlight leads, cost per lead, conversion rate, newsletter sign-ups, partner referrals, registrations, demo quotes, price quotes, or materials download. You'll also need to keep a close eye on KPIs such as Web inquiries per visit, call center volume, and support inquiries if you hope to measure how effective your online customer support efforts are.

These best practices save you time by getting down to the bottom line in a hurry. You can read much more about KPIs in Chapter 11.

Segment Your Visitors' Behavior

If you've boned up on your Web analytics vocabulary, you know that *segmentation* is the grouping of customers based on visitor behavior. Some people call these *groups clusters*. Still others call them *customer segments, visitor labeling,* or *visitor profiling*. Web analytics vendor WebTrends (www.webtrends.com) characterizes this tactic as a "powerful aspect of relationship marketing in which you target sub-sections or groups of customers who share a specific trait or set of behaviors."

Don't worry too much about what to call this tactic — just do it. Visitor segmentation has been used in the offline world for decades to increase customer retention and increase top line sales. Several, but not all, Web analytics applications make it oh-so-easy to implement this strategy online. (So be sure to ask about this feature before you plunk down your dollars.) You can segment your visitors by where they came from before they entered your site, by particular actions such as downloading a white paper, by what page they landed on inside your site, and more. The possibilities are virtually endless.

After you segregate your visitors into nice and neat categories, you can take a closer look at the activity of users in that segment, such as time spent on site and conversion rates. You might find that visitors who download a white paper from your site are twice as likely to become customers as those who don't. You might find that visitors who came to your site through a Google search behaved quite differently than visitors who came to your site through Yahoo!, MSN, or some niche search engine.

Check out these telling metrics to examine to determine which user groups are helping you pay the bills:

✔ Which group of visitors was most likely to convert?

✔ What content did they view?

✔ What promotional campaigns did they respond to?

✔ Are they return or first-time visitors?

✔ Do members of that group spend longer on your site than other segments?

Armed with this information, you can target these segments with special campaigns or make changes to the site based on perceived user preferences.

Know Your Navigation Report

Until the World Wide Web became mainstream, navigation reports were reserved for Christopher Columbus types who used them to avoid winding up on a deserted island where headhunters lay in wait of fresh trophies. Okay, so you won't shipwreck if you ignore your online navigation report, but you might very well miss out on some buried statistical treasure.

Also known as a *clickstream,* a *navigation report* reveals the order in which your visitors click through your Web site and how long they stay on each page. The report also shows at a glance the percentage of visitors who clicked each link as well as where those visitors came from, such as a search engine or a link partner. Reviewing this report can offer insights into which products, content, or other pages were most interesting to any given customer.

The navigation report, then, helps you determine which pages are the most popular. You can also calculate the return on investment on your pay per click (PPC) budget by comparing the traffic volumes that each search engine sent to a particular page. Maybe you're a bookstore trying to drive traffic to a landing page that features all your releases. The navigation report tells you in no uncertain terms whether your keywords and keyphrases generated traffic or whether you should go back to the drawing board. This same report shows you whether that clickstream flows through to the shopping cart and a sale was completed.

As you review your navigation report, put on your customer-colored glasses. You want to see a smooth flow through your site from one section to the next. It should be logical. If your navigation report shows that visitors are rapid-fire clicking through the pages on your site, perhaps the navigational elements of your site need some fine-tuning. Maybe your site hierarchy makes sense to you but confuses visitors. And confused visitors can be difficult to convert into paying customers.

Keep Up With Keyword Campaigns

With the potentially high cost of PPC campaigns, you'd be a fool not to use your Web analytics tools to provide additional insight into your PPC advertising. Also called *paid search,* this method retrieves search listings based on who paid the most money for keywords to appear at the top of the heap.

First, failing to track which keyphrases drive paying customers to your site could leave you with loads of traffic but no sales. If you are serious about paid search as a business-building strategy, you need to know what works — and what doesn't.

Second, you should track which PPC vendors provide the best value. Don't fall into the trap of the low-priced keywords that some PPC vendors offer. It doesn't matter whether you can buy traffic for a penny per click if none of that traffic converts. Use visitor segmentation to group your visitors by PPC vendor and compare the results to weed out the poor performers.

Some Web analytics programs, like ClickTracks (www.clicktracks.com), offer a *campaign report*. This eliminates some of the heavy data digging by showing you metrics such as how many users spent less than five seconds on the site. If they spent less than five seconds on the site, they saw nothing of interest and moved on. This report also offers an ROAS, or *return on advertising spend,* which is a ratio between the cost of a campaign and the revenue that it generates.

Third, watch your PPC search terms. With the introduction of *advanced matching* — displaying your PPC ads for keywords that are similar or related to the keywords you bid on — some advertisers are surprised to learn that they are paying for traffic that isn't helping their Web site goals.

To illustrate this point, pretend you want to sell bricks online. Yes, they are heavy, and the shipping costs are prohibitive (to put it politely). (We've seen worse ideas.) You launch PPC advertising campaign on several of the most popular search engines. You bid on the term, or keyword, *brick.* Because you sell many different colors, shapes, and sizes of bricks, you get a bright idea: Turn on advanced matching in case people search for *bricks, yellow bricks,* or *circular bricks.*

That might have seemed like a bright idea at the time, but your keyword reports belie your brains. Your Web analytics data show that you are also paying for visitors searching for free bricks, brick making, ceramic bricks, and other terms that you end up paying for through the nose. The problem is you don't sell any of those items — and you don't give them away for free, either. So the visitors comes to your site sand probably see nothing of value.

The takeaway: Advanced matching can be a good thing, or it can bankrupt your ad campaign in a flash. If you decide to experiment with this feature, keep a constant eye on your Web analytics to make sure you aren't wasting money on unrelated common words that people use in conjunction with your keywords of choice. Most search engines let you set *negative matches* on your PPC campaigns. With these, you could specifically exclude the words that are irrelevant to your potential visitors (like *free, making,* and *ceramic* in the preceding example) and save a bundle o' cash.

Optimize Your Landing Pages

On the World Wide Web, Home Sweet Home is not the name of the revenue game. What we mean by that is most of your traffic might not land on your home page. So although we recommend that you make your home page user-friendly and visually appealing, don't stop there. Every other page on your site should be just as pretty and easy to navigate as the home page.

Don't take our word for it. See for yourself. On your Web analytics report, you will notice that many users enter your site from pages other than the home page. Although in most cases, the home page is indeed the single most popular page on a site, you might find that most of your search traffic doesn't come directly to your home page. When it comes to Net surfers searching for information, most of them will land somewhere within the confines of the site. Consider each of those "somewheres" a landing page.

With only so many hours in the day, focusing too much energy on your home page could leave you with ineffective landing pages — the very pages where you display your products or make a pitch for your services. If you spend money on PPC campaigns that send visitors to your product pages, concentrating on landing pages makes even more sense.

- ✔ Test different headlines.
- ✔ Test different call to action sizes and placements.
- ✔ Test different product images.
- ✔ Test different copy lengths.
- ✔ Test various special offers.
- ✔ Try adding reviews and testimonials.

Calculate Visitor Conversion

Much has been said about conversion rates, and much more will be said in the future. In fact, we've said it before and we'll say it again: Converting visitors into customers (or qualified leads, subscribers, and so on) is the overarching purpose of most Web sites today. Sure, if you are merely blogging for fun or posting an old-fashioned online billboard for your company, calculating the conversion rate may not be on your Top 10 list of best practices. But for the vast majority of Web site owners, conversions are critical.

Your *conversion rate* is the percentage of visitors who complete a desired action. That could be buying a shirt, filling out a form, subscribing to a newsletter, or some other target activity. If your goal is to get people to fill out a form so you can build a mailing list, the conversion rate is the number visitors who fill out the form divided by your total number of visitors. If you are selling a shirt, your conversion rate is the total number of transactions divided by your total number of visitors. For a more in-depth look at conversion rates read Chapter 11 for the lowdown on understanding KPIs.

Don't worry about someone else's numbers. An outstanding conversion rate for one site might be a poor conversion rate for another. Just benchmark where you are at and compare the rates from week to week as you make changes to your site. If you still want to know some general rule, try this: If your conversion rate is less than one percent, your site could use some improvement. Your priority should be to invest time and energy into making site improvements.

Save Your Historical Data

Looking back at your traffic numbers from when you first launched your Web site five years ago can be fun — and even quite funny. Surely, your traffic has grown exponentially, and you have much more data to dissect today than you did way back when. Reviewing your early metrics is more than a stroll down Memory Lane, though — it's smart business because your historical data could hold keys to Web analytics success.

True, how your Web site performs today is what matters most. However, it's also absolutely true that looking back to last year's data — or even data from two, three, or five years ago — can illustrate trends, for better or worse. In fact, this historical perspective might be the only way to fully comprehend how serious those slightly downward trends in your KPIs really are.

Maybe you've been losing a fraction of a second in the average time spent on site each week for the past two years. Your monthly reports don't offer much cause for concern, adding the effects of that downward trend it over a year or two can send you reaching for the aspirin bottle and your Web designer's phone number.

By contrast, perhaps you've seen a net gain in a critical KPI, such as your conversion rate per repeat visitor. In that case, you should be celebrating instead of messing with the design too much. The point is this: Sometimes the only way to truly determine how well your site is performing is to put the data into historical context. For more reading on this topic, turn to Chapter 12.

Make Changes Gradually

Knowledge might indeed be power, but you have to use that power to make an effect. As you begin to put the power of behind-the-scenes visitor behavior in action, be sure to take it one step at a time. Say your traffic is anemic, your average time per visit is a split second, and your conversion rate is, well, non-existent. What's a Web site entrepreneur to do?

You might be tempted to do an entire site redesign — and in some cases, that's not a bad idea. Or maybe you just launched a site redesign, complete with eye-pleasing graphics, award-winning copywriting, and plenty of high-tech bells and whistles, but your metrics are worse than ever. You have little idea what you did to make it worse and probably no idea how to make it better.

No matter whether you are in dire straits or just want to get more from a site that is already performing well, your best practice is to start where you are and make changes gradually. With each set of changes, monitor your KPIs to see how your fiddling affected your site's vital signs over the course of a month. If the changes helped, hold steady. If they made matters worse, revert to the original game plan and set out to test another set of changes.

You could make all sorts of changes to your site that could pay dividends. The most important conceptual changes include the following:

- Make sure your visitors know what you're selling.

- Make sure your Web site is communicating your unique value proposition, or what makes your service/product/offering better than your competition.

- Build trust and credibility through testimonials, certifications, awards, and so on.

Commit to Continual Improvement

Your Web site is running like Michael Johnson in the 2000 Olympic Games — fast, furious, and profitably. Watch out! A busy schedule might lure you into a state of complacency, and your competitor could catch a second wind, come from behind, and steal the winner's wreath from right off your head. Instead of staring proudly at that gold medal in the trophy case, get back on the Web analytics track and try to break your own world's record for most unique visitors in a month, longest average time on site, or some other vital KPI that will boost your online success.

Web analytics is more than just a measurement tool; rather, it's an ongoing process of driving value from your Web site. Committing to continual improvement means measuring the effect of every change you make to the Web site. It means analyzing the performance of every new product, service, or content you add. Likewise, it means looking for areas where your KPIs are dropping off and also digging through the data to find out why.

Committing to continual improvement does not mean making changes to your Web site just for the sake of making changes to your Web site. Any time you enact a design change, remove content, add features, or make any other change — no matter how big or small — you should have a good reason. You should also forecast the anticipated impact of those changes. Are you moving the Subscribe Now button because the response has been poor? Then you would naturally expect that its new location should produce a greater conversion rate. Any and all changes you make should be in line with your business goals, and their effects should be measured.

Appendix

Web Analytics Glossary

A/B testing: Comparing visitor response to two different versions of your site and measuring the effect that each one makes on conversions.

abandonment: When a visitor leaves your site in the midst of a transaction.

acquisition: Attracting visitors to a Web site by using various advertising and marketing strategies.

actionable data: Information that offers an accurate foundation on which to make decisions about changes to your Web site, search engine marketing, or customer relationship management strategies.

Active Server Pages (ASP): A server-side scripting language developed by Microsoft to run on a Web server.

advanced matching: Displaying your paid search ads for keywords that are similar or related to the keywords you bid on.

affiliate marketing: An advertising system in which Web site owners, search engine marketers, and e-mail marketers promote companies in return for a commission on sales.

after-click tracking (ACT): Also called *path analysis, clickstream,* or *navigational analysis.* This is simply a study of the paths visitors take through your site.

aggregate data: A summary of the information that your Web analytics program collects.

Apache: Popular Web server software.

Application Programming Interface (API): A language and format that one software program uses to communicate with another software program.

application service provider (ASP): A company that charges a monthly fee to host applications; an alternative software delivery method in which customers rent rather than buy software.

authenticated user: Users who are required to log in, such as subscribers or members.

authentication: A process that requires users to enter a username or password to identify themselves to gain access to a Web site's resources.

average lifetime value (ALV): An individual visitor's lifetime value in monetary terms. ALV is determined by tracking past orders.

AWStats: A popular, free Web analytics application that displays traffic logs graphically.

bandwidth: The amount of data that is transferred to and from a Web site.

bandwidth allotted: The amount of data that a Web host allows a customer to transfer to and from a Web site in a given period of time. Customers may vary amounts for hosting accounts with varying bandwidth allotments.

banner ad: An advertisement that's displayed on a Web page.

benchmark: A clearly defined point of reference from which measurements can be made.

bounce rate: The percentage of entrances on any individual page that results in the visitor's immediate exit from the site.

browsing a directory: Viewing all the files within a particular subfolder.

bytes: A unit of measurement for data.

captcha: An acronym for Completely Automated Public Turing Test to Tell Computers and Humans Apart. Webmasters employ this method to tell computers and humans apart by requiring the user to view a code and type it in an entry box.

click fraud: When someone purposely clicks a paid search ad listing with no intention to buy.

clickstream: The recorded path a visitor takes through your Web site.

clickthrough rate (CTR): Typically used to calculate how often a banner ad is clicked compared with how many times it is viewed.

client-side: Programs that are installed on your computer, just like Microsoft Word or Adobe Photoshop.

control panel: A browser-based Web site management tool.

conversion: Closing the deal; when a visitor becomes a buyer, subscriber, or member; or takes some other desired call to action.

conversion rate: The percentage of visitors who complete a transaction; fill out a membership; or, in the case of lead generation, request additional information.

cookie: Small text files that allow a Web server to store information about visitors and recognize them when they return.

cross-sell: To sell related products or services over and above the original intended purpose.

dashboard: An area in your analytics application, usually the main page, that summarizes basic metrics such as the number of unique visitors and the most popular keywords for a Web site.

dedicated server: A server that you own or rent, which offers you full control.

delayed conversions: Conversions that start online but close offline.

dynamic IP address: An IP address that changes each time a user connects to the Internet.

dynamic pages: Pages that are generated by programming languages such as ASP, PHP, or ColdFusion.

entry page: The page at which the visitor enters a Web site.

exit page: The point at which the navigational path within the site ends; the page on which the visitor leaves the site.

filters: A method of narrowing the scope of a report by defining statistical ranges or data types that should or should not be included.

frequency capping: A feature that allows you to limit the maximum number of impressions/views of an ad that a visitor can see within a defined period of time.

guerilla marketing: Unconventional marketing tactics designed to get maximum results from minimal resources.

hit: A logged record of each time a Web server delivers a file to a visitor's browser.

hitbots: Also called *clickbots;* programs that automatically click paid search ads.

internal site search: A search feature on a Web site that searches only that Web site.

IP (Internet Protocol) address: A unique numeric code assigned by the user's Internet Service Provider (ISP).

JavaScript: A client-side scripting language developed by Netscape.

key performance indicators (KPI): Metrics that indicate how well a site is performing against goals.

keywords and **keyphrases:** The term or terms that searchers enter into the search box of a search engine.

landing page: A specific Web page at which a visitor first arrives in response to organic search or paid search initiatives.

logfile: A data file that records transactions that occurred on the Web server.

long tail: Keywords and keyphrases that individually don't account for much traffic but together can outnumber top keywords.

multivariate testing: A method for testing multiple versions of the same Web site to determine how visitors respond to content, design, and other elements. Multivariate testing is used in Web site or online advertising optimization efforts.

navigation: Clicking from one page to another within a Web site, or sometimes from one Web site to another.

newsgroup: A discussion group that is related to one topic.

nonhuman user: Any visitor that is not an actual person that uses a browser to navigate your site; a robot, a spambot, or some other automated script.

organic search: Unpaid, or natural, search listings.

page display: When a page successfully displays on the visitor's computer screen.

pageview: A record of each time a visitor views a Web page on a site.

paid search: *See* pay per click.

pay per click (PPC): Also called *paid search.* This method retrieves listings based on who paid the most money for keywords to appear at the top of the heap.

phishers: People who trick someone into giving them confidential information or doing something else he or she normally wouldn't do, typically through spam messages that appear legitimate.

ping: Using a program to test whether a particular network destination is online by sending a request and waiting for a response.

platform: The operating system that runs a computer.

predictive analytics: A type of data mining that focuses on predicting possibilities and trends.

proxy: A system that lets several users connect to the Internet through the same IP address at the same time.

query: On advanced Web analytics software, a question posed to the database to get answers to specific metric questions.

raw logfile: A data file that stores information on all requests made to a Web site.

Really Simple Syndication (RSS): A software system that lets users subscribe to content from their favorite Web sites and have it delivered to a feed reader that aggregates it in one convenient location.

referrer spam: A technique that sends traffic to a Web site using fake URLs that show up in the site referrer report. Referrer spam is largely targeted at blogs and sites that publish referrer statistics. The goal of referrer spam is to drive traffic to the spammer's site and increase page rankings in search engines.

referring page: The URL of the previous Web page from which a link was followed.

reverse DNS look-up: Translating IP numbers to domain names to uncode the true referrer.

robot: Also known as *Web crawlers, bots,* or *spiders.* A robot is an automated script or program that browses the Web.

RSS feed readers: Also called *aggregators.* RSS feed readers are software applications or remotely hosted services that collect syndicated content from various Web sites into one program for easy viewing.

search engine marketing (SEM): Increasing the visibility of a Web site in search engines through improving rank in organic listings, purchasing paid listings, or a combination of these and other search engine-related activities.

search engine optimization (SEO): A method of improving the rankings for relevant keywords in search results by making changes to the content or navigational structure of a Web site.

search engine spider: A program or automated script that crawls the Web to update search engine indexes.

segment: A customer group as defined by either a user's activities on a Web site or other strategic data.

segmentation: Grouping customers based on visitor behavior.

SEM: *See* search engine marketing.

SEO: *See* search engine optimization.

server-side application: Software installed on the Web site's server.

session: Also called a *visit.* A session is the period of time from when a visitor logs on to a site to when he exits.

shared server: Web servers that host multiple clients and potentially thousands of Web sites.

shopping cart abandonment rate: Rate at which visitors exits a Web site during the shopping cart process before completing the sale.

site map: Pages that link to all the other pages on the Web site.

site referrer: *See* referring page.

spam: Unsolicited e-mail.

spambot: Automated software programs that collect e-mail addresses for the express purpose of engaging in spam or selling e-mail address lists to spammers.

spiders: *See* search engine spider.

unique visitors: The number of individual people who visit your Web site.

Unix: An operating system well known for its reliability and scalability. Solaris, HP-UX, and AIX are popular Unix operating systems.

up-sell: To sell customers a higher-priced version of the product they intended to purchase.

visit duration: A record of how long an individual stayed on a site.

visitor segmentation: *See* segmentation.

Web 2.0: A loosely defined movement characterized by an ongoing transition of the World Wide Web from a collection of Web sites to a comprehensive computing platform that encourages user involvement and serves Web applications to end users.

Web analytics: Software that analyzes the behavior of site visitors.

Web counters: Scripts or software programs that indicate the number of online visitors.

Web crawlers: *See* search engine spider.

Weblog: Commonly known as *blogs*. These are online journals that require very little technical experience to set up and maintain.

Index

• S •

BUSINESS, CAREERS & PERSONAL FINANCE

Fundraising For Dummies
0-7645-9847-3

Investing For Dummies
0-7645-2431-3

Also available:
- Business Plans Kit For Dummies
0-7645-9794-9
- Economics For Dummies
0-7645-5726-2
- Grant Writing For Dummies
0-7645-8416-2
- Home Buying For Dummies
0-7645-5331-3
- Managing For Dummies
0-7645-1771-6
- Marketing For Dummies
0-7645-5600-2

- Personal Finance For Dummies
0-7645-2590-5*
- Resumes For Dummies
0-7645-5471-9
- Selling For Dummies
0-7645-5363-1
- Six Sigma For Dummies
0-7645-6798-5
- Small Business Kit For Dummies
0-7645-5984-2
- Starting an eBay Business For Dummies
0-7645-6924-4
- Your Dream Career For Dummies
0-7645-9795-7

HOME & BUSINESS COMPUTER BASICS

Laptops For Dummies
0-470-05432-8

Windows Vista For Dummies
0-471-75421-8

Also available:
- Cleaning Windows Vista For Dummies
0-471-78293-9
- Excel 2007 For Dummies
0-470-03737-7
- Mac OS X Tiger For Dummies
0-7645-7675-5
- MacBook For Dummies
0-470-04859-X
- Macs For Dummies
0-470-04849-2
- Office 2007 For Dummies
0-470-00923-3

- Outlook 2007 For Dummies
0-470-03830-6
- PCs For Dummies
0-7645-8958-X
- Salesforce.com For Dummies
0-470-04893-X
- Upgrading & Fixing Laptops For Dummies
0-7645-8959-8
- Word 2007 For Dummies
0-470-03658-3
- Quicken 2007 For Dummies
0-470-04600-7

FOOD, HOME, GARDEN, HOBBIES, MUSIC & PETS

Chess For Dummies
0-7645-8404-9

Guitar For Dummies
0-7645-9904-6

Also available:
- Candy Making For Dummies
0-7645-9734-5
- Card Games For Dummies
0-7645-9910-0
- Crocheting For Dummies
0-7645-4151-X
- Dog Training For Dummies
0-7645-8418-9
- Healthy Carb Cookbook For Dummies
0-7645-8476-6
- Home Maintenance For Dummies
0-7645-5215-5

- Horses For Dummies
0-7645-9797-3
- Jewelry Making & Beading For Dummies
0-7645-2571-9
- Orchids For Dummies
0-7645-6759-4
- Puppies For Dummies
0-7645-5255-4
- Rock Guitar For Dummies
0-7645-5356-9
- Sewing For Dummies
0-7645-6847-7
- Singing For Dummies
0-7645-2475-5

INTERNET & DIGITAL MEDIA

eBay For Dummies
0-470-04529-9

iPod & iTunes For Dummies
0-470-04894-8

Also available:
- Blogging For Dummies
0-471-77084-1
- Digital Photography For Dummies
0-7645-9802-3
- Digital Photography All-in-One Desk Reference For Dummies
0-470-03743-1
- Digital SLR Cameras and Photography For Dummies
0-7645-9803-1
- eBay Business All-in-One Desk Reference For Dummies
0-7645-8438-3
- HDTV For Dummies
0-470-09673-X

- Home Entertainment PCs For Dummies
0-470-05523-5
- MySpace For Dummies
0-470-09529-6
- Search Engine Optimization For Dummies
0-471-97998-8
- Skype For Dummies
0-470-04891-3
- The Internet For Dummies
0-7645-8996-2
- Wiring Your Digital Home For Dummies
0-471-91830-X

Separate Canadian edition also available
Separate U.K. edition also available

Available wherever books are sold. For more information or to order direct: U.S. customers visit www.dummies.com or call 1-877-762-2974.
U.K. customers visit www.wileyeurope.com or call 0800 243407. Canadian customers visit www.wiley.ca or call 1-800-567-4797.

WILEY

SPORTS, FITNESS, PARENTING, RELIGION & SPIRITUALITY

0-471-76871-5   0-7645-7841-3

Also available:

- Catholicism For Dummies
  0-7645-5391-7
- Exercise Balls For Dummies
  0-7645-5623-1
- Fitness For Dummies
  0-7645-7851-0
- Football For Dummies
  0-7645-3936-1
- Judaism For Dummies
  0-7645-5299-6
- Potty Training For Dummies
  0-7645-5417-4
- Buddhism For Dummies
  0-7645-5359-3

- Pregnancy For Dummies
  0-7645-4483-7 †
- Ten Minute Tone-Ups For Dummies
  0-7645-7207-5
- NASCAR For Dummies
  0-7645-7681-X
- Religion For Dummies
  0-7645-5264-3
- Soccer For Dummies
  0-7645-5229-5
- Women in the Bible For Dummies
  0-7645-8475-8

TRAVEL

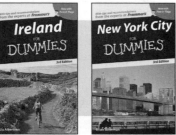

0-7645-7749-2   0-7645-6945-7

Also available:

- Alaska For Dummies
  0-7645-7746-8
- Cruise Vacations For Dummies
  0-7645-6941-4
- England For Dummies
  0-7645-4276-1
- Europe For Dummies
  0-7645-7529-5
- Germany For Dummies
  0-7645-7823-5
- Hawaii For Dummies
  0-7645-7402-7

- Italy For Dummies
  0-7645-7386-1
- Las Vegas For Dummies
  0-7645-7382-9
- London For Dummies
  0-7645-4277-X
- Paris For Dummies
  0-7645-7630-5
- RV Vacations For Dummies
  0-7645-4442-X
- Walt Disney World & Orlando
  For Dummies
  0-7645-9660-8

GRAPHICS, DESIGN & WEB DEVELOPMENT

0-7645-8815-X   0-7645-9571-7

Also available:

- 3D Game Animation For Dummies
  0-7645-8789-7
- AutoCAD 2006 For Dummies
  0-7645-8925-3
- Building a Web Site For Dummies
  0-7645-7144-3
- Creating Web Pages For Dummies
  0-470-08030-2
- Creating Web Pages All-in-One Desk
  Reference For Dummies
  0-7645-4345-8
- Dreamweaver 8 For Dummies
  0-7645-9649-7

- InDesign CS2 For Dummies
  0-7645-9572-5
- Macromedia Flash 8 For Dummies
  0-7645-9691-8
- Photoshop CS2 and Digital
  Photography For Dummies
  0-7645-9580-6
- Photoshop Elements 4 For Dummies
  0-471-77483-9
- Syndicating Web Sites with RSS Feeds
  For Dummies
  0-7645-8848-6
- Yahoo! SiteBuilder For Dummies
  0-7645-9800-7

NETWORKING, SECURITY, PROGRAMMING & DATABASES

0-7645-7728-X   0-471-74940-0

Also available:

- Access 2007 For Dummies
  0-470-04612-0
- ASP.NET 2 For Dummies
  0-7645-7907-X
- C# 2005 For Dummies
  0-7645-9704-3
- Hacking For Dummies
  0-470-05235-X
- Hacking Wireless Networks
  For Dummies
  0-7645-9730-2
- Java For Dummies
  0-470-08716-1

- Microsoft SQL Server 2005 For Dummies
  0-7645-7755-7
- Networking All-in-One Desk Reference
  For Dummies
  0-7645-9939-9
- Preventing Identity Theft For Dummies
  0-7645-7336-5
- Telecom For Dummies
  0-471-77085-X
- Visual Studio 2005 All-in-One Desk
  Reference For Dummies
  0-7645-9775-2
- XML For Dummies
  0-7645-8845-1